THE PERFECT FINISH

THE PERFECT FINISH

SPECIAL DESSERTS FOR EVERY OCCASION

BILL YOSSES
and Melissa Clark

photographs by Marcus Nilsson

W. W. NORTON & COMPANY
NEW YORK · LONDON

Frontispiece: Red Eye Devil's Food Cake.

For information about permission to reproduce
selections from this book, write to Permissions,
W. W. Norton & Company, Inc.,
500 Fifth Avenue, New York, NY 10110

For information about special discounts for bulk purchases, please contact
W. W. Norton Special Sales at specialsales@wwnorton.com or 800-233-4830

Manufacturing by Worzalla
Book design by Studio 421
Production manager: Devon Zahn

Library of Congress Cataloging-in-Publication Data

Yosses, Bill.
The perfect finish : special desserts for every occasion / Bill Yosses
and Melissa Clark ; photographs by Marcus Nilsson. — 1st ed.
p. cm.
Includes index.
ISBN 978-0-393-05953-3 (hardcover)
1. Desserts. I. Clark, Melissa. II. Title.
TX773.Y677 2010
641.8'6—dc22

2010006891

W. W. Norton & Company, Inc.
500 Fifth Avenue, New York, N.Y. 10110
www.wwnorton.com

W. W. Norton & Company Ltd.
Castle House, 75/76 Wells Street, London W1T 3QT

1 2 3 4 5 6 7 8 9 0

CONTENTS

ACKNOWLEDGMENTS

This book began to take shape during 2002 when Melissa Clark and I were writing a series of dessert recipes for the *New York Times*. I am grateful that I have such a meticulous and diligent partner who is able to capture the complexity of a great recipe yet put it into such understandable and mouth-watering terms.

There were so many different directions that the dessert world was traveling in at that time, and writing those articles with the talented Ms. Clark I started to review in my mind the places where and the people from whom I learned the most. Those people live throughout this book.

I am a Francophile. Some of the first memorable experiences for me happened in France, but soon enough I began to see that our American cuisine has a fast developing gastronomy of its own.

Though certainly not the first time my eyes were opened to possibilities, one stands out in my memory. A dessert I had at La Table d'Anvers in Paris, made by the pastry chef Philippe Conticini, opened my eyes to the possibilities of flavor. He used Cuban tobacco in an orange sauce. Cuban tobacco! And it was wonderful. Just a few tiny specks, but it was like a sharp chili and made the dish come alive. I later rushed to learn about this pastry man and read that he was looking to create "emotions in the mouth." I have never met Monsieur Conticini, but I love that phrase and I think it is the dessert maker's highest calling. The experience that is not only the affective pleasure of a delicious morsel but one that brings back a fond memory or taste experience that surprises and delights you.

Thanks to a handful of chefs who have mastered this ability to mix unusual flavors successfully, we are open to new adventures. The urge to experiment results in many failures, but gastronomy is for the adventurous and I admire the pluck of those wild dreamers. Some who I have known and worked with, such as Pierre Hermé and Robert Linxe, and others whose art I have tasted, such as Pierre Gagnaire and Joël Robuchon, teach volumes with every dish they serve.

This book tacks much closer to traditional shores, but always with a twist of eager anticipation for something new.

My first and best pastry teacher was a classicist, Jean-Pierre LeMasson, who was at Perigord Park Restaurant back in the 1980s. I owe my love of desserts to him. He was still open to learning new things after thirty years in the business, and he made sure that curiosity was the most important lesson learned in his kitchen. I was lucky enough to get advice from Nick Malgieri and Dieter Schorner, pastry chefs who are at the top of the pastry pyramid in my book, and who are never too busy for an encouraging word.

I was privileged to work in the kitchens of David Bouley for many years, and those were great times, devoted to the best ingredients and preparations. My sincere gratitude also goes to Joe Gurrera of Citarella, who is a walking encyclopedia on the tastes of New Yorkers.

In writing this book, great advice and wonderful support have been my lucky lot with the greatest of cookbook editors, Maria Guarnaschelli, who along with the W. W. Norton staff has forged this book into a finely tuned reality. I thank them sincerely. The meticulous testing done by Rebecca Adams, Jaimee Young, and Molly Killeen is without peer and Melanie Tortoroli has added greatly to the text and themes in the book. Art director Ingsu Liu gave the book a seamless elegance.

The photographs are beautiful, irresistible, luscious, and mouth watering, and the amazing artistry of photographer Marcus Nilsson is to blame. The glint of light on Baccarat crystal creates a beautiful setting for a cake—my thanks to Baccarat and to Katie DosSantos for supplying those pieces. Susan Sugarman was an inspired choice as food stylist, and she has a special knack for creating beautiful visuals. My agent and wonderful friend, Lisa Queen, has been there whenever needed as moral support, confidence builder, and judicious commentator.

My mother loved to bake. I am convinced she petitioned the Pope for some new holy days just so she could bring her cakes to the parties in the church basement. This book is dedicated to her. My life is made wonderful by my partner, Charlie. He wears many hats: life partner, best friend, critical taster, and he sings a mean karaoke. His support sees me through.

INTRODUCTION

After baking professionally for many years, most chefs have a pretty good repertoire and don't come across astounding recipes every day. Not because they are jaded, but because their experience has brought them into contact with so much wonderful food.

Coming across a new dish that wildly exceeds expectations is thrilling, and the source doesn't matter; home cooking, ethnic restaurant, neighborhood joint, organic, biodynamic, or molecularly gastronomic, we have all had that thought, that, "I just have to get that recipe."

This book is a compilation of winner recipes. Each one has something unique and stands out as the best in its class. They may be fancy or simple, French, American, Asian, or Latin inspired, but all have a unique character that sets them apart. For all their individuality, I chose recipes that are faithful to the American palate. Flavors, textures, and appearances that are familiar and even nostalgic, but in each case they are contemporary and fit our modern concept of dessert as a delicious but reasonable part of an overall healthy diet.

Desserts and baking have changed dramatically, and the interest in health and wellness certainly is a major influence. I use less sugar and butter and often replace some of the sugar with honey or other sweeteners such as maple syrup. I also add herbs as an interesting counterpart to the flavor combinations. Peaches and lemon verbena is one of my favorites. When the flavors are robust and layered, people don't miss the sugar; their taste buds have other things to satisfy them. Nut oils are a good substitute for butter and they carry less saturated fat, as well as having their own nutrients. I often replace some butter with a good oil such as almond, grapeseed, olive, or even walnut, as you will see in Crêpes Suzette with Dark Rum and Oranges (page 172).

It seems to me that desserts made with good ingredients, prepared with skill, and presented beautifully will always make people happy, and that is the purpose of this book. Desserts are the part of eating that says "pleasure" most succinctly.

Besides nutrition, pleasure is a worthy goal when eating, and in this book taste and gastronomic pleasure are the ultimate arbiters of a recipe's value.

It so happens that ingredients raised locally, artisanally, and humanely taste better 99 percent of the time, so I recommend seeking out those types of ingredients when buying groceries. And since farmers' markets are easier to find now, that is where I hope you will shop.

I am lucky to have started my cooking career in Paris, and especially to have found the purveyors of Rungis, the wholesale food market there. There is no better place to see the highest quality produce. Now, thirty years after my first visit to France, it is gratifying to see the farmers' markets in the United States begin to offer that level of quality.

Recently I helped start a farmers' market in Westport, Connecticut, with Michel Nischan, the eloquent spokesman for sustainability and local sourcing of foods. That market, which follows the French model, was an instant success. It seems only fitting that we should fashion our markets on those that have existed in France for centuries—after all, much of America's founding philosophy comes from the exchange of ideas between the "lumières" of eighteenth-century France and our own first statesmen, like Thomas Jefferson.

On a visit to Jefferson's estate, Monticello, I was amazed to discover that most of the vegetables in the thousand-foot garden there derive from our third president's heirloom seed stock. Peter Hatch is the affable gardener who has cultivated this garden for the past thirty-two years. He likes to quote Jefferson's prescription for healthy living, which is no different from what we counsel today: "I have lived temperately, eating little animal food and that, not as an aliment, so much as a condiment for the vegetables which constitute my principal diet." Jefferson's concern for gastronomy is well documented. In seeking a maître d' he considered the "indispensable qualifications" to be "honesty and skill in making the dessert." I like to think about Jefferson's attention to his kitchen and garden, and to remember that American cuisine, with its great bounty, was not always reliant on convenience and processed foods. I am thrilled to be in the food business at a point in history when American palates are returning to elemental tastes and good food.

I would love you to source the fruits for these recipes in farmers' markets, but I also tried to balance this book with three practical thoughts in mind; simplicity, convenience, and originality.

The recipes are fairly simple and require minimal skills and equipment; many of the ingredients are already found in a well-stocked kitchen, so they remain convenient. The last purpose, originality, was served by introducing a twist to the recipe, either technical or flavor wise, such as the Cardamom Nut Butterballs (page 233). In such recipes, I may send you out to look for some exotic ingredients, but there is usually an "optional" attached, so if you want to make the dessert *now*, you can.

It is that "now" that gave me the idea to organize the book according to how a reader may want to use it. For me, I am usually baking with a specific event or gathering in mind. So rather than divide the book in a formal way into doughs, batters, mousses, cakes, and so on, I used chapter divisions that mirror our daily lives and activities: "Pick Me Ups" for a quick fix of a sweet pleasure; "Restaurant Desserts You Can Make at Home" for the most refined and nuanced desserts.

Another feature that I included in the book are my "Chef's Notes." These are explanations in further depth, which are inserted directly next to the recipe concerned. This allows you to investigate further without flipping pages and losing your place, or getting batter on the book, which makes for sticky pages. I have tried to point out in these chef's notes a few secrets and simple tips that will help you make the recipe.

The headnotes have explanations of the recipes, often including the source or the person who first served it to me. These headnotes are also crucial because they go into the basic technique or reasoning behind a certain baking procedure. Additionally, this is where I can talk to you about the flavors that inspired the recipe and how to enhance those flavors either by a baking or culinary method, or merely through conservation and storage: tips which prolong freshness or sometimes help a dessert mature into a better-tasting dish.

My most fervent wish is to see your copy of this book stained and dirty with many uses and spills. It gives me a sense of pride to see the recipes I love shared and enjoyed by others. That is where the "now" comes in most strongly, I hope that as you peruse these desserts it will make you want to get into the kitchen and start right away.

There is everything you need on these pages to go step by step without hesitation and to arrive at a perfect finish, worthy of your friends and family.

THE PERFECT FINISH

COME FOR BRUNCH

In the not too distant American past, the morning meal—a stick to the ribs eggs-bacon-flapjacks affair—was arguably the most important meal of the day. It provided farmers with the energy to take them through their many strenuous chores, at the end of which they might have just a simple dinner or some bread. This American model is completely different from the European paradigm, where breakfast is more minimal, but no less compelling, consisting of freshly baked breads and other pastries, and the requisite hot milky coffee. In this chapter, I focus on the lighter and more pastry-centric European tradition. Sweet eye-openers like tender Feathery Jam-Filled Butter Cakes (page 25) and fragrant Orange Flower–Scented Kugelhopf (page 43) will lull you calmly yet delectably into your day, which is probably less strenuous than that of our farming forebears.

The recipes in this chapter are intended to be shared with others. I think it's a wonderful, intimate gesture to invite guests over for breakfast or brunch because it means you're making them a part of your morning ritual. Prepare your dough or batters in advance and then, just before your guests arrive, pop whatever you're making into the oven. Then enjoy these treats as they were meant to be enjoyed—steaming hot and spread with good butter and some fruit preserves. None of us has time to make bread every day, but these recipes can be saved for that getaway weekend in the country or that slow, no appointments weekend in January, when the yeasty aroma of bread will become a very happy memory. A well-made loaf of brioche is like a medal of honor—you won't need to do any boasting about it, your friends will do it for you.

Some of the best breakfast breads are, of course, the pillowy-soft yeasted kind, like my ethereal Buttery Brioche (page 32), which is a treat all on its own, but can be made extra special when served with a perfumed acacia honey. Although making yeasted bread such as brioche may seem labor-intensive and complicated, it really isn't. Most of the time the bread doesn't even require your attention because it will simply be rising somewhere while you do other things. There are ways you can incorporate the process of making bread into your daily routine so that it becomes less daunting. Bread making can be a great therapy—seeing the dough come together and take on a life of its own as the yeast begins to percolate is a satisfying experience. And, to save time, the dough can be frozen. Tightly triple wrap it to avoid freezer burn, and proof it up to 10 days later. Let it thaw in the refrigerator overnight, then bring it out in the morning to finish the rise.

Faster than yeast breads are the aptly named "quick breads" (made with chemical leaveners rather than yeast), such as Chewy Brown Sugar Date Walnut Loaf (page 31) and sweetly spiced Gingery Pumpkin Breakfast Bundt (page 27). These breakfast delights can be put together quickly in the morning. Scones and muffins are fast and easy yet very rewarding—try my light and airy Blueberry Angel Muffins (page 13) or the earthier Figgy-Prune Scones (page 19) for proof of that! These treats taste much better when freshly made, but since they don't usually take long, they are easy to plan for—add ripe seasonal fruit and you are good to go.

ORANGE SUPREME MUFFINS

The ideal muffin is moist with a crunchy top and soft crumb. It shouldn't be too rich in itself so that it can accommodate a pat of butter without getting weighed down. The texture should be spongy, with real resistance, somewhere between bread and cake. I tend to like lots of fruit in a muffin—essentially, for me, the muffin is a vehicle for the fruit. Traditional muffin batters are often too soft to support a fruit overdose, so I mix a little bread flour into the all-purpose flour. Bread flour contains more gluten, which gives bread dough its elasticity and structure. Adding a little to muffins makes a stronger batter that really lets me pack the fruit in. (If you don't have any bread flour on hand, you can use all-purpose only for a lovely, if softer, muffin.)

Muffins are best served warm with butter and juice and very good hot coffee. I'd like to put to rest the notion that there's something wrong with putting jam and butter on muffins—it may be gilding the lily a bit, but a hot Orange Supreme Muffin with melting butter and damson plum preserves accompanied by a cup of thick Colombian coffee can be awe inspiring.

Chef's Note For working these muffins in advance, I find paper baking cups very handy: I fill the ungreased cups with batter and then place the filled cups in muffin tins for baking. The advantage of this extra step is that I can freeze the batter-filled cups. Once they're frozen, I transfer the cups to a resealable plastic freezer bag and keep them on hand in case of surprise guests (you'll need to add a few minutes onto the baking time). The frozen batter lasts for several weeks in the freezer, well wrapped in plastic film.

ORANGES

Not to overstress the point, but the key word in Orange Supreme Muffin really isn't "muffin," it's "orange." The flavor of orange is remarkably delicate and tends to dissipate quickly, which is why professional bakers often add Grand Marnier or Cointreau to orange-flavored dishes. For these muffins, I get an intense flavor with the whole orange: the juice, the zest, and the segments (which the French call *suprèmes*; see photographs on page 8). You can increase the level of orange flavor easily by adding zest. The other ingredients, juice and segments, will affect the overall recipe and must be used with care. One final recommendation is to use a few drops of Boyajian brand orange oil, an excellent artisanal product (see Sources, page 275).

Recipe continues

Orange Supreme Muffin.

ORANGE SUPREME MUFFINS

Unsalted butter, for the muffin tin, optional

1¾ cups all-purpose flour (7.9 ounces, 224 grams)

¼ cup bread flour or all-purpose flour (1.12 ounces, 32.5 grams)

1 teaspoon baking powder (5 grams)

1 teaspoon baking soda (5 grams)

½ teaspoon salt (2.5 grams)

2 navel oranges (7 ounces, 198 grams)

12 tablespoons (1½ sticks) unsalted butter, melted (6 ounces, 171 grams)

½ cup half-and-half (4.25 ounces, 121 grams)

½ cup medium-flavored honey such as orange blossom or clover (6 ounces, 170 grams)

¼ cup packed light brown sugar (2 ounces, 57 grams)

3 large eggs (5.1 ounces, 145 grams), at room temperature

1. Position a rack in the center of the oven. Lightly grease a standard muffin tin, or use ungreased paper muffin cups.

2. Sift the all-purpose flour, bread flour or all-purpose flour, baking powder, baking soda, and salt into a large bowl and set aside.

3. In a small bowl, grate the zest from the oranges and set it aside. To supreme the oranges, use a sharp knife to cut the top and bottom off each orange. Stand one of the oranges up on a cutting board and cut the peel and white pith away from the fruit, following the curve with your knife, so that the segments are exposed. Hold the peeled fruit over a bowl and cut out the segments, letting them fall into a bowl along with the juice and discarding the seeds. Repeat with the second orange. (See photographs on page 8.)

4. Preheat the oven to 375°F. Add the melted butter, half-and-half, honey, brown sugar, eggs, and reserved orange zest and segments to the dry ingredients. Mix together with a wooden spoon or large whisk until just smooth.

5. Divide the batter among the muffin cups so that each is two-thirds full. Bake on the center rack until the muffins are puffed and golden and a cake tester inserted in the center of a muffin comes out clean, about 45 minutes. Transfer the muffins to a wire rack to cool slightly before serving warm.

HOW TO SUPREME AN ORANGE.

1. After cutting off the top and bottom, slide a sharp knife down the outside of the orange, leaving no white pith.

2. Carefully slide the knife in between the segments.

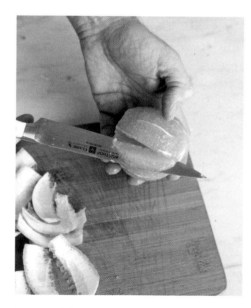

3. Pop out the supreme.

4. Continue around the entire fruit.

BANANA COCONUT STREUSEL MUFFINS

Bakers tend to be held prisoners of the seasons, so it's valuable to have recipes that can be made year-round. Good bananas are always available, and they're a natural paired with sweet shreds of coconut. When baking with bananas, riper is definitely better. The ideal baking banana is covered with black dots and is very soft and dark yellow on the inside. Don't worry if you think they are overripe because that's what will give you really intense banana flavor. The combination of oil and ripe banana makes this muffin flavorful and also keeps it moist for days. (See photograph on page 2.)

Chef's Note Unless otherwise specified, chiffon cakes and oil-based quick breads and muffins should be made with a neutral-tasting vegetable oil. Both safflower and grapeseed oil fit the bill. I tend to use safflower since it is more affordable.

MAKES 9 STANDARD-SIZE MUFFINS
SPECIAL EQUIPMENT: 12-CUP STANDARD-SIZE MUFFIN TIN, ICE CREAM SCOOP

½ cup dry grated unsweetened coconut (1.5 ounces, 43 grams)

2 packed tablespoons light brown sugar (.95 ounce, 21 grams)

1 cup plus 2 tablespoons all-purpose flour (5 ounces, 142 grams), plus additional for the muffin tins

⅛ teaspoon salt, plus a pinch for the streusel (.8 gram)

2 tablespoons cold unsalted butter, sliced (1 ounce, 28 grams)

6 tablespoons granulated sugar (2.6 ounces, 75 grams)

2 teaspoons baking powder (9.8 grams)

¼ cup neutral oil, preferably safflower or grapeseed (1.87 ounces, 53.75 grams), plus additional for the muffin tins

¾ cup mashed overripe bananas (about 2 small, 6 ounces, 170 grams)

¼ cup whole milk (2.1 ounces, 60 grams)

1 large egg, at room temperature, lightly beaten (1.7 ounces, 48 grams)

1. Position a rack in the center of the oven and preheat to 350°F. Lightly grease nine cups of a standard muffin tin with oil or nonstick cooking spray, then dust them with flour, or use ungreased paper muffin cups.

2. To make the streusel, in a bowl stir together the coconut, brown sugar, 2 tablespoons of the flour, and a pinch of salt. Add the butter and rub the mixture together with your fingers or a pastry cutter until you have large crumbles about the size of a pea. Set aside.

Recipe continues

Banana Coconut Streusel Muffin.

3. In a large bowl, whisk together the remaining cup of flour, the granulated sugar, baking powder, and the remaining 1/8 teaspoon salt.

4. In a small bowl, stir together the 1/4 cup of oil with the mashed bananas, milk, and egg until they are well combined. Add the banana mixture to the flour mixture and stir until just combined.

5. Using an ice cream scoop, fill the prepared muffin cups halfway. Top the muffins with streusel, dividing the streusel evenly among the muffins. Fill the three empty cups halfway with tap water to prevent the muffin tin from warping. Bake the muffins on the center rack until they rise and are golden and bounce back when pressed, about 30 minutes. Let cool in the tin for about 15 minutes and serve warm. (Leftovers can be wrapped in foil and stored in the refrigerator for up to 4 days, then re-warmed in a 350°F oven for 10 minutes before serving.)

SIFTING

Although most all-purpose flour these days is pre-sifted, cake flour tends to clump and requires sifting, but the most important reason to sift dry ingredients is for an even distribution. Baking powder, baking soda, and spices all need to be dispersed evenly throughout the recipe. You don't need a triple-tier hand sifter—just pass the dry ingredients through a fine mesh sieve into a bowl or onto parchment paper.

Blueberry Angel Muffin.

BLUEBERRY ANGEL MUFFINS

These muffins have so much going for them. Not only do they happen to be fat free, they're also a cake, small and fruit filled. Thus they allow you to tap into the psychic pleasure of eating cake—a virtuous cake—for breakfast, with your nice cup of coffee. For the most stupendous results, make these muffins just a few hours before you serve them; they will be buoyantly fluffy, with only a tiny bit of pleasing chewy resistance before they melt in your mouth, leaving the amazing flavors of blueberries and vanilla lingering on your tongue.

If you somehow manage to have muffins left over, toast them before serving. They can even be frozen, then toasted. The toasted muffins won't have that same airy texture, but they'll still be tasty. In fact, Melissa likes to spread toasted blueberry muffins with butter—a good antidote if you miss the fat in angel food!

Chef's Note In order to keep the muffins light, once you beat the egg whites to their peak volume, you don't want to disturb the batter any more than necessary. That's why I toss the vanilla and berries together in a bowl, then fold half of them into the batter and top the muffins with the rest, rather than mixing in the vanilla earlier and stirring all the berries in, as you might in a conventional blueberry muffin recipe. (If you want to know more about meringue, the key to this muffin's fluffiness, see the discussion of meringue on page 15.) The goal is to avoid crushing the airiness—better to mix the berries in less evenly than to lose all that lift.

MAKES 12 STANDARD-SIZE MUFFINS

SPECIAL EQUIPMENT: 12-CUP STANDARD-SIZE MUFFIN TIN, SIFTER, ELECTRIC MIXER, CAKE TESTER

Recipe continues

Nonstick cooking spray, for the muffin cups

⅔ cup cake flour (2.67 ounces, 76 grams)

½ cup confectioners' sugar (2 ounces, 57 grams)

¼ teaspoon salt (1.25 grams)

1¼ cups blueberries (6.5 ounces, 185 grams)

2 teaspoons vanilla extract (8 grams)

8 large egg whites (7 ounces, 200 grams), at room temperature

Pinch of cream of tartar

½ cup granulated sugar (3.5 ounces, 99 grams), plus 6 teaspoons additional for sprinkling

Finely grated zest of 1 lemon

1. Position a rack in the center of the oven. Lightly grease a standard-size muffin tin with nonstick cooking spray, or use ungreased paper muffin cups.

2. Sift the cake flour, confectioners' sugar, and salt onto a piece of parchment or waxed paper and set aside. In a small bowl, toss the blueberries with the vanilla.

3. In a clean bowl of an electric mixer fitted with the whisk attachment, beat the egg whites and cream of tartar on medium-low speed until frothy. Add 1 tablespoon of the granulated sugar and beat at medium until soft peaks form. Beat in the remaining granulated sugar, and raise the speed to high. Beat until stiff peaks form. While the eggs are beating, preheat the oven to 375°F.

4. When you have stiff peaks, stop the machine and remove the bowl. Immediately sprinkle the dry ingredients and lemon zest over the egg whites and fold in with a rubber spatula, working carefully to avoid deflating the whites. Fold in half of the blueberries.

5. Divide the batter among the muffin cups so that each is two-thirds full. Top each muffin with a few more blueberries and sprinkle each with 1/2 teaspoon granulated sugar.

6. Bake on the center rack until the muffins are lightly golden and a cake tester inserted in their centers comes out clean, 20 to 25 minutes. Remove the muffins from the tin as soon as they come out of the oven and transfer them to a wire rack to cool for 15 minutes. Serve within 4 hours.

Meringue is the eighth wonder of the world, and a kitchen miracle. What other ingredient can expand ten times its volume? After all, it is 90 percent air! A few tips:

1. Egg whites a few days old make better meringues.

2. The bowl and the whites themselves must be impeccably clean, that is, no residue on the bowl and no yolks broken into the egg whites.

3. Room temperature whites yield meringue with a strong body.

4. A pinch of cream of tartar and a little sugar to start the meringue off are helpful, the cream of tartar (acid) loosens protein bonds and helps them to re-form as bubbles, with air trapped inside.

5. The smaller the bubbles, the stronger the meringue.

6. A good test for a stiff meringue is that it should hold up a coin (a quarter) on its surface.

7. Very stiff meringue will hold up an egg on its surface.

The ultimate meringue is whipped by hand in a copper bowl. The finest mesh of bubbles and the strongest, creamiest meringue you have ever seen.

FLUFFY GOLDEN WAFFLES

My friend Rick Jakobson once made these waffles for me, and they are unforgettable. Rick is from Sweden, where they know good breakfast recipes and they know their waffles, though the two don't overlap as they do here. You see, in Europe, waffles are served as a sweet snack or dessert rather than breakfast. I like them any time, with any kind of topping, as long as they are light and crisp outside, soft and steaming inside, as these certainly are. Making waffles with yeast gives the texture a little extra chewiness and snap that can soak up the syrup and remain crisp. The flavor is more pronounced, with a depth of complexity that regular waffles lack. Using a preheated waffle iron ensures that the crust is crunchy and golden brown. Sometimes I like to add a tablespoon of malt powder or malt syrup to the batter to give it a touch of malty earthiness, though I make that optional here.

If you're serving these for breakfast, there's no better topping than good butter and maple syrup. If you have time, you might want to reduce the maple syrup by a third in a small pan over medium heat while the waffles bake. Reducing the syrup gives it a thicker, richer texture and more intense maple flavor. Ripe seasonal fruit, whipped cream, honey and jam are also excellent waffle-toppers, depending on what you have on hand and what your mood dictates. To make these into a dessert, try topping them with ice cream and hot fudge sauce.

Chef's Note You will notice that this recipe has two leaveners: yeast and baking soda. They combine to make a lighter waffle. The yeast in this recipe supplies not only volume but also a chewier texture and deeper tangy flavor. See page 35 if you want to know more about yeast. The baking soda adds more air.

MAKES ABOUT 10 (7-INCH) HEART-SHAPED WAFFLES OR
4 (7-INCH) SQUARE WAFFLES

SPECIAL EQUIPMENT: WAFFLE IRON, SIFTER, ELECTRIC MIXER, LADLE,
11-BY-17-INCH BAKING SHEET (OPTIONAL)

Vegetable oil, for brushing waffle iron

2½ teaspoons (1 envelope) active dry yeast (.25 ounce, 7 grams)

½ cup lukewarm water

2 cups all-purpose flour (8.5 ounces, 242 grams)

1 tablespoon sugar (.4 ounce, 10 grams)

1 tablespoon malt powder (.25 ounce, 10 grams) or 1 tablespoon malt syrup (1 ounce, 30 grams), optional

1 teaspoon salt (5 grams)

2 cups milk (16 ounces, 454 grams)

8 tablespoons (1 stick) butter (4 ounces, 115 grams), melted

2 large eggs (3.4 ounces, 96 grams), separated, at room temperature

1½ teaspoons baking soda (10 grams)

Butter and maple syrup, for serving

1. In a small bowl, combine the yeast with 1/2 cup of lukewarm water and 2 tablespoons of the flour. Allow the mixture to rest for 15 minutes.

2. Sift the remainder of the flour, the sugar, malt, if using, and salt into a large bowl. Stir in the milk and melted butter. Add the yeast mixture and stir together until the batter is smooth.

3. Cover the bowl with plastic wrap and allow it to rest at room temperature for 2 hours or until it begins to bubble. Refrigerate for 2 hours or overnight.

4. Preheat the waffle iron and brush with vegetable oil if it is not nonstick. Take the batter out of the refrigerator.

5. In a small bowl, lightly beat the eggs. Add the eggs and the baking soda to the batter and stir to combine.

6. Brush the waffle iron with oil. Fill the waffle iron by ladling in the batter until it has spread to 1/2 inch from the edge. Close and bake until the waffle stops steaming and is nicely browned. Serve immediately on warm plates with butter and warm maple syrup. Or, if you want to serve them all together, transfer the waffles as they are baked to an 11-by-17-inch baking pan in a 250° F oven to keep them warm. 250 degrees is the ideal temperature to keep baked goods warm without drying them out. Place two cooling racks on a baking sheet and put the hot waffles on them. Stacking the waffles creates steam, which makes them soggy.

BILL'S AIRY CRÈME FRAÎCHE PANCAKES

These fluffy, tender pancakes will simply melt in the mouth. I use crème fraîche or sour cream to give them a subtle tanginess balanced by the caramel sweetness of brown sugar and just a touch of vanilla. They are very delicate, so make sure you really see tiny bubbles break the surface before flipping. You might find that maple syrup overpowers the lightly sour nuance of the crème fraîche. In that case, a sprinkle of confectioners' sugar and a pat of melting butter are all the gilding these pancakes need. The optional malt gives an earthy background flavor.

MAKES 28 (4-INCH) PANCAKES
SPECIAL EQUIPMENT: BLENDER, HEATPROOF SPATULA

4 large eggs (7 ounces, 200 grams), at room temperature

2 cups crème fraîche or sour cream (13.5 ounces, 390 grams)

1 cup cake flour (4 ounces, 113 grams)

2 tablespoons packed light brown sugar

2 teaspoons vanilla extract (8 grams)

¾ teaspoon salt

1 teaspoon baking soda

2 teaspoons malt powder or 2 teaspoons malt syrup, optional

Canola oil, for the skillet

1. Crack the eggs into the blender and pulse briefly to break up. Add the crème fraîche, flour, brown sugar, vanilla, salt, baking soda, and malt powder or malt syrup and blend until smooth.

2. Place a 12-inch skillet over medium heat and warm until very hot. Brush or spray lightly with canola oil.

3. Drop the pancake batter 1/8 cup (2 tablespoons) at a time into the hot pan, making 4 pancakes at one time. When the pancakes are covered with bubbles and slightly puffy, flip them using a heatproof spatula. The pancakes will bake to a chocolatey brown if using the malt.

4. Cook for another 30 seconds and slide the pancakes onto a plate. Keep them warm by covering with a sheet of foil and continue to cook the remaining pancakes.

FIGGY-PRUNE SCONES

Scones are the haiku of pastry because with the least visible effort, you will achieve the most exquisite results. The whole point is to do as little as possible—scones are made from just a few ingredients, and the baker uses minimal movements, touching the dough as little as possible. If you could just stare at the dough and make it come together, that would be the perfect way to make a scone! I've seen people just absolutely go into a trance making scones, handling the dough gently and rhythmically. Your aim is to incorporate the butter into the flour without developing any gluten whatsoever. I learned in bread baking that even the lightest movement will activate the gluten in the flour. Sometimes all you need to do is pick up a piece of dough and turn it over to develop elasticity. Keep the temperature of all the ingredients cool and definitely mix gently.

In this recipe, figs add a pleasing crunch and prunes add a moist sticky sweetness, and they combine with the buttery, delicate scones to create a harmony of textures. Of course, if you feel like it, you can also substitute other dried fruit, such as raisins, dried cherries, dried apricots, or dates. Or make the scones without any fruit at all. The base dough is tender, flaky and just sweet enough on its own.

MAKES 8 (3-INCH) ROUND SCONES
SPECIAL EQUIPMENT: 11-BY-17-INCH BAKING SHEET, ELECTRIC MIXER, ICE CREAM SCOOP

1⅓ cups all-purpose flour (6 ounces, 170 grams)

¼ cup sugar, plus 1 tablespoon for sprinkling (2.2 ounces, 62.5 grams)

½ tablespoon baking powder (7.35 grams)

½ teaspoon salt (2.5 grams)

6 tablespoons unsalted butter, chilled and cut into ½-inch cubes (3 ounces, 85 grams)

½ cup dried pitted prunes, coarsely chopped (3 ounces, 85 grams)

½ cup dried figs, coarsely chopped (2.13 ounces, 62 grams)

¼ cup heavy cream (2 ounces, 57 grams), plus additional for brushing

1 large egg (1.7 ounces, 48 grams), at room temperature

1. Position a rack in the center of the oven and preheat to 375°F. Line a baking sheet with parchment paper.

2. Sift the flour, 1/4 cup sugar, baking powder, and salt onto a piece of parchment or waxed paper and set aside.

Recipe continues

3. Place the butter in the bowl of an electric mixer fitted with the paddle attachment. Add the prunes, figs, cream, and egg. Sprinkle the flour mixture over the butter mixture and mix on slow to medium speed until the dough just comes together. Do not overmix.

4. Use an ice cream scoop or tablespoon to portion out 8 equal balls of dough on the parchment paper.

5. Brush the scones with heavy cream and sprinkle them with the remaining tablespoon of sugar. Bake on the center rack until firm and golden, about 25 minutes. With a spatula, lift them onto a wire rack to cool for at least 10 minutes, then serve warm.

APPLE AND WHITE CHEDDAR SCONES

These simple scones echo the delightful sweet-savory contrast of that classic American pairing: apple pie and cheddar cheese. There are times when you want something savory in the morning, or perhaps in the later morning as you start to transition into lunch, and cheddar lends just the right balance to these crumbly, apple-studded pastries. Before I mix them into the dough, I pre-bake the apple wedges slightly so they're soft enough to blend easily with the scone mixture without becoming mushy—it's a treat to find pockets of apple flavor.

For this recipe, I shape the dough in an untraditional way—patting it into a round, then cutting it into wedges—so that no dough is wasted. The wedges are irresistibly fragrant when they're a little warm; eat them shortly after baking, or reheat them a bit in the oven.

MAKES 6 (2½-INCH) WEDGE-SHAPED SCONES
SPECIAL EQUIPMENT: 11-BY-17-INCH BAKING SHEET, SIFTER, ELECTRIC MIXER,
ROLLING PIN, PASTRY BRUSH

2 firm, tart apples such as Granny Smith, Macoun, or Pippin (about 1 pound, 454 grams)

1½ cups all-purpose flour (6.75 ounces, 195 grams), plus additional for work surface

¼ cup sugar, plus 1½ tablespoons for sprinkling (2.2 ounces, 62.5 grams)

½ tablespoon baking powder (7.35 grams)

½ teaspoon salt (3.35 grams), plus additional for egg wash

6 tablespoons unsalted butter (3 ounces, 85 grams), chilled and cut into ½-inch cubes, plus additional for the baking sheet

½ cup sharp white cheddar cheese (about 2.25 ounces, 65 grams), shredded

¼ cup heavy cream (2 ounces, 57 grams)

2 large eggs (3.4 ounces, 96 grams), at room temperature

1. Position a rack in the center of the oven and preheat to 350°F. Line a baking sheet with parchment paper.

2. Peel and core the apples, cut them into sixteenths, and place them in a single layer on the lined baking sheet. Bake the apples until they take on a little color and feel dry to the touch, about 20 minutes, then transfer to a bowl and let cool. Leave the oven on.

Recipe continues

Apple and White Cheddar Scones, cooling on a rack.

3. Sift the flour, sugar, baking powder, and salt onto a piece of parchment or waxed paper and set aside.

4. Place the butter in the bowl of an electric mixer fitted with the paddle attachment. Add the apples, cheese, cream, and one of the eggs. Sprinkle the flour mixture over the butter mixture and mix on low speed until the dough just comes together. Do not overmix.

5. Generously flour a work surface, place the scone dough on it, and sift a light layer of flour over the top of the dough. Use a rolling pin to gently roll the dough into a 1 1/4-inch-thick, 6-inch circle. Cut the circle into 6 wedges (2 1/2-inches wide at their outer edge) and transfer them to the baking sheet, leaving at least 2 inches between each scone.

6. In a small bowl, beat the remaining egg with a pinch of salt. Brush the scones with the egg wash and sprinkle them with the remaining tablespoon of sugar. Bake on the center rack until firm and golden, about 30 minutes. With a spatula, lift them onto a wire rack to cool for 10 minutes, then serve warm.

Feathery Jam-Filled Butter Cakes.

FEATHERY JAM-FILLED BUTTER CAKES

I like to make these cakes because they are quick crowd pleasers. The crumb has an irresistibly buoyant texture, and a light, lemony flavor that is also nicely suited to teatime (though don't even think about dunking them in your cup of tea, as the airy treats will simply dissolve between your fingers). These are a breakfast dessert—not a muffin. The jam in the batter makes this an inside-out breakfast cake.

I prefer to gently swirl in the jam rather than fold it in completely. Not only does this make for a prettier presentation, but it also distributes the flavor unevenly, which I find is the fun of it—some bites are intensely jammy, while others are more about the soft buttery cake. And both are irresistible.

Chef's Note Jellies and jams are convenient and delicious time-savers in baking. They can be used in layer cakes to replace a filling or in baked goods such as these cakes. Just be sure to incorporate them into the batter—don't apply them to the surface. Jams exposed directly to oven heat will burn.

MAKES 12 CAKES

SPECIAL EQUIPMENT: 12-CUP STANDARD MUFFIN TIN, ELECTRIC MIXER,
CAKE TESTER, PASTRY BRUSH

2 cups cake flour (16 ounces, 450 grams)

2 teaspoons baking powder (10 grams)

Finely grated zest of 1 lemon

¼ teaspoon salt (1.25 grams)

8 tablespoons unsalted butter (4 ounces, 127 grams), plus additional for pan

½ cup sugar (6 ounces, 170 grams)

2 large eggs, lightly beaten (3.4 ounces, 94 grams)

1 teaspoon vanilla extract (4 grams)

⅓ cup whole milk (2.8 ounces, 80.6 grams)

½ cup seedless fruit jam (5.2 ounces, 75 grams)

GLAZE

⅓ cup confectioners' sugar (1.3 ounces, 38.35 grams)

2 teaspoons lemon juice (.3 ounce, 5 grams)

¾ teaspoon finely grated lemon zest

1. Preheat the oven to 350°F. Grease a 12-cup standard muffin tin with butter. In a bowl, whisk together the flour, baking powder, lemon zest, and salt.

Recipe continues

2. In the bowl of an electric mixer fitted with the paddle attachment, beat together the butter and sugar on medium-high speed. Add the eggs one at a time, then beat in the vanilla.

3. Reduce the speed to medium-low. Add the flour mixture in three additions, alternating with the milk. Fold in the jam in three or four strokes, until just incorporated.

4. Divide the batter among the cups of the prepared tin. Bake until golden on top and a cake tester inserted in the center of each cake comes out clean, about 25 minutes. Let the cakes cool for 5 minutes in the pan.

5. While the cakes cool, prepare the glaze: Whisk together the sugar, egg white, milk, and lemon zest. Turn the cakes onto a wire rack set over a rimmed baking sheet. Using a pastry brush, brush the tops of each cake generously with the glaze. Turn the cakes over and brush the bottoms with the glaze. Let cool completely.

GINGERY PUMPKIN BREAKFAST BUNDT

Fresh ginger is the secret to this intense pumpkin quick bread dressed up in a bundt pan. It is zestier and more vibrant than your typical pumpkin bread. Although it's marvelously moist and light on the day you bake it, I love to panfry day-old slices in some butter and a sprinkling of brown sugar. It gives a crusty glaze to the surface, and warms it. This cake is an excellent keeper and will last for a week. The texture will compact slightly as it sits, but the flavor gets even stronger and deeper.

MAKES 1 BUNDT CAKE TO SERVE 10 TO 12
SPECIAL EQUIPMENT: 2-QUART BUNDT PAN, ELECTRIC MIXER, SPATULA, CAKE TESTER

Nonstick cooking spray, for the pan

3⅓ cups all-purpose flour (18 ounces, 492 grams)

2 teaspoons baking soda (10 grams)

1½ teaspoons salt (7.5 grams)

1 teaspoon ground cinnamon (2 grams)

½ teaspoon baking powder (2.45 grams)

2⅔ cups dark brown sugar, packed (15.5 ounces, 450 grams)

4 large eggs (6.8 ounces, 193 grams), at room temperature

12 tablespoons (1½ sticks) unsalted butter (6 ounces, 171 grams), melted

1 (15-ounce) can pumpkin puree

1 tablespoon freshly grated fresh ginger (.6 ounce, 17 grams)

⅔ cup coarsely chopped toasted walnuts (2.5 ounces, 80 grams)

⅔ cup golden raisins (2.5 ounces, 80 grams)

1. Preheat the oven to 350°F. First, brush with soft butter, then spray a 2-quart Bundt pan with cooking spray as an extra precaution—this batter is quite sticky.

2. Sift the flour, baking soda, salt, cinnamon, and baking powder into a medium bowl.

3. In the bowl of an electric mixer fitted with the paddle attachment, beat the brown sugar, eggs, and melted butter until light and fluffy, about 5 minutes. Scrape the inside of the bowl. Beat in 2/3 cup water. Add the pumpkin and ginger and beat to combine.

4. Add half the flour mixture and beat at a low speed just until it is moistened. Scrape down the inside of the bowl and add the remaining flour mixture. Beat until just combined.

5. Using a spatula, fold in the walnuts and raisins. Scrape the batter into the prepared pan and bake for 80 to 90 minutes, until a cake tester inserted in the middle comes out clean. Allow the cake to cool completely in the pan before turning out.

BANANA–SOUR CREAM LOAF

The secret of this recipe is the incredible ability of sour cream to produce a moist cake that will keep. Because of the bananas, which count as liquid, this cake also develops a soft crumb that marries well with its moist texture.

Chef's Note This recipe fits a standard 9-by-5-inch loaf pan, but can be used to fill the disposable paper molds available now. These ovenproof paper molds go directly into the oven on a sheet pan and bake for only 35 minutes.

MAKES 1 (9-INCH) LOAF TO SERVE 8

SPECIAL EQUIPMENT: 2-QUART (9-BY-5-INCH) LOAF PAN, ELECTRIC MIXER, SPATULA, CAKE TESTER

2¾ cups all-purpose flour (12.4 ounces, 357.5 grams), plus additional for pan

1 teaspoon baking soda (5 grams)

1 teaspoon baking powder (5 grams)

½ teaspoon salt (2.5 grams)

2 large eggs (3.4 ounces, 96 grams), at room temperature

1½ cups mashed ripe bananas (10.75 ounces, 305 grams, about 3)

½ cup sour cream (3.75 ounces, 110 grams)

1⅓ cups sugar (10.4 ounces, 295 grams)

12 tablespoons (1½ sticks) unsalted butter (6 ounces, 175 grams), plus additional for pan

1 cup chopped pecans, lightly toasted (3.5 ounces, 100 grams)

1. Preheat the oven to 350°F. Lightly grease and flour a 2-quart (9-by-5-inch) loaf pan.

2. Sift the flour, baking soda, baking powder, and salt into a medium bowl. In a separate bowl, lightly beat the eggs and combine with the bananas and sour cream.

3. In the bowl of an electric mixer on a high speed, beat together the sugar and butter until fluffy, about 2 minutes.

4. Scrape down the inside of the bowl and add a third of the banana mixture. Beat on low speed just to combine. Scrape down the inside of the bowl and add a third of the flour mixture. Beat on low speed just to combine. Add the remainder of the banana and flour mixtures in thirds, scraping down the inside of the bowl between each addition. Be careful not to overmix.

5. Using a spatula, fold in the pecans and scrape the batter into the prepared pan. Bake for 1 hour 15 minutes to 1 hour 20 minutes, until a cake tester inserted in the center of the loaf comes out clean. Allow the loaf to cool in the pan, then turn out.

Banana–Sour Cream Loaf in mini-loaf paper molds.

Chewy Brown Sugar Date Walnut Loaf.

CHEWY BROWN SUGAR DATE WALNUT LOAF

This bread comes together in less than 20 minutes, and it's the kind of unexpected retro treat everyone is always happy to find in a breadbasket at brunch. The dates make this loaf stay moist for a long time, so it is still delectable 4 to 5 days later. And the brown sugar gives it a deep butterscotch flavor. Thinly sliced and toasted, this bread is also a great accompaniment to a cheese plate. For classic cream cheese and date-nut sandwiches, spread thin slices with a thick layer of cream cheese.

MAKES 1 (9-INCH) LOAF TO SERVE 8

SPECIAL EQUIPMENT: 9-BY-5-INCH LOAF PAN, CAKE TESTER

1 cup coarsely chopped, pitted Medjool dates (see Sources, page 275) (about 12 large dates, 6.7 ounces, 191 grams)

1 cup packed dark brown sugar (8.4 ounces, 239 grams)

8 tablespoons (1 stick) unsalted butter (4 ounces, 113 grams), plus additional for the pan

1 teaspoon baking soda (5 grams)

1 large egg (1.7 ounces, 48 grams), at room temperature

1 teaspoon vanilla extract (4 grams)

1½ cups all-purpose flour (6.75 ounces, 195 grams)

1 cup coarsely chopped toasted walnuts (4 ounces, 113 grams)

Pinch of salt

Cream cheese, for serving

1. Position a rack in the center of the oven and preheat to 350°F. Use some of the butter to grease a 9-by-5-inch loaf pan.

2. In a saucepan, combine the dates, sugar, and butter with 1 cup water and bring to a boil. Take the pan off the heat and stir in the baking soda.

3. Transfer the date mixture to a large bowl and beat in the egg and vanilla. Stir in the flour, walnuts, and salt and scrape into the loaf pan.

4. Bake on the center rack until a cake tester inserted into the center of the loaf comes out clean, 50 to 60 minutes. Let cool in the pan for 10 minutes, then slide a thin knife or offset spatula around the sides of the pan and turn it over to unmold the loaf onto a wire rack. Allow the loaf to cool on the rack for a few more minutes, then serve warm, with cream cheese.

BUTTERY BRIOCHE

I first ate brioche in the late 1970s, when I was apprenticing with pastry chef Jean-Pierre LeMasson at a restaurant in New York called Perigord Park. On Saturday mornings, I would arrive at work at 6 A.M., and Jean-Pierre would have brioche coming out of the oven just as I came through the door. We'd start our day sitting in the cozy kitchen, the smell of yeast in the air, drinking coffee and eating the warm bread with tangy Normandy butter and apricot preserves we'd pilfered from the pantry. It was bliss.

Brioche tastes as if someone decided to see how rich a bread they could make, while still keeping it technically a bread. It's extremely versatile, somewhere between a bread and a savory dessert, equally at home with foie gras and marmalade. And its flavor is not imposing, so it's a perfect canvas to brush with almond syrup and cook for French toast, to soak with chocolate or vanilla custard and bake into bread pudding, or to simply toast and spread with anything you like.

You can think of brioche as a kind of pound cake, made light and fluffy from yeast. You begin by working the flour and eggs in a mixer for a solid 20 minutes to develop the gluten before adding the butter. This creates a mesh of protein in the dough, enabling it to support all of the butter you're going to add. If there's a trick to brioche, it's making sure that the mixing of the flour and eggs is thorough. Once the dough is well mixed, when you add the butter it will incorporate into the dough within 5 minutes (before the butter gets too warm and makes the dough look slick and greasy).

It might be helpful to give you a breakdown of the technique for brioche:

Step 1. Combine all ingredients except butter

Step 2. Develop gluten (20 minutes)

Step 3. Add butter and beat to incorporate

Step 4. Let rest

Step 5. Chill (this makes the dough less sticky to handle)

Step 6. Shape and let rise until doubled (about 2 hours)

Step 7. Bake (about 50 minutes)

This simple recipe relies on good, rich ingredients. For an especially delectable brioche, I recommend using butter with a very low moisture content, often called European or creamy style. Standard butter is 80 percent butterfat; the lower moisture butters I prefer contain from 82 to 86 percent butterfat. My preference is cultured butter from Normandy called Beurre Échiré.

In this recipe, I use enough yeast to ensure that the project is fun, without the drudgery of sitting around all day while the dough slowly rises. There isn't too much yeast, which can cause the finished brioche to taste raw and overwhelmingly yeasty, but there's enough to lend a pleasant aroma and flavor. I also like to add an almost undetectable amount of ground cinnamon, which tempers the yeast flavor. If you didn't know the cinnamon was there, you probably couldn't detect it, but its subtle, sweet spiciness does enhance that lovely, fresh-baked aroma.

When baked, brioche is still very soft, without a thick crust—the outside of the brioche is browned yet pliable, and the center stays tender and pale. It's important to remove the loaf from the pan immediately, so that steam doesn't form as it cools, making the walls of the brioche soggy.

MAKES 1 (9-INCH) LOAF TO SERVE 8
SPECIAL EQUIPMENT: 9-BY-5-INCH LOAF PAN, ELECTRIC MIXER FITTED WITH THE DOUGH HOOK, PASTRY BRUSH, CAKE TESTER

3 tablespoons whole milk (1.6 ounces, 45.4 grams)

2 teaspoons (1 envelope) active dry yeast (.25 ounce, 7 grams)

2¼ cups all-purpose flour (10 ounces, 283 grams), plus additional for board

5 large eggs (8.5 ounces, 241 grams), at room temperature

1½ tablespoons sugar (.75 ounce, 21 grams)

1 teaspoon salt (5 grams)

½ teaspoon ground cinnamon (2.5 grams)

6 tablespoons cold unsalted low-moisture butter, preferably containing at least 82 percent butterfat, such as Beurre Échiré or Plugra (3 ounces, 85 grams), cut into ¼-inch slices (See Sources, page 275), plus additional for pan

1. Cut a square of parchment paper to fit the bottom of a 9-by-5-inch loaf pan. Butter the pan and then also butter the parchment (or use a nonstick spray).

2. Heat the milk in a microwave or in a small pan until it is just warm to the touch. Place the yeast in the bowl of an electric mixer fitted with the dough hook and add the milk. Mix briefly to combine. Mound the flour over the milk and yeast and let sit for 15 minutes.

3. In a bowl, whisk together 4 of the eggs with the sugar, 1/2 teaspoon of the salt, and the cinnamon. Add this mixture to the flour and mix on low speed, turning the mixer on and off so you don't overmix, until combined.

4. Run the mixer on medium speed, occasionally stopping the mixer to scrape down the bowl and dough hook, until the dough comes together and begins to pull away from the sides of the bowl, about 20 minutes. If it sticks to the sides of the bowl it is not yet ready.

Recipe continues

5. With the mixer still running, add the butter and continue to mix until the butter is incorporated and the dough is shiny, but not wet. (If you overmix here, the dough may become wet and greasy—if this happens, add 1 tablespoon of flour and mix for an additional 30 seconds.)

6. Dust a large clean bowl with flour, place the dough in the bowl, and cover tightly with plastic wrap. Let sit at warm temperature (85°F) until the dough begins to rise, about 45 minutes to 1 hour (it should expand by at least 20 percent). Freeze the dough for 1 hour or refrigerate overnight to make it easier to handle.

7. Turn the dough onto a floured surface. Flour your hands and roll the dough into a ball, and then into an 8-inch-long log. Place the dough in the center of the prepared loaf pan.

8. In a small bowl, whisk the remaining egg. Use a pastry brush to paint the top of the dough with this egg wash. Place the pan in a warm, draft-free, humid environment. (For example, microwave a small bowl of water, then place the brioche in the microwave and close the door, or place the brioche in a closed oven with a shallow pan of warm water—the environment should not exceed 140°F. Remove the dough before preheating the oven.) Let rise until the dough is doubled in size, 2 to 3 hours. It will come up to nearly the top of the pan when ready.

9. Meanwhile, position a rack in the center of the oven and preheat to 350°F. Bake the brioche on the center rack until the crust is golden brown, a cake tester stuck into the side of the loaf comes out clean, and the bottom of the loaf sounds hollow when tapped, 50 minutes to 1 hour. Immediately remove the loaf from the pan and let cool on a wire rack for at least 1 hour. Serve warm or at room temperature. (Store any leftovers in a bread box or bread bag, or wrapped in a clean dishcloth at room temperature for up to 2 days, or make it into Almond Bostock, page 39).

YEAST

There are two kinds of yeast: active dry and fresh. The fresh kind is called brewer's yeast and is available in the dairy section of some grocery stores. Active dry yeast is easier to find. I have no problem with active dry yeast; its convenience outweighs any drawbacks. Fresh yeast lasts only a few weeks in the refrigerator and gets slimy when frozen. However, the flavor of fresh brewer's yeast is superior, I think, so if you can find it, use it. Most of the recipes in this book use a single envelope of active dry yeast, .25 ounce or 7 grams.

It is best to avoid letting the salt and sugar of a yeasted recipe come into contact with the yeast early on, which can inhibit its development. Give the yeast a chance to grow and bubble a little first. And remember that yeast grows best at 90°F to 140°F. Cooler is too cold for it to grow and hotter will kill it. It is best to stay under 120°F, to be safe.

A convenient way to mix a recipe is to add yeast and warm liquid to the bottom of the bowl, cover them with some flour, and then add the other ingredients, including the salt and sugar, resting them on top of the flour. Let this sit for 15 minutes and cracks will form in the surface of the flour. This means the yeast is starting to "work." From there you can start mixing.

BRIOCHE "TOQUE" WITH DRIED CHERRIES AND ORANGE ZEST

This is a novelty bread—essentially my standard brioche, but in a whimsical shape. You may not want to go to the trouble if you're just making brioche for yourself, but if you're entertaining, or you want to amuse the kids, or if you just want to make things a little more festive, this adds some excitement. I bake it in a coffee can, which is almost always available, but if you have a cylindrical terrine mold, that works beautifully, too. In this recipe the brioche rises above the top of the can and bulges out like a floppy, old-fashioned chef's toque. Not that brioche needs enhancing, but in the style of lavish holiday breads like kugelhopf and panettone, I add some dried cherries and candied orange rind. Anything you add to brioche should be dry, since liquid or fresh fruit is too heavy and would collapse the dough's structure. Dried fruits like golden raisins or chopped prunes or apricots, nuts, candied ginger, and citrus zest are all delightful ways to dress up the bread. For additional crunch and sweetness, I like to sprinkle the top of the toque with pearl sugar, those puffed sugar balls that are often put on panettone or other sweet Italian breads and pastries (see Sources, page 275).

MAKES 1 LOAF TO SERVE 8

SPECIAL EQUIPMENT: ZESTER, RIMMED 11-BY-17-INCH BAKING SHEET, 1-POUND METAL COFFEE CAN, ELECTRIC MIXER FITTED WITH A DOUGH HOOK, PASTRY BRUSH

1 cup sliced blanched almonds (3 ounces, 85 grams)

3 tablespoons whole milk (1.6 ounces, 45.4 grams)

2 teaspoons (1 envelope) active dry yeast (.25 ounce, 7 grams)

2¼ cups all-purpose flour (10 ounces, 283 grams), plus additional for board

5 large eggs (8.5 ounces, 241 grams), at room temperature

1½ tablespoons sugar (.66 ounce, 18.75 grams)

½ teaspoon ground cinnamon (2.5 grams)

6 tablespoons cold unsalted low-moisture butter (3 ounces, 85 grams), preferably containing at least 82 percent butterfat, such as Beurre Échiré or Plugra (3 ounces, 85 grams), cut into ¼-inch slices (see Sources, page 275), plus additional for the pan

1 cup dried sour cherries (see Sources, page 275) (6 ounces, 170 grams)

Grated zest of 1 orange

1. Position a rack in the center of the oven and preheat to 350°F. Spread the almonds in a single layer on a rimmed 11-by-17-inch baking sheet and toast them on the center rack in the oven, tossing once, until they are fragrant and golden brown, about 6 minutes. Transfer to a plate to cool. Turn off the oven.

2. Use a can opener to remove the top and bottom from a 1-pound metal coffee can, and brush the inside with softened butter or use a nonstick spray. Line a baking sheet with parchment paper and place the can on end on the baking sheet.

3. Heat the milk in a microwave or in a small pan until it is just warm to the touch. Place the yeast in the bowl of an electric mixer fitted with the dough hook and add the milk. Mix briefly to combine. Mound the flour over the milk and yeast and let set for 15 minutes.

4. In a bowl, whisk together 4 of the eggs with the sugar and the cinnamon. Add this to the flour and mix on low speed, turning the mixer on and off so you don't overmix, until combined.

5. Run the mixer on medium speed, occasionally stopping the mixer to scrape down the bowl and dough hook, until the dough comes together and begins to pull away from the sides of the bowl, about 20 minutes.

6. With the mixer still running, add the butter and continue to mix until the butter is incorporated and the dough is shiny, but not wet. (If you overmix, the dough may become wet and greasy—if this happens, add 1 tablespoon of flour and mix for an additional 30 seconds.) Add the almonds, cherries, and orange zest and mix to incorporate.

7. Dust a clean bowl with flour, place the dough in the bowl, and cover tightly with plastic wrap. Let sit in a warm place until the dough begins to rise, 45 minutes to 1 hour (it should expand by at least 20 percent). Freeze the dough for 1 hour or refrigerate overnight.

8. Turn the dough onto a floured surface. Flour your hands and roll the dough into a ball. Place the ball inside the coffee can. Place the can on end on the baking sheet in a warm, draft-free, humid environment. (For example, microwave a small bowl of water, then place the brioche in the microwave and close the door, or place the brioche in a closed oven with a shallow pan of warm water—the environment

Recipe continues

should not exceed 140°F. Remove the dough before preheating the oven.) Let sit until the dough has risen and extended beyond the top of the coffee can, 1 to 2 hours.

9. Meanwhile, position a single rack as low as possible in the oven, and remove the other racks. Preheat the oven to 350°F. In a bowl, whisk the remaining egg. Use a pastry brush to gently paint the top of the dough with this egg wash. Bake on the center rack for 45 minutes, until the top of the brioche is golden brown. Loosen any attached dough with a paring knife by running the knife around the sides of the can, and let it cool on a wire rack for at least 1 hour. Serve warm or at room temperature. (Store any leftovers in a bread box or bread bag, or wrapped in a clean dishcloth at room temperature for up to 2 days).

ALMOND BOSTOCK

Bostock, an indulgent French use for leftover brioche, is a good way to use your newly minted brioche-making skills. The recipe transforms plain brioche into something between a great breakfast and a spectacular dessert—a showstopper on any menu. Slices of syrup-soaked bread spread with almond cream are baked until they develop a wonderfully crusty surface that crackles beneath your fork to reveal a creamy, fragrant center.

The almond flavor comes from orgeat, a syrup used in Italian bars and cafés, where it is poured over ice or mixed with soda water to make a refreshing almond-flavored soft drink. Orgeat has a wonderfully natural almond flavor that enhances the subtle taste of almond flour. If you can't find orgeat, use orange flower water or rose water.

MAKES 8 TO 10 SLICES

SPECIAL EQUIPMENT: RIMMED 11-BY-17-INCH BAKING SHEET, PASTRY BRUSH, OFFSET SPATULA

8 tablespoons (1 stick) unsalted butter, softened (4 ounces, 113 grams), plus additional for the baking sheet

1 cup sugar (7 ounces, 198 grams)

2 large eggs (3.4 ounces, 96 grams), at room temperature

1 cup almond flour (see Sources, page 275) or finely ground blanched almonds (3.7 ounces, 107 grams)

2 tablespoons orgeat (almond) syrup (1.5 ounces, 42.5 grams) or orange flower water or rose water (orange flower water and rose water: .35 ounce, 10 grams) (see Sources, page 275)

1 (9-inch) loaf day-old brioche (use store-bought or follow recipe on page 32), sliced ½ inch thick

⅔ cup sliced blanched almonds (2 ounces, 57 grams)

1. Position a rack in the center of the oven. Butter a rimmed 11-by-17-inch baking sheet. To make the almond cream, in the bowl of an electric mixer fitted with the paddle attachment, cream the butter with 1/2 cup of the sugar. Beat in the eggs one at a time, and then the almond flour or ground almonds. Beat for a minute to lighten the texture.

2. To make the almond (or orange flower water or rose water) syrup, combine the remaining 1/2 cup sugar with 1/2 cup water in a small saucepan and bring to a boil, stirring until the sugar has dissolved. Take the pan off the heat and add the orgeat or orange flower water or rose water.

Recipe continues

Almond Bostock.

3. Preheat the oven to 350°F. Arrange the brioche slices on the baking sheet and brush them generously with the almond syrup. Use an offset spatula to spread about 3 tablespoons of almond cream onto each slice of brioche, mounding it slightly in the center. Sprinkle 2 teaspoons of sliced almonds over each slice.

4. Bake on the center rack until a golden brown crust forms on top, about 30 minutes. Serve warm.

Orange Flower–Scented Kugelhopf.

ORANGE FLOWER–SCENTED KUGELHOPF

Simply put, kugelhopf is a spectacular display of your baking prowess. It's so round and big—you get major points if you take this on. It's also delicious, like a brioche, but studded with raisins and almonds. Native to Germany, Austria, and Alsace, the cake is made in a special kugelhopf mold, though a Bundt or an angel food cake pan works just as well. It is usually adorned with a sprinkle of sugar, but I soak mine in an orange flower syrup to moisten it and imbue it with fragrant sweetness.

Chef's Note Orange flower water, sometimes called Neroli, is one of many essential oils used in baking and cooking, mostly in southern France and the Mediterranean. Made from the flowers of the bitter orange tree, it can be used in scones, marshmallows, or flavored breads such as in this recipe. Bergamot and rose water are two other essential oils that work well in baking. Use them sparingly, almost imperceptibly, for best results, and use only the highest quality sources such as Mandy Aftel of Aftelier. She has high-quality, food-safe essences of scented geranium, pepper, violet, and grapefruit oil (see Sources, page 275).

MAKES 1 LOAF TO SERVE 8 TO 10

SPECIAL EQUIPMENT: ELECTRIC MIXER FITTED WITH THE DOUGH HOOK, KUGELHOPF MOLD
(OR A BUNDT OR ANGEL FOOD PAN)

1 cup raisins (5.1 ounces, 144 grams)

Dark rum, such as Myers's, for covering

½ cup plus 2 tablespoons whole milk (5.3 ounces, 151.25 grams)

2 envelopes dry active yeast (.5 ounce, 14 grams)

3½ cups all-purpose flour (15.75 ounces, 455 grams)

¼ cup plus 1 tablespoon sugar (2.2 ounces, 62.5 grams)

½ teaspoon salt (2.5 grams)

2 large eggs (3.4 ounces, 96 grams), at room temperature

1 large egg yolk (.6 ounce, 18.6 grams)

8 tablespoons (1 stick) unsalted butter, softened (4 ounces, 113 grams)

ORANGE SYRUP

1¼ cups granulated sugar (8.75 ounces, 250 grams)

1 cup confectioners' sugar (4 ounces, 113 grams)

1 teaspoon orange flower water (see Sources, page 275) (3.3 grams)

Recipe continues

FOR THE DOUGH

1. The night before preparing the kugelhopf, boil 2 cups water and pour over the raisins. Allow to soak for 5 minutes, then drain. Cover the raisins with good, dark rum and soak overnight.

2. In a small saucepan heat the milk until very warm to the touch; let cool for 30 seconds. Add the yeast to the bowl of an electric mixer fitted with the dough hook. Pour in the warm milk. Cover the yeast mixture completely with the flour, then add the sugar and salt and allow to rest, without stirring, for 15 minutes in a warm (85°F) place to activate the yeast. It is important to cover the yeast with flour so it does not come into direct contact with the sugar or salt yet.

3. Mixing the dough on slow speed, add the whole eggs and yolk. Mix until the dough becomes shiny and pulls away from the sides of the bowl, about 15 minutes. The dough must develop sufficient elasticity to incorporate the butter.

4. Add the butter, mixing on medium speed until fully incorporated. Strain the raisins, place them on a towel to dry, and add them to the dough. Mix until combined, but do not overmix or the raisins will break down and turn the dough blue.

5. Remove the dough from the bowl, cover with plastic wrap, and put into the freezer for 15 minutes to slow the yeast down.

6. Transfer the dough from the freezer to a floured work surface. Push out the air from the dough, turning it over frequently so it doesn't stick to the table. Transfer the dough to a bowl, cover with plastic wrap, and allow to rise in a warm place (95 to 110°F) for 1 to 2 hours, or until doubled in volume.

7. When the dough has doubled in volume, transfer it to a floured surface and push out the air again. Roll it into a ball by flouring your hands and shaping the dough in a clockwise motion, smoothing the surface as you go.

8. Shape the dough into a ring and place it in a well-buttered 2-quart kugelhopf mold (or a Bundt or angel food pan). Press the two ends of the ring together in the pan. Cover with plastic wrap to prevent the dough from drying out, and allow it to rise again in a warm place until doubled, about 45 minutes.

9. Position a rack in the middle of the oven and preheat to 375°F. Bake the kugelhopf for 60 minutes, or until the top is fully browned and sounds hollow when tapped on the bottom.

FOR THE SYRUP

1. In a small saucepan combine the sugars, 1 cup water, and the orange flower water and boil until the sugars have dissolved.

2. Remove the loaf from the oven, turn it out of the mold onto a rack set over an 11-by-17-inch baking sheet to catch any syrupy drips, and very slowly pour the warm syrup over the kugelhopf immediately while it is still warm.

PICK-ME-UPS

While fancy layer cakes and elaborately arranged tarts can be impressive, there's something to be said for the unassuming cookie—a bite-size treat that you can just pop in your mouth when you're craving a little something. They are satisfyingly attractive and utterly charming without being fussy. They also look so elegant in their own right that they require little or no decoration to make a dramatic appearance at a special occasion. A carefully arranged platter of Chocolate Peanut Crinkles (page 59), Mini-Muffin Financiers (page 78), Rosemary-Scented Date-Nut Bars (page 71), or Pepper and Spice Dark Chocolate Cookies (page 53) would be a wonderful way to please a variety of palates and showcase your versatile baking abilities at a dinner party. What's more, they can be baked and arranged hours before your guests arrive with no last minute finishing touches required.

These are also great desserts to serve at a party because even if everyone's too full at the end of the meal to eat a rich dessert, they won't pass up a taste of something sweet with their coffee or tea, perhaps accompanied by some fresh fruit.

Besides serving these nibbles at parties, you can also use them as great gifts or even wedding favors. Simply place some in a cellophane bag, tie with a nice ribbon, and you're set to go. People will be impressed, particularly with treats like Extra-Bittersweet Chocolate Brownies (page 65) and Blood Orange Squares (page 73) and will appreciate the effort and care you put into their gift.

These desserts are appealing not only because of their size but also because of their flavors. Since they're so small, they have to deliver a lot of intensity and satisfaction in a tiny package. I use unusual and robust ingredients like essential oils, black sesame seeds, and pink peppercorns to add unexpectedly delightful nuances. Even many of the more familiar-seeming recipes are not the childhood sweets they appear. Marshmallows gain sophistication from fragrant drops of rose water; chocolate wafer cookies pack a zing from chile powder; and chocolate chip cookies get an elegant makeover from the addition of suave hazelnut butter.

A final note on these recipes: They are all fairly easy to make in advance, with the exception of a few of the more cakelike treats such as the madeleines and financiers. (Even with those, you can prepare the batters ahead and bake them at the last minute, or at most a few hours ahead.) Candies will keep well when stored in a tin, and many cookies grow better with age as long as they are stored properly in a container with a tight-fitting lid. It is also extremely convenient to make a batch of cookie dough, form it into a log, and store it in the freezer. That way, when you're rushing, you can simply slice the log and have fresh cookies in no time.

CHOCOLATE CHUNK
COOKIES WITH NUTELLA

This is my homage to David Leiderman and the amazing company he founded (but no longer owns), David's Cookies. It was a wonderful concept. Lured in from the street by the scent of baking, you were greeted by the sight of warm, gooey chocolate chip cookies coming off a conveyor belt directly from the oven. Eating those cookies was a religious experience for me and has shaped my idea of what the perfect chocolate chip cookie should be—crisp around the edges, soft and buttery in the center, and suffused with large chocolate chunks and a butterscotch flavor from the combination of brown sugar and vanilla.

My recipe, however, has a secret ingredient that I don't think David used in his cookies (though I'm not sure, he might have at one time). I add a little bit of natural Nutella or hazelnut paste to the dough. It helps keep the cookies chewy and flexible, and also gives an overall subtle nutty taste. If you want to add chopped nuts for more flavor and for texture, don't be too cautious about mixing different varieties; I think nuts, in general, all go well together.

Chef's Note Of course, eating these cookies right out of the oven is the best, but they'll hold for 3 to 4 days, well wrapped, because of the moisture in the Nutella or hazelnut paste. If you like a chewier cookie, underbake them a little. If you like crisp, then bake away!

MAKES 4 DOZEN (2½-INCH) COOKIES

SPECIAL EQUIPMENT: 2 RIMMED 11-BY-17-INCH BAKING SHEETS, SIFTER, ELECTRIC MIXER

2⅓ cups all-purpose flour (10 ounces, 283 grams)

1 teaspoon baking soda (5 grams)

1 teaspoon salt (5 grams)

8 tablespoons (1 stick) unsalted butter (4 ounces, 113 grams)

1 cup granulated sugar (7 ounces, 198 grams)

½ cup packed light brown sugar (4 ounces, 113 grams)

¼ cup unsweetened Nutella or hazelnut paste (see Sources, page 275) (1.75 ounces, 50 grams)

2 large eggs (3.4 ounces, 96 grams), at room temperature

1 vanilla bean, split lengthwise and seeds scraped and reserved, or 1 teaspoon vanilla extract (4 grams)

12 ounces bittersweet chocolate (preferably 60 to 66 percent cacao content), coarsely chopped into ¼-inch pieces or larger (3 cups, 340 grams)

½ cup coarsely chopped nuts, such as walnuts, pecans, or hazelnuts, optional (2 ounces, 57 grams)

Recipe continues

1. Position the oven racks in the top and bottom third of the oven and preheat to 375°F. Line two rimmed 11-by-17-inch baking sheets with parchment paper or nonstick liners.

2. Sift the flour, baking soda, and salt onto a piece of parchment or waxed paper and set aside.

3. In the bowl of an electric mixer fitted with the paddle attachment, cream the butter and sugars. Add the Nutella or hazelnut paste and beat until smooth. Beat in the eggs one at a time, and the vanilla bean seeds or vanilla extract, scraping down the bowl as needed.

4. Gradually add the flour mixture to the butter mixture and combine at low speed until the dough comes together. Stir in the chocolate pieces and, if desired, the nuts. Drop heaping tablespoons of the dough 2 inches apart onto the prepared cookie sheets, flattening them slightly by hand. At this point the raw cookies can be frozen, well wrapped, for up to a month.

5. Bake, turning the sheets from back to front and switching them between the top rack and the bottom halfway through, until lightly browned, 8 to 10 minutes. Cool the cookie sheets on wire racks before removing the cookies with a spatula. Store in an airtight tin for up to 1 week.

FLAT AND CHEWY CHOCOLATE CHIP COOKIES

I know, I know. I just said that the previous recipe makes the best chocolate chip cookies ever. And to my taste, it does. But that doesn't negate the deliciousness of this recipe one bit. It's perfect for chocolate chip cookie purists who don't want anything like nut paste interfering with their enjoyment. Thin, chewy, and redolent of that traditional trinity—brown sugar, butter, and vanilla—these cookies are the original, and for many people the best, vehicle for big chunks of melted chocolate. Chopped walnuts are optional here. (See photograph on page 46.)

MAKES ABOUT 8 DOZEN SMALL (1½- TO 2-INCH) COOKIES
SPECIAL EQUIPMENT: 2 RIMMED 11-BY-17-INCH BAKING SHEETS, ELECTRIC MIXER

2 cups all-purpose flour (8.5 ounces, 242 grams)

2 teaspoons salt (10 grams)

1¼ teaspoons baking soda (6.25 grams)

½ pound (2 sticks) unsalted butter (8 ounces, 227 grams), plus additional for the baking sheets

1½ cups packed light brown sugar (12 ounces, 339 grams)

¼ cup granulated sugar (1.75 ounces, 50 grams)

2 large eggs (3.4 ounces, 96 grams), at room temperature

1 tablespoon vanilla extract (12 grams)

14 ounces bittersweet chocolate (preferably 60 to 66 percent cacao content), coarsely chopped (about 2 cups, 400 grams), or Nestlé chocolate chips

2 cups walnuts, coarsely chopped, optional (5.7 ounces, 168 grams)

1. Grease two rimmed 11-by-17-inch baking sheets.

2. In a medium bowl, combine the flour, salt, and baking soda. Set aside.

3. In the bowl of an electric mixer fitted with the paddle attachment, cream together the butter and sugars at medium speed until light and fluffy, about 3 minutes. Add the eggs one at a time, and continue to mix until incorporated. Beat in the vanilla.

4. Add the flour mixture to the butter mixture, mixing in a little at a time, until combined. Using a rubber spatula or wooden spoon, fold in the chocolate, and the walnuts, if using.

5. Cover the bowl with plastic wrap and refrigerate for 1 hour.

Recipe continues

6. When ready to bake, position the oven racks in the top and bottom thirds of the oven and preheat to 350°F.

7. Scoop out 1 tablespoon of dough and roll into a ball. Transfer to one of the prepared baking sheets. Repeat with the remaining dough, placing the cookies about 1 1/2 inches apart. (If you run out of space on the sheets, you may need to bake the cookies in batches.) Bake the cookies, turning the baking sheets from back to front and switching them between the top rack and the bottom halfway through, until golden brown, 8 to 10 minutes. Let cool until the cookies are slightly firm, about 5 minutes, then use a metal spatula to transfer the cookies to wire racks to cool completely. Store in an airtight tin for up to 1 week.

CHOCOLATE CHIPS: MELTED OR NOT?

You will notice two different looking cookies from the same recipe in the photograph on page 46. The cookies on the left were made with a premium chocolate, chopped by hand. The ones on the right were made with chocolate chips. Premium chocolate has more cacao, which melts easily. Chocolate chips such as Nestlé Toll House Morsels contain stabilizers, which prevent them from melting.

PEPPER AND SPICE DARK CHOCOLATE COOKIES

Fiery black pepper adds a little heat and brings the chocolate in these cookies back to its origins in Mexico. Historically, chocolate was always mixed with chile peppers and taken as a drink by the Aztecs. And to this day, in the rural areas of South America, cooks still grind cocoa beans with nuts and spices. The natural oils in the cocoa and nuts hold the mixture together in a disk, which is then scraped and shaved in the mornings to make hot cocoa.

This cookie is reminiscent of that sandy, crumbly disk. I keep the texture somewhat coarse by using whole peppercorns and cinnamon sticks and grinding them at the last minute. Then I add lightly crushed pink peppercorns so you get an overall background heat that's enlivened with sharper peppery bursts with a slightly floral, piney note. Refrigerating the dough overnight helps it keep its crumbly texture after baking. It's a pleasant surprise.

MAKES ABOUT 3 DOZEN COOKIES

SPECIAL EQUIPMENT: SPICE GRINDER OR CLEAN ELECTRIC COFFEE GRINDER, MORTAR AND PESTLE, 2 (11-BY-17-INCH) BAKING SHEETS

1 teaspoon black peppercorns (1.66 grams)

1 cinnamon stick

1½ cups all-purpose flour (6.4 ounces, 181.5 grams)

⅔ cup Dutch-processed unsweetened cocoa powder (2 ounces, 57 grams)

1½ teaspoons baking powder (7.35 grams)

1 teaspoon ground allspice (1.25 grams)

¼ teaspoon salt (1.25 grams)

⅛ teaspoon ground ginger (.2 gram)

Pinch of ground mace

Pinch of cayenne pepper

¼ teaspoon pink peppercorns (.33 gram)

12 tablespoons (1½ sticks) unsalted butter, softened (6 ounces, 170 grams)

¾ cup packed light brown sugar (6 ounces, 170 grams)

1 large egg (1.7 ounces, 48 grams), at room temperature

2 teaspoons vanilla extract (8 grams)

Granulated sugar, for sprinkling

1. In an electric spice grinder or clean electric coffee grinder, grind the black peppercorns and cinnamon stick to a medium-fine powder. Sift the ground spices, flour, cocoa powder, baking powder, allspice, salt, ginger, mace, and cayenne onto a piece of parchment or waxed paper and set aside.

Recipe continues

Pepper and Spice Dark Chocolate Cookies.

2. Using a mortar and pestle or the flat side of a knife, crush the pink peppercorns. Place the pink pepper in the bowl of an electric mixer fitted with the paddle attachment, and add the butter and brown sugar. Beat until creamy and smooth, scraping down the sides of the bowl. Beat in the egg and vanilla.

3. Add the spice-flour mixture to the butter mixture and mix on low speed until just combined. Transfer the dough to a piece of plastic wrap and roll it into a 1 1/2-inch-diameter log. Wrap well and refrigerate overnight.

4. The next day, position the oven racks in the top and bottom thirds of the oven and preheat to 375°F. Line two baking sheets with parchment paper or nonstick liners. Using a thin-bladed knife, slice the cookies into 1/4-inch-thick coins and place them on the baking sheets 1/2 inch apart. Sprinkle each cookie with a pinch of granulated sugar. Bake, turning the sheets from back to front and switching them between the top rack and the bottom halfway through, until the cookies are just firm to the touch, about 8 minutes. Allow the cookies to cool on the baking sheets for 5 minutes to firm up, then use a spatula to transfer them to wire racks to cool completely. Store in an airtight container for up to a week.

Double Chocolate Cookies.

DOUBLE CHOCOLATE COOKIES

These are about as rich as a cookie can get without turning into a brownie. But with the textural contrast of their sweet, crisp-crackling exterior dissolving into bittersweet puddles when you bite in, I like them even better than brownies. My secret is using two chocolates: dark and milk. Melted high-quality dark chocolate is added to the dough in place of cocoa powder, giving the cookie a truer chocolate flavor. Chopped milk chocolate is then added, intensifying the whole chocolate experience. When cool, they look like a cookie should, but take a taste and you'll think you're sinking your teeth into a molten chocolate soufflé. But trust me, these tasty treats are a lot easier than making a soufflé (and they travel better, too)!

MAKES 40 COOKIES
SPECIAL EQUIPMENT: SIFTER, ELECTRIC MIXER WITH PADDLE ATTACHMENT,
2 (11-BY-17-INCH) BAKING SHEETS

⅔ cup cake flour (2 ounces, 60 grams)

1 teaspoon baking powder

¼ teaspoon salt

1½ cups sugar (12 ounces, 336 grams)

4 tablespoons (½ stick) unsalted butter (2 ounces, 60 grams)

4 large eggs (8 ounces, 220 grams), at room temperature

1 teaspoon vanilla extract

4 cups chopped dark (70 to 72%) chocolate (1 pound, 464 grams), melted and still warm

3½ cups chopped milk (50 to 55%) chocolate (14 ounces, 400 grams)

1. Sift together the flour, baking powder, and salt into a small bowl. In the bowl of an electric mixer using the paddle attachment, cream the sugar and butter. Add the eggs one at time and the vanilla and continue to beat at medium speed until combined.

2. Scrape down the sides of the bowl and add the flour mixture, beating to combine. Mix in the melted chocolate until combined and stir in the chopped milk chocolate.

3. When you are ready to bake the cookies, preheat the oven to 350° F. Lightly grease two baking sheets with butter or line with parchment paper. Using two tablespoons, drop the dough onto the pans with 12 cookies per pan, 2 inches apart. Bake for 10 to 12 minutes, until the tops of the cookies are glossy and cracked. Cool the cookies on the pan for 5 minutes, then transfer to wire racks to cool completely before serving. Store the cookies in an airtight container. They are best right out of the oven, but will last for a day or two.

Chocolate Peanut Crinkles.

CHOCOLATE PEANUT CRINKLES

These profoundly chocolaty, chewy cookies are not to be missed. With their white, crackled, confectioners' sugar coating, they resemble the ordinary kind of chocolate crinkle cookies you might see on buffets at Christmas. But the similarity stops there. With a soft, fudgy interior and a brittle-sugar coating, they gently crunch before immediately melting on the tongue like soft chocolate ganache. If you don't have peanuts, feel free to use whatever baking-appropriate nuts you have on hand—hazelnuts, walnuts, pecans, or almonds would work just as well in this recipe. Serve these cookies within 2 days of baking, preferably with a glass of cold milk or cup of hot tea. You will most certainly be worshipped.

MAKES ABOUT 3 DOZEN (1¾-INCH) COOKIES

SPECIAL EQUIPMENT: FOOD PROCESSOR FITTED WITH THE BLADE ATTACHMENT, ELECTRIC MIXER FITTED WITH THE PADDLE ATTACHMENT, 2 (11-BY-17-INCH) BAKING SHEETS

⅔ cup toasted, skinned unsalted peanuts (1.9 ounces, 56 grams)

2 tablespoons granulated sugar (.87 ounce, 25 grams)

6 ounces bittersweet chocolate (preferably 60 to 66 percent cacao content), chopped (about 1 cup, 170 grams)

2¾ cups all-purpose flour (12.4 ounces, 357.5 grams)

2 tablespoons Dutch-processed unsweetened cocoa powder (.4 ounce, 11.5 grams)

2 teaspoons baking soda (10 grams)

¾ teaspoon salt (3.75 grams)

1½ cups light brown sugar (12 ounces, 342 grams)

8 tablespoons (1 stick) unsalted butter, softened (4 ounces, 112 grams), plus additional for the pan

2 large eggs (3.4 ounces, 96.5 grams), at room temperature

¼ cup whole milk (2.1 ounces, 60 grams)

1 teaspoon vanilla extract (4 grams)

¾ cup confectioners' sugar (3 ounces, 85.5 grams)

1. In the bowl of a food processor fitted with the blade attachment, finely chop the nuts with the granulated sugar. In the top of a double boiler or in a bowl set over (not in) a pot of simmering water, melt the chocolate.

2. In a large bowl, sift together the flour, cocoa powder, baking soda, and salt. In the bowl of an electric mixer fitted with the paddle attachment, cream the brown sugar and butter until light and fluffy. Add the eggs one at a time, until incorporated. Beat in the melted chocolate, stopping the mixer to scrape down the sides before beating again. Mix in the milk and vanilla. Mix in the flour mixture in three additions. Fold in the nuts.

Recipe continues

3. Form the dough into a ball and cover tightly with plastic wrap. Refrigerate the dough for 3 hours or overnight.

4. When you are ready to bake the cookies, preheat the oven to 350° F. Grease two 11-by-17-inch baking sheets with the unsalted butter. Place the confectioners' sugar in a wide, shallow bowl. Scoop out a heaping tablespoon of dough and roll into a ball. Coat generously with sugar and transfer to a baking sheet. Repeat with the remaining dough and sugar.

5. Bake the cookies, turning the baking sheets from back to front and switching them between the top rack and the bottom halfway through, until cracked but not completely firm, 12 to 15 minutes. Let cool on the baking sheet so they can firm up a bit, about 2 minutes, then use a spatula to transfer to a wire rack to cool. These can be stored in an airtight container for up to 2 days.

GINGER MOLASSES COOKIES

These chewy, triple ginger cookies are my twist on the traditional holiday favorite gingersnap, but with a moist rather than crisp crumb. Of course, ginger and spice should not be a flavor combo reserved only for the month of December. In fact, I love to make them up whenever I'm feeling a little run down. That burst of ginger is a head-clearing boost, perfect for the end of a heavy meal or sluggish afternoon. They are a true pick-me-up in cookie form.

MAKES 40 COOKIES

SPECIAL EQUIPMENT: ELECTRIC MIXER, RUBBER SPATULA, RIMMED BAKING SHEET

2½ cups all-purpose flour (12 ounces, 340 grams)

1 teaspoon baking soda (.25 ounce, 5 grams)

¾ teaspoon ground ginger

¾ teaspoon ground cinnamon

¾ teaspoon ground cloves

¾ teaspoon salt

½ pound (2 sticks) unsalted butter, at room temperature (8 ounces, 226 grams)

2 cups dark brown sugar, packed (8 ounces, 226 grams)

1 large egg (1.75 ounces, 50 grams)

¼ cup molasses (2.5 ounces, 70 grams)

1 tablespoon plus 1 1/2 teaspoons fresh ginger, grated (1 ounce, 28 grams)

¾ cup chopped candied ginger (4 ounces, 120 grams), plus additional for garnish if desired

Turbinado or granulated sugar, for rolling

1. In a medium bowl, sift together the flour, baking soda, ground ginger, cinnamon, cloves, and salt. In the bowl of an electric mixer using the paddle attachment, cream together the butter and sugar until light and fluffy. Scrape down the sides of the bowl, then add the egg, molasses, and fresh and candied ginger and beat to combine.

2. Add the flour mixture all at once, and beat on low speed until the dry ingredients are just incorporated. Using a rubber spatula, fold in the ginger pieces.

3. Wrap the dough in plastic and chill for at least 1 hour and up to overnight.

Recipe continues

4. Preheat the oven to 350° F. Place the turbinado sugar in a shallow bowl. Roll the dough into 1-inch balls and coat them in the sugar. Place the balls on a rimmed baking sheet 1 inch apart. If you like, sprinkle the tops of the cookies with more candied ginger. Bake for 12 to 15 minutes until the cookies are just set (they will still be a little soft). Transfer the cookies to a wire rack to cool. Store in an airtight container.

Ginger Molasses Cookies, ready to go into the oven.

Ginger Molasses Cookies.

Extra-Bittersweet Chocolate Brownies.

EXTRA-BITTERSWEET CHOCOLATE BROWNIES

Here are the fudgy brownies that will be stiff competition for the Intense Chocolate Pound Cake with Dark Chocolate Glaze on page 149 at that buffet table. This is a great recipe that's simple enough to memorize, just in case you decide to whip them up on the fly at a friend's house. The key to this recipe is to underbake the brownies. You don't necessarily want to see the batter ripple like a custard when you wiggle the pan, but when you insert a cake tester, it should come out with moist brownie crumbs clinging to it (just as long as it's not slick and very wet). What makes these brownies special is the ratio of flour to chocolate. Little flour, lots of chocolate. There's just enough flour to hold the brownie together without a hint of cakiness. Wrapped and frozen they last a month. 10 to 20 seconds in the microwave will bring them back to life.

MAKES 24 (2-BY-2-INCH) BROWNIES TO SERVE 12 TO 24
SPECIAL EQUIPMENT: 9-BY-13-INCH BAKING PAN, SIFTER, DOUBLE BOILER, ELECTRIC MIXER, CAKE TESTER

½ cup all-purpose flour (2.25 ounces, 65 grams)

½ teaspoon salt (2.5 grams)

7 ounces bittersweet chocolate (preferably 60 to 66 percent cacao content), coarsely chopped (1¼ cups, 196 grams)

14 tablespoons unsalted butter (7 ounces, 198 grams), plus additional for the pan

4 large eggs (6.8 ounces, 193 grams), at room temperature

1 cup sugar (7 ounces, 198 grams)

2 cups coarsely chopped toasted walnuts, optional (8 ounces, 227 grams)

1. Position a rack in the center of the oven. Butter a 9-by-13-inch baking pan.

2. Sift the flour and salt onto a piece of parchment or waxed paper and set aside.

3. In a double boiler set over steaming but not boiling water, melt the chocolate with the butter. (Alternatively, use a microwave at 50 percent power and stir every 10 seconds.)

4. In the bowl of an electric mixer fitted with the whisk attachment, beat the eggs and sugar at high speed until light colored and mousselike, 6 to 8 minutes. It will have tripled in volume.

Recipe continues

5. Preheat the oven to 350°F. Scrape the chocolate-butter mixture into the egg mixture and mix on low speed until incorporated. Sprinkle the flour mixture over the batter and fold in using a rubber spatula, adding the walnuts halfway through folding, if using.

6. Scrape the batter into the pan, level the top with the spatula, and bake on the center rack until just set in the center, about 25 minutes—a cake tester inserted into the middle will emerge with moist crumbs clinging to it. (For even fudgier brownies, take the pan out when the batter is still molten, like custard, in the center, about 20 minutes.) Let cool in the pan and cut into squares.

PECAN TOFFEE BARS

These indulgent treats are like mini pecan pies in bar form. The crisp, buttery short-bread crust holds a gooey filling that, once baked, sets into toffee, helping the bars keep their shape during transport.

This recipe is a good opportunity to use molasses, which is a classically American ingredient—one of those things American desserts can be proud of. Molasses is unfiltered, unrefined sugar cane extract and brings with it a full range of fruity flavors.

Although toasting nuts before baking with them is a common practice for bringing out their flavor, you might notice that we don't call for toasting the pecans here. The reason is that they'll actually toast while the bars bake.

MAKES 4 DOZEN (1½-INCH) BARS
SPECIAL EQUIPMENT: 9-BY-13-INCH BAKING PAN, PASTRY CUTTER

SHORTBREAD CRUST

3 cups all-purpose flour (13.5 ounces, 390 grams), plus additional for rolling

¾ pound (3 sticks) unsalted butter, chilled and cut into cubes (12 ounces, 340 grams), plus additional for the pan

½ cup sugar (3.5 ounces, 99 grams)

¾ teaspoon salt (3.75 grams)

PECAN FILLING

1½ cups sugar (10.5 ounces, 300 grams)

1 cup dark corn syrup (11.5 ounces, 328 grams)

½ cup molasses (5.6 ounces, 161 grams)

4 large eggs (6.8 ounces, 193 grams), at room temperature

3 tablespoons unsalted butter, melted (1.5 ounces, 42.6 grams)

1 teaspoon vanilla extract (4 grams)

Pinch of salt

2½ cups pecans (12.5 ounces, 355 grams)

FOR THE CRUST

1. Position a rack in the center of the oven and preheat to 350°F. Grease a 9-by-13-inch baking pan. In a medium bowl, using a fork or pastry cutter, combine the flour, butter, sugar, and salt until the mixture resembles coarse crumbs.

2. Press the dough into a ball, gathering up all the crumbles. On a floured surface, roll out the dough to a 9-by-13-inch rectangle about 1/8 inch thick. Press it into the bottom of the baking pan, pushing the dough out to the edges of the pan (but

Recipe continues

Pecan Toffee Bars.

not up the sides of the pan). Prick the dough all over with a fork and cover with aluminum foil, pressing the foil down into the corners. Bake on the center rack until it has become slightly golden when you lift up the foil, about 30 minutes. Transfer to a wire rack to fill, leaving the oven on.

FOR THE FILLING
In a large bowl, mix together the sugar, corn syrup, molasses, eggs, butter, vanilla, and salt. Stir in the pecans to combine. Spread the filling evenly over the hot crust.

TO BAKE AND SERVE
Return the pan to the oven and bake on the center rack until the mixture is set and no longer moves to the side when the pan is tilted, about 30 minutes. Transfer the pan to a wire rack to cool, cut into bars, and serve.

Rosemary-Scented Date-Nut Bars.

ROSEMARY-SCENTED DATE-NUT BARS

Shortbread crusts are ideal as a pick-me-up because they are sturdy enough to hold together, but still melt in your mouth when you take a bite. For this sophisticated recipe, I recommend Medjool dates, which are fat, moist, and practically candied in their own sugary juices. The rosemary, a savory herb, tempers the sweetness just enough to please just about everyone.

Chef's Note Dates are a terrific fall-winter ingredient for baking since they hold in moisture and are available when the summer fruits peter out. Medjool dates are the best. They are harvested from September until November but last much longer in the refrigerator, well covered. They have a particular affinity for citrus and make a great salad addition. Orange segments, dates, endive, pecans, and radishes in a light honey dressing = delicious.

MAKES ABOUT 20 (2-INCH) BARS
SPECIAL EQUIPMENT: FOOD PROCESSOR, 9-BY-13-INCH BAKING PAN

SHORTBREAD CRUST

12 tablespoons (1½ sticks) unsalted butter, chilled and cubed (6 ounces, 170 grams)

1½ cups all-purpose flour (6.75 ounces, 19.5 grams)

½ cup confectioners' sugar (2 ounces, 57 grams)

¼ teaspoon salt (1.25 grams)

DATE-NUT FILLING

2 cups pitted Medjool dates coarsely chopped (see Sources, page 275) (about 24 large, 13.4 ounces, 382 grams)

1¼ cups all-purpose flour (5.3 ounces, 151.25 grams)

1½ cups packed light brown sugar (12 ounces, 339 grams)

¼ cup coarsely chopped walnuts (1 ounce, 28 grams)

1 teaspoon finely minced fresh rosemary leaves (about 1 gram)

¼ teaspoon ground cardamom (.3 gram)

½ teaspoon baking powder (2.45 grams)

¼ teaspoon salt (1.25 grams)

4 large eggs, lightly beaten (6.8 ounces, 193 grams), at room temperature

Recipe continues

FOR THE CRUST

Position a rack in the center of the oven and preheat to 350°F. In a food processor, pulse together all the ingredients for the shortbread until it just begins to hold together in large pieces. Turn the dough out into a 9-by-13-inch baking pan and press it into a single layer covering the bottom, but not the sides, of the pan. Smooth the crust with a rubber spatula. Bake on the center rack, rotating the pan halfway through, until golden and firm to the touch, 20 to 25 minutes. Remove from the oven and place on a rack to cool.

FOR THE FILLING

In another bowl, stir together all the filling ingredients except the eggs. Whisk in the eggs until combined. Spread the filling over the baked shortbread.

TO BAKE

Bake on the center rack until the filling is just set, about 20 minutes. Cool in the pan, then cut into bars.

BLOOD ORANGE SQUARES

This is considered a Sicilian version of classic lemon squares. You can find blood oranges in the market in the late fall months. The blood orange lends a beautiful orange-pink color to the curd, and the lime juice tempers the tartness of the orange. I prefer using limes here instead of lemons because they have a mellow edge and blend more harmoniously with the blood oranges.

Though these squares are not quite as sturdy as pound cakes and brownies, you can still cut them into pieces and move them around without much trouble. A handy trick is to bring a little confectioners' sugar with you to sprinkle on before serving. It'll cover up any little nicks or scratches, and it makes a handsome presentation. If you don't have one of those metal sugar shakers for transport, you can pack the sugar in a salt shaker. Just make sure to cover the holes with a piece of tape for the journey.

MAKES 20 (2-BY-2-INCH) SQUARES, ENOUGH FOR 10 TO 20 SERVINGS
SPECIAL EQUIPMENT: ZESTER, FOOD PROCESSOR, 9-BY-13-INCH BAKING PAN

SHORTBREAD CRUST

- 12 tablespoons (1½ sticks) unsalted butter, chilled and cubed (6 ounces, 170 grams)
- 1½ cups all-purpose flour (6.75 ounces, 195 grams)
- ½ cup confectioners' sugar (2 ounces, 57 grams)
- ¼ teaspoon salt (1.25 grams)

BLOOD ORANGE FILLING

- 1½ cups granulated sugar (10.5 ounces, 300 grams)
- 2 tablespoons all-purpose flour (.56 ounce, 16.25 grams)

- ½ teaspoon baking powder (2.45 grams)
- Finely grated zest of 1 lime
- Finely grated zest of 1 blood orange
- Pinch of salt
- 4 large eggs (6.8 ounces, 193 grams), at room temperature
- ⅓ cup freshly squeezed lime juice (2 to 3 limes) (2.9 ounces, 83.3 grams)
- 1 cup freshly squeezed blood orange juice (8 ounces, 225 grams)

FOR THE CRUST

Position a rack in the center of the oven and preheat to 350°F. In a food processor, pulse together all the ingredients for the shortbread until the mixture just begins to hold together in large pieces. Turn the dough out into a 9-by-13-inch baking pan and

Recipe continues

press it into a single layer covering the bottom of the pan. Smooth the top with a rubber spatula. Bake on the center rack, rotating the pan halfway through, until golden and firm to the touch, 20 to 25 minutes. Remove from the oven and reserve.

FOR THE FILLING

In a large bowl, whisk together the sugar, flour, baking powder, citrus zests, and salt. In another bowl, whisk together the eggs and citrus juices. Pour the liquid ingredients into the dry ingredients in two additions, whisking until smooth. Spread the filling over the baked shortbread.

TO BAKE

Bake on the center rack until it is just set, about 15 minutes. Cool in the pan, then cut into squares.

Blood Orange Squares.

LINZERTORTE

Linzertorte is a European dessert that Americans recognize and love. It is named for the Austrian city of Linz, where it is believed to have been invented, and most variations include an almond crust and jam filling—usually raspberry jam is favored in this country, though black currant is more common in Austria. I find an all-raspberry filling too sweet, so I prefer to use a combo of sweet raspberry and tart red currant jam, which gives the filling a particularly bright color and flavor. (But you can make it all raspberry if you like, either seedless or with seeds as is your preference. Apricot jam and a citrus marmalade are delicious here as well.) An interesting twist in this recipe is that the dough is made with hard-cooked egg yolk, as in Austria. The yolk makes the texture of the crust extra crumbly and a little moister than usual.

I agonized about putting this recipe in the "I'll Bring Dessert" chapter, but I didn't want people looking for cookies to miss it. This hybrid between a tart and a cookie can be cut into squares and picked up. If you're taking it with you, bring the tart in its pan, and cut just before serving.

MAKES 1 (9-INCH) TART TO SERVE 8 TO 10
SPECIAL EQUIPMENT: FOOD PROCESSOR (IF USING GROUND ALMONDS), SIFTER,
ELECTRIC MIXER, 9-INCH TART PAN WITH REMOVEABLE BOTTOM, ROLLING PIN, BAKING SHEET

ALMOND CRUST

2½ cups all-purpose flour (11.2 ounces, 319 grams), plus additional for rolling

½ cup almond flour or finely ground almonds (1.85 ounces, 53.5 grams)

1½ teaspoons ground cinnamon (7 grams)

1 teaspoon baking powder (5 grams)

¼ teaspoon fleur de sel (see Sources, page 275) (.6 gram)

2 large, hard-cooked eggs (3.4 ounces, 96 grams)

½ pound (2 sticks) unsalted butter (8 ounces, 228 grams), plus additional for the pan

10 tablespoons confectioners' sugar (2.5 ounces, 72 grams)

1 teaspoon dark rum (4.67 grams)

JAM FILLING (see headnote)

½ cup raspberry jam (5.25 ounces, 150 grams)

½ cup red currant jam (5.25 ounces, 150 grams)

1 cup heavy cream, whipped, for serving, optional (8.12 ounces, 232 grams)

FOR THE CRUST

1. Sift the all-purpose flour, almond flour or ground almonds, cinnamon, baking powder, and fleur de sel onto a piece of parchment or waxed paper and set aside.

2. Peel the egg and remove the white and discard. Press the yolk through a sieve into a bowl.

3. In the bowl of an electric mixer fitted with the paddle attachment, cream the butter and confectioners' sugar at medium speed until smooth, about 5 minutes, scraping down the sides occasionally.

4. Add the cooked yolk to the butter mixture, then slowly add the flour mixture and rum until well incorporated, scraping down the sides of the bowl occasionally.

5. Wrap the dough in a piece of plastic film, shape it into a ball, and push it down to form a circle 2 inches high and 8 inches in diameter. Refrigerate for at least 2 hours.

6. Butter a 9-inch tart pan with removeable bottom. Sprinkle flour on a work surface and flour a rolling pin. Remove the dough from the refrigerator and roll the dough out to a 3/16-inch-thick round about 11 inches in diameter. Carefully wrap the dough around the rolling pin and transfer it to the tart pan. If the dough breaks, you can patch it by pressing the pieces back together. Press the dough over the bottom and up the sides of the tart pan. Reserve the scraps and form them into a small ball. Gently roll out to a 3/16-inch-thick rectangle to be used for the top lattice and cut into 8 to 12 strips of equal width. If the strips become too soft to handle, place in the refrigerator for 15 minutes, or until firm.

FOR THE FILLING, ASSEMBLY, AND BAKING

1. If using both raspberry and currant jam, stir them together in a bowl. Spread the jam in the tart shell. Carefully arrange half the dough strips on the tart shell at equal distance from each other; pinch the ends onto the crust. If the strips break during handling, simply piece them together; they will fuse during baking. Refrigerate the tart for 2 hours or overnight.

2. Position a rack in the center of the oven and preheat to 350°F. Place the tart on top of a baking sheet lined with parchment paper. Bake on the center rack until golden brown, about 45 minutes.

3. Transfer to a wire rack to cool slightly before lifting up the tart pan's base through the sides of the pan and either placing it on a serving plate or very gently sliding the tart off the pan's base onto a plate. Serve warm or at room temperature with unsweetened whipped cream, if desired. Once cooled they can be cut into small, bite-sized pieces.

MINI-MUFFIN FINANCIERS

There are probably hundreds of recipes for financiers, and with good reason. These golden, buttery little almond cakes are irresistible! They are also quite easy and satisfying to make. Since they have about a 24-hour life span once baked, it's best to make the batter ahead, up to 7 days, and keep it in a closed container in the fridge; then you can simply bake them whenever you get a craving. They are terrific still warm from the oven. The batter is transportable, so you can bake them to order on site. Using a mini-muffin tin means you don't have to use special financier pans.

MAKES 2 DOZEN (1¼-INCH) CAKES

SPECIAL EQUIPMENT: FOOD PROCESSOR (IF USING GROUND ALMONDS), SIFTER,
ELECTRIC MIXER, TWO 12-CUP MINI MUFFIN TINS, OFFSET SPATULA

8 tablespoons (1 stick) unsalted butter (4 ounces, 113 grams), plus additional for the pan

1 cup confectioners' sugar (4 ounces, 113 grams)

½ cup almond flour (see Sources, page 275) or finely ground blanched almonds (1.85 ounces, 53.5 grams)

6 tablespoons all-purpose flour (1.6 ounces, 45.4 grams)

¼ teaspoon baking powder (1.2 grams)

5 large egg whites, lightly beaten (5 ounces, 142 grams), at room temperature

1 teaspoon full-flavored honey, such as lavender (see Sources, page 275) (.25 ounce, 7 grams)

¼ teaspoon vanilla extract (1 gram)

1 cup raspberries, blueberries, or pieces of dried fruit (7 ounces, 198 grams)

1. In a heavy pan over medium heat, melt the butter and allow it to cook until the milk solids settle and stick to the bottom of the pot and are golden brown and slightly caramelized, about 7 minutes. Let cool.

2. Sift the confectioners' sugar, almond flour or ground almonds, all-purpose flour, and baking powder into the bowl of an electric mixer fitted with the whisk attachment. Mix on low speed, then add the egg whites, honey, and vanilla, and mix on low speed, scraping down the bowl, until combined. Add the melted butter and mix until incorporated. Cover the bowl and refrigerate for at least 2 hours or overnight.

3. When you are ready to bake the financiers, position a rack in the center of the oven and preheat to 400°F. Butter two 12-cup mini muffin tins. Fill the muffin cups about two-thirds full with the batter, and place two raspberries or blueberries, or one piece of dried fruit on each one. Bake on the center rack until golden brown around the edges and firm in the center, about 16 minutes. Let cool in the pans for

5 minutes, then run a thin knife or offset spatula around the sides of the muffin cups or financier molds and turn the financiers out onto wire racks. Serve warm or let cool on the rack and serve later that same day.

Mini-Muffin Financiers with raspberries.

ACACIA HONEY MADELEINES

Madeleines are at their zenith baked to order and served warm. But what's great about this recipe is that you can make the batter up to 3 days in advance, freeze it, and defrost it later. For guests, you could prepare the batter up to 4 hours ahead, pour it into the molds, and hold it in the fridge until it's time to bake them. This recipe is especially fun to use for experiments with all the artisanal honey that is available now, like tupelo, or Tasmanian leatherwood!

MAKES 2 DOZEN (2-INCH) CAKES
SPECIAL EQUIPMENT: 2 MADELEINE MOLD TRAYS, ELECTRIC MIXER,
PASTRY BAG FITTED WITH A PLAIN TIP

MADELEINES

- 2 tablespoons unsalted butter, softened (1 ounce, 28 grams), for greasing the molds
- 1¼ cups all-purpose flour (5.3 ounces, 151.25 grams)
- ½ cup plus 1 tablespoon confectioners' sugar (2.25 ounces, 64.7 grams)
- 1½ teaspoons baking powder (7.35 grams)
- ¼ teaspoon salt (1.25 grams)
- 3 large eggs (5.1 ounces, 145 grams), at room temperature
- ¼ cup acacia honey or other good-quality honey (see Sources, page 275) (3 ounces, 85 grams)

- 8 tablespoons (1 stick) unsalted butter, melted and cooled (4 ounces, 113 grams)
- 2 tablespoons whole milk (1 ounce, 28 grams)

GLAZE

- ½ cup confectioners' sugar (2 ounces, 60 grams)
- 3 tablespoons freshly squeezed lemon juice (1.5 ounces, 40 grams)
- 1 teaspoon honey (.4 ounce, 10 grams)

1. Position a rack in the center of the oven. Butter two madeleine mold trays with the softened butter.

2. In the bowl of an electric mixer fitted with the paddle attachment, briefly combine the flour, confectioners' sugar, baking powder, and salt.

3. Slowly add the eggs and honey, mixing on medium speed until just incorporated. Add melted butter and milk, and mix until the batter is smooth. The batter can be transferred to a container and frozen for up to 3 days at this point. If the batter is frozen, thaw overnight in the refrigerator.

4. Preheat the oven to 350°F. Using a teaspoon, fill the madeleine molds two-thirds of the way up. The filled pans can be loosely covered and refrigerated for up to 4 hours at this point.

5. Bake on the center rack until the madeleines have puffed and are lightly browned, 12 to 14 minutes. Allow them to cool slightly, then unmold.

6. To make the glaze, place the sugar, lemon juice, and honey in a small saucepan and bring to a boil over a medium heat. Brush the warm glaze over the ruffled side of the madeleines and return them to the oven to set the glaze. Serve warm, or allow them to cool, then wrap.

STRAIGHT FROM THE OVEN

It's perhaps the most iconic image of baking there is: A warm apple pie resting on the windowsill, its buttery-brown fragrance wafting through the neighborhood. The recipes in this chapter are meant to evoke just such an instinctual response—that visceral reaction that stems from traditional, homespun American desserts. Of all the recipes in this book inspired by American classics (and there are many), these are perhaps the most nostalgic. Fruit pie, bread pudding, you've seen them all before, and you're always happy to see them again because of their simple, familiar goodness. That's been updated in many cases in this chapter with a modern-day twist.

These are the kind of great-tasting desserts that are at their most delectable straight out of the oven, or at least made and served that same day. With pies, tarts, and cobblers, the butter in the crust is still tender and melts in your mouth, and the heat brings out the flavor and texture of the filling to perfection. Of course, all warm goodies are even better with ice cream or whipped cream spooned over the top to highlight that inimitable contrast between warm fruit, flaky, crisp pastry, and cool, melting cream.

These homey desserts will make you feel truly accomplished when you remove them, bubbling and golden, from the oven. Not even the fanciest garnish or icing can beat the flavor of a warm dessert. This said, you needn't plan your whole day around making them. Many of these recipes, such as the Upside-Down Cranberry-Caramel Cake (page 85) and Chocolate Brioche Pudding (page 87), can be baked several hours or even a day ahead and reheated for five or ten minutes at 350°F. Still others, such as the Individual Maple Apple Tatins (page 103), can be partially prepared in advance, refrigerated, and then baked at the last minute.

But none of the advance preparation will detract from that final moment when your guests bite into something warm, comforting, and delightfully old-fashioned. And if anyone remarks that your dessert reminds them of something their grandmother used to make, you've earned the highest compliment there is.

UPSIDE-DOWN CRANBERRY-CARAMEL CAKE

When you want an easy and quick dessert, upside-down cake is your choice. This recipe riffs on the American classic Pineapple Upside-Down Cake. The cranberries are available year round, and the caramel balances the tartness of the fruit. (See photograph on page 82.)

MAKES 1 (9-INCH ROUND) COBBLER
SPECIAL EQUIPMENT: ONE 9-INCH ROUND CAKE PAN, SIFTER, ELECTRIC MIXER, OFFSET SPATULA

Unsalted butter or cooking spray, for the baking pan

⅔ cup packed light brown sugar (5 ounces, 142 grams)

12 tablespoons (1½ sticks) unsalted butter, melted (6 ounces, 171 grams)

1 tablespoon unsulphured molasses

2 cups all-purpose flour (8.5 ounces, 242 grams)

1 cup sugar (7 ounces, 198 grams)

2 teaspoons baking powder (9 grams)

1 teaspoon salt (5 grams)

3 large eggs (5.1 ounces, 150 grams), at room temperature

1 cup sour cream (8.5 ounces, 242 grams)

2 cups fresh or frozen cranberries (8 ounces, 230 grams)

1. Position a rack in the center of the oven and preheat to 375°F. Grease a 9-inch round cake pan with butter, and cover the bottom with parchment paper cut to size.

2. In a medium saucepan over medium heat, combine the brown sugar with 4 tablespoons of the melted butter, the molasses, and 1/4 cup water. Bring to a boil, stir well, and pour into the prepared cake pan.

3. For the batter, sift the flour, sugar, baking powder, and salt onto a piece of parchment or waxed paper and set aside.

4. In the bowl of an electric mixer fitted with the whisk attachment, beat the eggs and sour cream together at medium speed until well blended. Scrape down the inside of the bowl and pour in the remaining 8 tablespoons (1/2 cup) of melted butter. Beat until the butter is fully absorbed. Add the flour mixture and beat together until smooth.

Recipe continues

5. Add the cranberries to the cake pan, gently pressing the fruit into an even layer with no gaps. Pour the batter on top of the cranberries and smooth with a spatula. Bake on the center rack until golden, 45 minutes. Remove from the oven and let cool in the pan for 15 minutes. While the cake is still warm, run a thin knife or offset spatula around the inside of the pan, then invert over a flat platter, shaking lightly until the cake releases onto the plate. Remove the parchment paper. Best served warm.

Upside-Down Cranberry-Caramel Cake.

CHOCOLATE BRIOCHE PUDDING

Eggy brioche, soaked in creamy custard imbued with intense bittersweet chocolate, is quite possibly the most pleasing vehicle for chocolate there is—especially when you serve it meltingly warm from the oven. Although bread pudding originated as a way for frugal home cooks to use up their leftover stale bread, this refined version is good enough to warrant buying a loaf just for this purpose. Brioche works particularly well because its light, open texture absorbs the maximum amount of custard without becoming too soggy. You could also use challah, though the pudding will be a bit heavier and more compact.

Chef's Note If you're making this in advance, bake it, let it cool completely, and store well wrapped in the refrigerator for up to 5 days. Bring to room temperature for at least 30 minutes (and up to 2 hours) before reheating it. Cover the pan with foil and reheat for 12 to 15 minutes at 350°F before serving. Or reheat single portions for about 5 to 10 minutes at 350°F.

MAKES 1 (9-BY-13-INCH) PUDDING TO SERVE 8
SPECIAL EQUIPMENT: 9-BY-13-INCH BAKING DISH, FINE-MESH SIEVE, LARGE ROASTING PAN

2 cups whole milk (17 ounces, 484 grams)

2 cups heavy cream (16.24 ounces, 464 grams)

1 cup sugar (7 ounces, 198 grams)

8 large eggs (13.6 ounces, 386 grams), at room temperature

12 ounces bittersweet chocolate (preferably 60 to 66 percent cacao content), coarsely chopped (about 2 cups, 340 grams)

About 8 cups day-old brioche or challah, cut into 1-inch cubes (12 ounces, 340 grams)

1. In a medium saucepan over medium-high heat, combine the milk, cream, and sugar. In a large mixing bowl, whisk the eggs together. When the milk mixture has come to a boil, slowly pour a third of it into the eggs, whisking constantly. Pour in the remaining milk mixture and whisk until combined.

2. Add the chopped chocolate, stirring until the chocolate is melted, then strain the mixture through a fine-mesh sieve.

Recipe continues

3. Position a rack in the center of the oven and preheat to 325°F. Spread the brioche cubes out in a greased 9-by-13-inch Pyrex baking dish. Cover with the chocolate custard and allow the brioche to soak for about 30 minutes, or until softened and most of the liquid is absorbed. (It may take longer, depending on how dry the brioche is.) Push the cubes into the mixture occasionally to submerge them.

4. Place the baking dish inside a large roasting pan. Fill the roasting pan one-third full with water, to prevent the custard from overheating.

5. Bake on the center rack for 60 to 70 minutes, or until the custard moves as a single mass without waves or ripples when the pan is jiggled. Let rest for at least 30 minutes before serving.

STONE FRUIT GALETTE

I love the homespun look of an open-faced fruit galette shaped free form right in the pie pan. In the summer, when the market is bursting with fresh plums and other stone fruits, there's nothing more enticing than their plummy, jammy juices barely contained in a golden flaky crust.

You can use a variety of plums in this galette, depending on what you find. I recommend sugar plums, but mirabelle, greengage, Italian prune, Santa Rosa, and damson are equally wonderful. Other stone fruits such as apricots, peaches, nectarines, and cherries can be used instead of, or along with, plums if you want to get creative. Apricots are a particularly fitting substitute (or addition), since they have the same amount of juice as plums and they turn a lovely deep orange color with a dark caramelized top when baked. Always taste your fruit before adding the sugar. If the fruit seems on the tart side and you like a sweet pie, use the greater amount of sugar. But if your fruit is sweet, use the lesser amount.

If you like to fuss as I do, paint the edges of the piecrust with a little heavy cream and a generous sprinkle of turbinado or granulated sugar. They give this otherwise very rustic pie a shiny, sparkly "too good to be true" coating that crunches delightfully when you take a bite.

MAKES 1 (9-INCH) GALETTE
SPECIAL EQUIPMENT: 9-INCH PIE PAN, LARGE SAUCEPAN

ALL-BUTTER PIECRUST

1¼ cups all-purpose flour (6.25 ounces, 180 grams)

¼ teaspoon salt

10 tablespoons (1¼ sticks) unsalted butter, preferably a high-fat, European-style butter like Plugra, chilled and cut into ½-inch pieces (5 ounces, 140 grams)

2 to 5 tablespoons ice water (.75 to 1.75 ounces, 20 to 50 grams)

STONE FRUIT FILLING

1¾ pounds plums, halved and pitted (908 grams)

1¼ to 1½ cups light brown sugar, packed (10 to 12 ounces, 260 to 340 grams)

½ teaspoon salt

¼ teaspoon ground cardamom

¼ teaspoon ground cinnamon

¼ cup cornstarch (1 ounce, 30 grams)

1 tablespoon unsalted butter, chilled and diced (.5 ounce, 10 grams)

Heavy cream, for brushing

Turbinado sugar, for sprinkling

Recipe continues

Stone Fruit Galette.

FOR THE PIECRUST

1. In a food processor, briefly pulse together the flour and salt. Add butter and pulse until the mixture forms chickpea-size pieces (3 to 5 one-second pulses). Add ice water 1 tablespoon at a time, and pulse until the mixture is just moist enough to hold together.

2. Form the dough into a ball, wrap with plastic, and flatten into a disk. Refrigerate at least 1 hour before rolling out and baking.

FOR THE FILLING

1. Roll out the cold pie dough between two pieces of plastic wrap to 1/8-inch thickness. Line the pie pan with the dough (discard the plastic wrap), leaving a 1-inch overhang. Chill the dough for at least 30 minutes and up to overnight.

2. In a large saucepan, lightly toss together the plums, brown sugar, salt, cardamom, and cinnamon. Allow the fruit mixture to stand for 20 minutes.

3. Preheat the oven to 400°F. Place the saucepan over medium heat and sift in the cornstarch while stirring. Cook the fruit mixture, stirring occasionally, for 3 to 4 minutes, until the cornstarch is completely dissolved and the mixture has thickened slightly.

4. Scrape the fruit mixture into the pie pan, dot with the butter, and fold the overhanging pie dough over the edges of the pan, tucking it into the fruit. Brush the edges with the heavy cream and sprinkle with the turbinado sugar. Place the pie on a foil-lined baking sheet and bake for 25 minutes, or until the edges begin to turn golden.

5. Lower the temperature to 350°F. Continue to bake for an additional 35 to 40 minutes, until the center of the pie is bubbling. Allow to cool and set for at least 2 hours before serving.

CANDIED BACON PEACH COBBLER

The best argument for buying seasonal and local fruit is the peach. Peaches never seem to ripen properly when they are picked early and shipped across country. Though the local season may last only a few weeks, the tree-ripened peach, juicy and tender, makes my summer complete. If you want to prolong the peach dessert season, you can buy from an organic orchard near San Francisco called Frog Hollow Farms (see Sources, page 275). Their orchard has many varieties of peaches that blossom at different times from June to August. Their peaches are like the best ones you have ever tasted at a roadside farm stand. The addition of candied bacon to the crust here adds an earthy saltiness that packs a wallop when paired with luscious, sweet peaches.

MAKES A 9-INCH SQUARE BAKING DISH TO SERVE 6

SPECIAL EQUIPMENT: RIMMED BAKING SHEET, FOOD PROCESSOR, 9-INCH SQUARE BAKING DISH, PASTRY BRUSH

COBBLER BISCUITS

- 4 strips bacon (4 ounces, 113 grams)
- ¼ cup light brown sugar (1.75 ounces, 50 grams)
- 1⅔ cups all-purpose flour (7.75 ounces, 220 grams)
- 3½ tablespoons granulated sugar (1.75 ounces, 50 grams)
- 1½ tablespoons baking powder (.5 ounce, 20 grams)
- ⅛ teaspoon salt
- 6 tablespoons (¾ stick) unsalted butter, cubed (3 ounces, 85 grams)
- ⅔ cup plus 1 tablespoon heavy cream (6.5 ounces, 190 grams)

FRUIT FILLING

- 1½ cups granulated sugar (12 ounces, 340 grams)
- ¼ cup cornstarch (1 ounce, 33.75 grams)
- 3 pounds (1352 grams) peaches, peeled, pitted, and sliced into eighths
- 2 tablespoons honey (1.5 ounces, 45 grams)
- 1 teaspoon vanilla extract (5 grams)
- 1 teaspoon ground cinnamon

Demerara sugar, for sprinkling

FOR THE COBBLER BISCUITS

1. To prepare the cobbler biscuits, preheat the oven to 350°F. Place the bacon strips on a rimmed baking sheet lined with foil. Sprinkle half the brown sugar on top of the slices, then flip and sprinkle the other side with the remaining sugar. Bake until crisp, 20 to 25 minutes. Transfer the strips to a wire rack to cool.

2. Place the flour, granulated sugar, baking powder, and salt in a food processor fitted with the blade attachment and pulse to combine. Add the butter and run the motor until a coarse meal forms. Crumble in the candied bacon pieces and pulse briefly to combine. With the motor running, slowly drizzle in 2/3 cup of the cream until a soft dough forms.

3. Turn the dough out onto a lightly floured surface and gently knead to form a ball. Using your fingers, pinch off 2-inch pieces of dough and flatten into 1 1/2-inch thick rounds. You should get 9 rounds. Wrap the rounds in plastic and refrigerate while you make the fruit filling, or up to 2 days.

FOR THE FRUIT FILLING

1. Sift the sugar and cornstarch together into a large bowl. Add the peach slices and toss well to coat with the sugar mixture.

2. In a 2-quart saucepan over medium-high heat, combine the honey, vanilla, and cinnamon with 1/3 cup water and bring to a boil. Add the peach mixture and simmer, stirring occasionally, until the sauce thickens slightly, about 5 minutes.

TO ASSEMBLE AND SERVE

Preheat the oven to 350°F. Scrape the peach mixture into a 9-inch square baking dish and top with biscuit rounds. Brush the biscuit rounds with the remaining tablespoon of cream and sprinkle with the Demerara sugar. Bake until the biscuits are golden brown and the fruit is bubbling, 45 to 50 minutes. Allow to cool 20 to 30 minutes before serving.

Pie is probably the best example of a straight-from-the-oven dessert, and the key to a great pie is a great crust. Especially challenging with double-crust pies is keeping the bottom crust crisp when you don't pre-bake it and you're filling it with juicy fruits. Here are a few tips for getting around all that.

• First, I recommend the 1–2–3 method for mixing the dough: it's foolproof!

Step 1. Put the butter, lard, cream, sugar, and salt in the mixer and mix together briefly.

Step 2. Add one third of the flour and mix thoroughly.

Step 3. Add the last two thirds of the flour and mix just to incorporate.

Mixing in a third of the flour with the butter, lard, cream, sugar, and salt prevents the dough from forming gluten. This is because the high ratio of fat coats the flour so the gluten strands can not strengthen and adhere to one another. In Step 3, mix the rest of the flour as little as possible to keep that pesky gluten from forming.

• Another tip is to use a black pie pan, which transfers the heat better and helps crisp up the bottom. A Pyrex glass pie dish works nearly as well and has the advantage of letting you see the color of the bottom crust so you know when it's done. Avoid disposable aluminum foil pans, which aren't as good at conducting heat.

• Brush the raw pie dough on the bottom with a little egg white before adding the filling; it will act as a barrier and prevent some of the moisture from seeping through into the crust.

• Placing the pie on the bottom oven rack or, even better, atop a baking stone will help ensure a nice, crisp pastry.

• Since you can't break through a pie to check, your signal for doneness is to look for good golden-brown coloration over the entire top. The pie needs to thoroughly bake before you remove it from the oven. I find that many people underbake desserts in general. Just because a baked good is lightly browned on top doesn't mean that the interior is cooked through.

• In terms of shortening for the dough I favor a combination of butter, for its sweet, mellow flavor, and a small amount of lard, which contributes to tenderness and flakiness. In my experience, a little lard is the perfect addition for a piecrust, and I don't think you can ever get a truly flaky crust without some. The lard and butter combination has all the good flavor of the butter and the crunchy flakiness of the lard. It's just right.

• Once you have the technique for the crust mastered, you could use any fruit for the filling. Just take care not to add more binder than I specify, such as cornstarch, tapioca, or flour (I prefer cornstarch because it's almost imperceptible). My ideal pie has a juicy filling that's thickened just enough to take on a velvety texture.

We have come to expect a white, uncooked bottom crust under our pies and stopped being surprised by it, but a well-baked crust is not unattainable. This method pre-bakes the bottom crust, which is lined with aluminum foil and baking beads to hold it in place, then adds the filling and covers with the raw top dough, using egg wash to seal the baked bottom to the unbaked top crust.

A slice of Flaky Nectarine Pie (see recipe on page 97).

Flaky Nectarine Pie.

FLAKY NECTARINE PIE

In this pie, I use nectarines because they have a certain distinctive sour and tangy acidic flavor that I think pairs particularly well with the brandy and the brown sugar in the filling. Pre-cooking the filling with the cornstarch reduces the amount of liquid and activates the binding qualities of the starch before it goes into the pie shell. This prevents the fruit juices from soaking into the piecrust. Although this pie is scrumptious warm, I like to let it cool just to room temperature so the cornstarch has a chance to set up and lend some shape to the slices. Serve it plain, or with whipped cream, or à la mode, with a scoop of vanilla ice cream. (See photograph on page 95.)

MAKES 1 DOUBLE-CRUSTED 9-INCH PIE TO SERVE 8
SPECIAL EQUIPMENT: ELECTRIC MIXER, COLANDER, 9-INCH BLACK STEEL OR PYREX PIE PAN, RIMMED 11-BY-17-INCH BAKING SHEET, ROLLING PIN, PASTRY BRUSH, BAKING BEADS

CRUST

20 tablespoons (2½ sticks) unsalted butter, chilled and cubed (10 ounces, 283 grams)

7 tablespoons heavy cream (3.5 ounces, 100 grams)

3 tablespoons rendered lard (or use more butter) (1.25 ounces, 40 grams)

3¾ cups all-purpose flour (15 ounces, 425 grams), plus additional for rolling the dough

3 teaspoons granulated sugar (.4 ounce, 11 grams)

1¼ teaspoons salt (5 grams)

FILLING

8 cups (about 7) ripe nectarines, unpeeled, pitted, and cut into 1-inch chunks (35 ounces, 980 grams)

1 tablespoon freshly squeezed lemon juice (.54 ounce, 15.6 grams)

½ cup granulated sugar (3.5 ounces, 99 grams)

¼ cup packed light brown sugar (2 ounces, 57 grams)

⅛ teaspoon salt (.8 gram)

4 tablespoons cornstarch (1.5 ounces, 45 grams)

1 tablespoon brandy (.25 ounces, 7 grams)

1 teaspoon vanilla extract (4 grams)

1 egg white, beaten (1 ounce, 28 grams), at room temperature

1½ teaspoons Demerara or granulated sugar (1.5 ounces, 42 grams)

FOR THE CRUST

In the bowl of an electric mixer fitted with the paddle attachment, beat the butter, cream, and lard until smooth. In another bowl, thoroughly mix together the flour, sugar, and salt. Add about a third of the flour mixture to the butter and beat until the mixture comes together like a fairly wet dough. Add the remaining flour and

Recipe continues

mix until the dough just begins to come together. Turn the dough out on a floured surface and gently knead it into a smooth ball. Divide the dough in half, wrap each piece tightly in plastic wrap, and flatten into disks. Refrigerate for at least 2 hours or overnight (or up to 3 days).

FOR THE FILLING

1. In a large bowl, toss together the nectarines and lemon juice. Add the sugars and the salt, and gently mix to combine without mashing the nectarine chunks. Set aside to macerate for about 30 minutes.

2. Return the nectarines to the bowl and add the cornstarch, mixing until it has completely dissolved. Stir in the brandy and vanilla. Reserve.

TO ASSEMBLE AND BAKE

1. On a lightly floured surface, roll out both disks of dough to a 1/4-inch thickness and fold in half. Then re-roll to rounds about 12 inches in diameter and 3/16 inch thick (about the thickness of two quarters). This will create the layers of flakiness in your pie dough. Transfer one round of dough to a black steel or Pyrex 9-inch pie pan, and trim the edges so they are even with the rim of the pie pan. Place the second round on a flat baking sheet and put it in the freezer. This will become the top of the pie.

2. Freeze the dough in the pie pan for 1 hour. When ready to bake, preheat the oven to 425°F. Remove the pie pan from the freezer and line the dough with aluminum foil. Fill with baking beads, dried beans, or uncooked rice. Bake for 30 minutes. Allow to cool. When cool, preheat the oven again to 350°F.

3. Pour the nectarine filling into the pre-baked pie shell. Use a pastry brush to moisten the edges of the bottom pie crust with some of the egg white. Remove the top dough from the freezer and place over the fruit. Press down around the edges with your fingers to seal and tuck any excess dough under the edges. With a paring knife, cut 12 slits in the center of the raw dough, barely piercing it, to create air vents. Then, brush the top dough with the remaining egg white and sprinkle with Demerara or granulated sugar.

4. Bake on an aluminum-foil-covered rimmed 11-by-17-inch baking sheet on the center rack until the pie is deeply golden and you can see the thick juices bubbling through the vent, for 1 hour. Let cool before serving.

INDIVIDUAL APPLE TARTS

I guarantee that if you prepare these exquisite pastries, everyone will guess that you picked them up at some fabulous, Parisian-style pâtisserie. They just seem too professional and perfect to be homemade. These tarts are a bit reminiscent of miniature tart Tatins, but with a crust that flaunts the crisp, sugar-brittle texture of a palmier crowned with shining, tender, sliced apples. The vanilla glaze painted over the apples caramelizes as it bakes, giving the slices a beautiful, burnished sheen. I prefer to use a mix of apple varieties for the most complex flavor, but if you choose to use one variety, make it a tart one, such as Winesap or Granny Smith, to provide contrast for all the sweetness in the pastry.

If you have the time, homemade puff pastry will really make these little tarts extra special (see Classic Puff Pastry, page 101). Making your own puff pastry is a surprisingly simple procedure (it's easy, but it does require a bit of time) that gives an absolutely unbeatable flaky and golden result. Otherwise, just make sure to use high-quality, all-butter purchased puff pastry, such as Dufour, which is sold in easy to use 1-pound sheets and yields far superior flakiness and richness when compared with brands that use butter substitutes and contain trans fats.

Chef's Note Apples, pears, and many other fruits turn brown when their flesh is exposed to the air, due to oxidation. There are several ways to prevent this. Here we use melted butter to seal the sliced fruit off from the air. Another method is to sprinkle the fruit lightly with powdered vitamin C (1 teaspoon for 3 pounds of fruit). The vitamin C, an antioxidant, will slow down oxidation and keep the colors vibrant. Do not overuse it, though—the taste will be too tart.

MAKES 5 INDIVIDUAL SERVING TARTS
SPECIAL EQUIPMENT: 11-BY-17-INCH BAKING SHEET, PARCHMENT PAPER,
5-INCH ROUND COOKIE CUTTER, PASTRY BRUSH

1 (14-ounce) package puff pastry (397.25 grams)

2 tablespoons corn syrup (1.4 ounces, 41 grams)

1¼ pounds mixed variety apples (about 3), peeled, cored, and sliced ⅛ inch thick (20 ounces, 567 grams)

1 cup confectioners' sugar (4 ounces, 114 grams)

8 tablespoons (1 stick) unsalted butter (4 ounces, 113 grams), melted

1 vanilla bean, seeds scraped

Recipe continues

1. Preheat the oven to 350°F and position a rack in the bottom of the oven. Line an 11-by-17-inch baking sheet with parchment.

2. On a lightly floured surface unfold the pastry. Using a 5-inch round cookie cutter, cut out five rounds of dough, 1/4 inch thick. Transfer the rounds to the baking sheet.

3. Prick the dough all over with a fork and brush each round lightly with corn syrup. Layer the apple slices closely together on top of each round, fanning them out from the center. Repeat with a second layer of apples, fanning them in the opposite direction. Brush with melted butter to prevent discoloration. Transfer the tray to the refrigerator to set for 10 minutes.

4. Meanwhile, in a medium saucepan, combine the confectioners' sugar, the remaining butter, and the vanilla bean seeds. Simmer until the sugar and butter are melted. Whisk to fully combine.

5. Brush the top of each tart with some of the sugar mixture. Transfer the pan to the oven and bake, basting with the sugar mixture every 10 minutes, until the pastries are puffed and golden, about 60 minutes. Let cool for 5 minutes before serving.

CLASSIC PUFF PASTRY

Although good-quality, purchased puff pastry works just fine for baking, there is something very satisfying about making your own. It is a bit of a labor of love, but well worth it—you can truly taste the freshness in the buttery, flaky homemade version.

I find that a mix of all-purpose flour and cake flour yields a perfectly tender, well-structured pastry, but if you only have all-purpose, that will work fine too.

One important thing to remember: As you perform a roll-in (the pastry term for incorporating the butter into the dough), it is important to maintain as symmetrical a sheet as possible, both in diameter and thickness. This will allow for a final pastry that will puff up evenly when baked. After you've made it once or twice, you'll find the technique as simple as can be (and maybe even easier than running to the store for a frozen brand!).

Chef's Note Starting with cold butter is key in this recipe, as it will soften a good deal as you work with it. Warm butter won't create the airy pockets that give puff pastry its trademark flakiness. If you begin to find the rolling out process a bit arduous, hang half of the dough over the edge of a work table—gravity will help stretch the dough and will keep you from overworking it.

MAKES 3 POUNDS OF PUFF PASTRY

SPECIAL EQUIPMENT: ELECTRIC MIXER FITTED WITH THE PADDLE ATTACHMENT, ROLLING PIN, RULER

1¼ pounds (5 sticks) unsalted butter, chilled and cut into small pieces (20 ounces, 565 grams)

3 cups all-purpose flour (17 ounces, 484 grams)

1 cup cake flour (4 ounces, 113 grams)

2 teaspoons salt (10 grams)

1 cup cold water (8 ounces, 225 grams)

1. Place 1/4 pound (1 stick) of the butter in the bowl of an electric mixer fitted with the paddle attachment. Beat the butter on low until it is slightly softened. Add the flours and salt all at once. Increase the speed to medium. Once the flour and butter are incorporated, slowly drizzle in the cold water. Mix until the dough forms a loose ball, about 3 minutes. If the dough seems dry, add 1 tablespoon of water at a time until it comes together.

Recipe continues

2. On a lightly floured surface, roll the dough into a ball; slice a large X in its top. Cover with plastic wrap and refrigerate for at least 2 hours and up to 24 hours—the longer it chills the more supple the dough becomes.

3. Remove the remaining 1 pound (4 sticks) butter and the dough from the refrigerator. Arrange the butter on a lightly floured surface; cover loosely with plastic wrap and pound the butter gently with a rolling pin until slightly softened. Remove the plastic wrap and continue to work the butter with your hands until you have one uniform piece with a smooth, putty-like consistency. Using your hands, shape the butter into a 5-by-9-inch rectangle. Set aside.

4. Place the dough cut side up, on a lightly floured surface. Using a rolling pin, roll out the dough into a 12-by-15-inch rectangle that is 1 inch thick.

5. Use a wide spatula to transfer the butter rectangle onto the center of the dough. Fold all four sides of the dough over the butter like an envelope: first the right flap of butter, followed by the left, top, and bottom. Press together the dough seams, then smooth the dough gently with your palm to eliminate any air bubbles. Continue dusting off excess flour. Flip the dough so that it lies seam side down.

6. Start rolling out the dough. First roll from the center of the dough to the edge farthest away from you. Roll the top, then the bottom, and then the sides until the dough is about 1 foot long and about 8 inches wide. Carefully flip the dough (cradling it on your forearms if necessary). Continue rolling the dough until it is 24 inches long and 8 inches wide.

7. Look at the dough and, in your mind, divide it into thirds. Grabbing the 8-inch edge on the right, fold two-thirds of the way down the dough. Pat it down gently. Grab the left edge and lift to place it evenly over the top. Make sure that you keep the edges square. Congratulations—this is your first turn.

8. Repeat the process. (If, during the second turn, or any subsequent turns, the dough feels elastic because it's being worked too much, refrigerate it for an hour before doing another turn.) After you've finished the second turn, press two fingers into the top of the dough to indicate how many turns you've completed. (It's amazing how easily you can forget.)

9. Refrigerate the dough, wrapped in plastic on a baking sheet, after every two turns and let it rest for an hour. Complete a total of six turns. Let rest, well wrapped in the refrigerator, for at least 30 minutes before rolling out and baking. To freeze, roll out the pastry 1/2 inch thick. Well-wrapped frozen puff pastry will last up to 1 month.

INDIVIDUAL MAPLE APPLE TATINS

This one definitely deserves a place in the canon of top-ten straight-from-the-oven desserts. I've Americanized my version of tarte Tatin by using maple syrup instead of caramel as a sweet base for the apples, which gives this a nuttier flavor than most.

There are two keys to success here. The first is to bake the puff pastry fully so it's a crunchy cap for the apples. The second is to pack your apples in very tightly, since they'll lose 30 to 40 percent of their volume as they bake. In order to come up with a really tight and beautiful tart at the end, take your time peeling and slicing the apples as evenly as possible.

MAKES 6 INDIVIDUAL TARTS

SPECIAL EQUIPMENT: BAKING SHEET, 6 (8-OUNCE) RAMEKINS, 9-BY-13-INCH BAKING PAN

8 ounces all-butter puff pastry (227 grams) (homemade, page 101, or store-bought)

½ cup confectioners' sugar (2 ounces, 57 grams)

½ cup granulated sugar (3.5 ounces, 99 grams)

7 tablespoons unsalted butter, softened (3.5 ounces, 99 grams)

½ cup maple syrup (see Sources, page 275) (3.5 ounces, 99 grams)

6 Golden Delicious, Mutsu, or Granny Smith apples, peeled, cored, and cut into eighths (3 pounds, 1.36 kilograms)

1. Position a rack in the center of the oven and preheat to 375°F. Roll out the puff pastry to 1/8 inch thick and prick it all over with a fork. Cut out six rounds a little larger than a 6-ounce ramekin diameter.

2. In a small bowl, combine the sugars. Sprinkle them evenly over the puff pastry rounds, then transfer the rounds to a baking sheet. Bake the rounds on the center rack until golden brown, about 20 minutes. If the sugar is not completely glossy, put the pastry under the broiler for a few seconds.

3. Grease six 8-ounce ramekins with 1/2 tablespoon butter each. In a large saucepan over medium-high heat, bring the maple syrup to a boil. Reduce the heat and simmer vigorously until the mixture reduces to a thick, molasses-type consistency, about 10 minutes. Add the remaining 4 tablespoons (1/2 stick) butter and bring the mixture to a boil. Remove from the heat and divide the syrup mixture among the greased ramekins.

Recipe continues

Individual Maple Apple Tatins.

4. Arrange the apple pieces in the ramekins, packing them in tightly. Place the ramekins in a baking pan and pour hot water into the pan to come halfway up the sides of the ramekins. Cover with aluminum foil and bake on the center rack until the apples are easily pierced with a fork, about 40 minutes.

5. Uncover and bake for another 15 minutes to add color. Remove the baking pan from the oven, and then transfer the ramekins to a dish towel spread out on the countertop. Place the baked puff pastry rounds on top of the apples—you will have to crush them a little to make sure they lie flat—and carefully invert each hot ramekin onto a plate to serve. Serve warm.

6. To give the tatin that shiny brûlée surface, sprinkle the apples on the top of the inverted tart with sugar and brown with a blowtorch.

Chef's Note These can be prepared in advance up to the point when the apples can be easily pierced with a fork. Wrap the tarts well and refrigerate for up to 2 days, then pop them in the oven for 15 to 20 minutes to add a little color and heat up before serving.

I'LL BRING DESSERT

Some of my most vivid memories of parties past involve scenarios where someone came to the door with some gorgeous creation that they'd made. While the idea of making a dessert that is unusual and stunning yet easy to transport to a dinner party may seem daunting, it really doesn't have to be. Bringing a homemade dessert not only makes a mark, but also is a thoughtful gesture that any host is sure to appreciate. Even the simplest of sweets can seem pretty impressive when they're homemade.

All the desserts in this chapter are based on classics—each with a special little twist. Mamie Eisenhower's Cheesecake with a Chocolate Crust (page 118), a thin but luscious cheesecake adapted from the 1950s recipe, is taken to another level with the combination of a sweet and crisp chocolate crust, which holds a rich, smooth cream cheese interior, infused with a hint of lemon. Gingerbread Bundt with Freshly Ground Spices (page 123) is a tender spice cake with a decided intensity and character from the freshly ground spices and a simple citrus glaze. The Pine Nut Tart with Rosemary (page 134) is a sophisticated take on the rich, nutty flavors found in pecan pie to create a truly original treat.

These desserts offer tantalizing flavor combinations, and they have the advantage of not being fussy. They are showstoppers yet are sturdy enough to survive a car ride. Rich and memorable, the aptly named Deepest, Darkest Chocolate Pudding (page 109) is ideal for situations where you need to whip up something delicious in a hurry—it requires no assembly and can be easily dressed up with a dollop of whipped cream. Many of these desserts benefit from being made in advance, their ingredients melding and their textures becoming even finer after a day or two. One shining example is the elegant Tiramisù Slices with Espresso Cream (page 132). A combination of mascarpone, ladyfingers, and espresso, the flavors get more integrated as the dessert sits for a few days in the fridge.

To show up with a dessert that proudly showcases your baking prowess you'll want your creation to look its best when it's finally unveiled. When you're traveling, the key to a good presentation is to carefully pack your creation so that it arrives at its destination in mint condition. See the Chef's Notes throughout this chapter for tips on how to bring specific recipes. An inspired dessert, transported with care, always meets with enthusiastic appreciation.

DEEPEST, DARKEST CHOCOLATE PUDDING

Of all the desserts you could bring to a dinner party, chocolate pudding is the homiest, most crowd pleasing, and most fun. And this is the richest of its kind! You can chill the pudding in attractive single-serving dishes or choose a really pretty bowl to transport it—use a fun, colorful bowl for a casual dinner or, for a really elegant presentation, take out those crystal bowls that don't get used much.

Make sure your host knows you'll need some fridge space when you arrive, or else bring along a cooler so you can serve the pudding totally chilled. Plan to whip plenty of good cream there, as well.

MAKES 8 (6-OUNCE) SERVINGS

SPECIAL EQUIPMENT: SIFTER, FOOD PROCESSOR, 8 (6-OUNCE) RAMEKINS OR TEACUPS, OR A LARGE DECORATIVE BOWL

6 tablespoons sugar (2.6 ounces, 75 grams)

4 tablespoons Dutch-processed unsweetened cocoa powder (1 ounce, 28.5 grams)

4 tablespoons cornstarch (1 ounce, 28.5 grams)

¼ teaspoon fine sea salt (1.25 grams)

1 large egg (1.7 ounces, 48 grams), at room temperature

2 large egg yolks (1.2 ounces, 37.2 grams), at room temperature

6 ounces bittersweet chocolate (preferably 60 to 66 percent cacao content) (about 1 cup, 170 grams)

2½ cups whole milk (20 ounces, 562 grams)

½ cup heavy cream (4 ounces, 114 grams)

1 vanilla bean, split lengthwise, seeds scraped and reserved, or 1 teaspoon vanilla extract (4 grams)

2 tablespoons unsalted butter, softened (1 ounce, 28 grams)

Softly whipped cream, for serving

About ½ pound bittersweet chocolate for curls

1. Sift the sugar, cocoa powder, cornstarch, and salt onto a piece of parchment or waxed paper. Place the egg and yolks in a bowl, sprinkle the sugar mixture over them, and whisk to combine. Add a few tablespoons of milk to soften the mixture.

2. In a food processor fitted with the blade attachment, pulse the chocolate until it is finely chopped.

3. Over medium heat, bring the milk and vanilla bean seeds or vanilla extract to a boil. Whisking constantly, gradually pour the hot milk over the egg mixture. Return

Recipe continues

this liquid to the saucepan, continuing to whisk constantly, and cook over low heat, stirring, until the mixture has thickened and just begun to bubble, about 5 minutes (one visible bubble is sufficient!).

4. Immediately pour this custard into the food processor with the chocolate, add the butter, and run until smooth, about 1 minute.

5. Pour the pudding into eight 6-ounce ramekins or teacups, or one large decorative bowl. Let cool, cover, and refrigerate for at least 4 hours, or up to 2 days, and serve with whipped cream or chocolate curls.

Making chocolate curls with a vegetable peeler.

Deepest, Darkest Chocolate Pudding.

SOFT ALMOND CAKE WITH FRESH RASPBERRIES

An adaptation of the tender, very buttery little almond flour cakes called financiers, this is a dessert I learned to make while working at Au Vieux Four, an old wood-fired bakery in Tours, France. The owner, a ninth-generation baker named Jacques Mahou, who mentored me, primarily made bread, but he had a little sideline of super desserts, including this one. It's very much the type of straightforward, quickly mixed dessert a French bread maker bakes along with the bread. Before serving, it is garnished with fresh fruit, which makes this very transportable dessert colorful and light at any time of year. Replace the raspberries used here with seasonal fruits in the spring, summer, and fall, or with imported tropical fruits in the winter.

Chef's Note It's always a good idea to bring materials for touch-ups, such as extra confectioners' sugar to sprinkle over a travel-worn cake such as this one.

MAKES 1 (9-INCH) CAKE TO SERVE 8
SPECIAL EQUIPMENT: FOOD PROCESSOR (IF USING GROUND ALMONDS),
9-INCH SPRINGFORM PAN, CAKE TESTER, SIFTER

2 cups almond flour (see Sources, page 275), or finely ground blanched almonds (7.4 ounces, 214 grams)

1½ cups cake flour (6 ounces, 180 grams)

1 teaspoon baking powder (5 grams)

6 large eggs (10.2 ounces, 289 grams), at room temperature

¾ cup medium-flavored honey such as orange blossom or clover (9 ounces, 255 grams)

¾ cup granulated sugar (5.25 ounces, 150 grams)

½ cup plus 2 tablespoons whole-milk plain yogurt or crème fraîche (5 ounces, 142 grams)

½ pound (2 sticks) unsalted butter, melted (8 ounces, 227 grams)

¼ cup raspberry jam (2.6 ounces, 75 grams)

2 pints fresh raspberries (9 ounces, 255 grams)

Confectioners' sugar, for dusting

1. In a bowl, whisk together the almond flour or ground almonds, cake flour, and baking powder. In a large bowl, whisk together the eggs, honey, granulated sugar, and yogurt or crème fraîche until just combined. While whisking, to the egg mixture add one-third of the butter and one-third of the flour mixture. Repeat twice. Cover the bowl with plastic wrap and refrigerate overnight so the moist ingredients are fully absorbed by the flour, firming up the batter. (This batter will keep well in a tightly covered bowl in the refrigerator, for up to 7 days. If desired, place in an airtight container and freeze for up to 1 month.)

2. The next day, or when you are ready to bake the cake, position a rack in the center of the oven, preheat the oven to 350°F, and butter the 9-inch springform pan. Scrape the thickened batter into the pan. Bake on the center rack until the top is golden brown and a cake tester inserted into the center comes out clean, about 1 hour.

3. Place the cake on a rack and let cool completely in the pan (for at least 1 hour), then remove the sides of the pan, slide the cake onto a serving platter, then carefully remove the bottom of the pan. Just before serving, spread the raspberry jam over the top of the cake and cover the surface with upright fresh raspberries, blackberries, or blueberries. Sift confectioners' sugar over the top.

Grand Old-Fashioned Blueberry Jelly Roll (Roulade).

GRAND OLD-FASHIONED
BLUEBERRY JELLY ROLL (ROULADE)

Like apple pie and chocolate cake, this is one of those homey desserts with no pretensions. If you want to make this for a small gathering you can easily halve the recipe, making a thinner roll. The baking time will be 10 to 12 minutes.

The secret to making an easily rollable cake is adding extra eggs and egg yolks to the batter. The eggs keep the cake light, moist, and supple, which is what you need to be able to roll a sponge cake that doesn't crack.

You can fill this basic sponge with anything from a fruit filling, as I use here, to jam to mousse to whipped cream, or even Nutella. If you use jam, choose a dark-colored one (or mixture of a couple of jams) to contrast with the light-colored cake, so when you cut into the roll you get a most attractive spiral. It's a good way to finish those half-empty jars of jam hanging out in the back of your fridge.

Chef's Note This simple cake travels perfectly. Just wrap it in plastic and then in foil. A sprinkling of confectioners' sugar is nice but not strictly necessary here. A jelly roll is charmingly plain and lasts 5 days in the fridge well covered.

MAKES 1 (4-BY-11-INCH) CAKE TO SERVE 8 TO 10

SPECIAL EQUIPMENT: ZESTER, 11-BY-17-INCH JELLY ROLL PAN OR RIMMED 11-BY-17-INCH
BAKING SHEET, SIFTER, ELECTRIC MIXER, OFFSET SPATULA

ROULADE SPONGE CAKE

Unsalted butter for the pan

12 large eggs (21 ounces, 600 grams)

1 teaspoon vanilla extract

⅓ cup granulated sugar (90 grams, 3 ounces)

¼ teaspoon cream of tartar

½ cup plus 1 tablespoon all-purpose flour (85 grams, 3 ounces)

BLUEBERRY FILLING

2 pints fresh or frozen blueberries (about 4 cups, 21 ounces, 600 grams)

Finely grated zest and freshly squeezed and strained juice of 1 orange

5 tablespoons confectioners' sugar (1.25 ounces, 36 grams)

5 tablespoons cornstarch, sifted with the sugar (1.25 ounces, 36 grams)

Recipe continues

FOR THE ROULADE SPONGE CAKE

1. Separate the eggs, reserving all of the yolks and 6 of the whites. The remaining 6 whites can be stored in the fridge for another purpose. In the bowl of an electric mixer, whisk the egg yolks with the vanilla and half the sugar until it quadruples in volume and turns pale yellow, about 10 minutes on high speed.

2. In a separate mixing bowl using a clean whisk attachment, beat the egg whites on medium speed until they start to foam. Add the cream of tartar and remaining sugar little by little and continue to beat until stiff peaks form, about 10 minutes, to make a meringue.

3. Preheat the oven to 400°F. Line an 11-by-17-inch rimmed baking sheet or jelly roll pan with parchment paper and use some of the butter to grease the top and sides of the sheet pan thoroughly.

4. Fold one-third of the meringue into the egg yolk mixture, then fold in the rest, until the mixture is no longer streaked with meringue. Sift the flour over the meringue in two stages, folding gently after each addition.

5. Pour the batter onto the prepared baking sheet and smooth with an offset spatula. Bake for 15 minutes, or until a cake tester inserted in the center of the cake comes out clean and the cake is a pale golden color. Let the cake cool in the pan, then immediately cover the pan in plastic wrap, so the cake doesn't dry out. Refrigerate until needed or overnight.

FOR THE FILLING

In a saucepan, combine the blueberries, orange zest and juice, confectioners' sugar, and cornstarch. Bring to a boil and reduce the liquid until slightly thickened, about 5 minutes. Let cool to room temperature.

TO ASSEMBLE AND SERVE

Remove the plastic wrap from the pan and slide the cake onto a clean kitchen towel sprinkled with confectioners' sugar. Spread the cooled blueberry filling over the cake so that the filling is thinner at the edges (the filling will spread a little as the cake is rolled). Starting at a long end of the cake, use the towel to lift the cake from underneath. Tucking the edge in and peeling away the towel as you go, roll tightly away from you. Transfer the jelly roll to a flat serving plate, seam side down. Cut crosswise into 1/2-inch-thick slices and serve.

HOW TO ROLL AN OLD-FASHIONED BLUEBERRY JELLY ROLL.

1. Roll from the long end.

2. Use the towel to lift.

3. Roll to the edge.

4. Reshape with the towel.

5. Elongate evenly.

6. Grand Old-Fashioned Blueberry Jelly Roll.

MAMIE EISENHOWER'S CHEESECAKE WITH A CHOCOLATE CRUST

Mamie Eisenhower published a lot of recipes during Ike's presidency, among them Million-Dollar Fudge, her best-seller, and this one, which I think is even better. I categorize cheesecake as a flan—meaning that it's a baked custard, and to remain creamy and soft it must not be cooked too rapidly or for too long. The flan/cake needs to be removed from the oven when its center is still slightly wobbly. When gently shaken, the whole cake should undulate in a mass (like a Jell-O mold), which indicates that the eggs have set with the liquids and cream cheese. Baked to this point and no further, the cake will be smooth and creamy once cooled. To achieve this texture, also be sure to beat the cream cheese and sugar together until completely smooth before adding other ingredients. (Once you add the eggs it's nearly impossible to remove lumps, except by forcing the batter through a sieve, which can get messy.)

If you adhere to these directions, you will be rewarded with a lush, velvety, slightly tangy cheesecake sitting on a thick layer of chocolate cookie crumb.

This version is low in the pan, light and moist, and gives equal billing to the chocolate cookie crust.

Chef's Note Cake carriers can go a long way in helping to protect your desserts, and I think they're worth having if you like to bake. In a pinch, a sturdy cardboard box or wine crate will do just fine. Within your cake carrier or box, place your cake or tart on a cake plate or cardboard round spread with a bit of corn syrup or honey to prevent the dessert from sliding around. Then use double-stick tape on the bottom of the plate or round so that everything stays put inside the container. To ensure that the top of your dessert doesn't get crushed, use toothpicks to prop up aluminum foil, plastic wrap, and box tops. Generally, it's advisable to use a container that's bigger and sturdier than you think you'll need, so you can place it on a car seat and drive (slowly and carefully!) without any worries.

Recipe continues

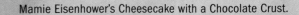
Mamie Eisenhower's Cheesecake with a Chocolate Crust.

MAMIE EISENHOWER'S CHEESECAKE WITH A CHOCOLATE CRUST

MAKES 1 (10-INCH) CAKE TO SERVE 8 TO 10

SPECIAL EQUIPMENT: ZESTER, FOOD PROCESSOR, COOKIE SHEET, 10-INCH SPRINGFORM PAN, ELECTRIC MIXER, OFFSET SPATULA

COOKIE CRUST

- 1 package (9 ounces) Nabisco Famous Chocolate Wafer cookies

- 4 tablespoons (½ stick) unsalted butter, melted (2 ounces, 57 grams)

  Unsalted butter, for the pan

CHEESECAKE

- 2 packages full-fat cream cheese (16 ounces, 454 grams), at room temperature

- ½ cup sugar (3.5 ounces, 99 grams)

- 3 large eggs (5.1 ounces, 145 grams), at room temperature

- 1 cup sour cream (8.5 ounces, 242 grams)

  Freshly grated zest and juice of 1 lemon

FOR THE CRUST

1. Position a rack in the center of the oven and preheat to 275°F. In the bowl of a food processor, pulse the cookies to fine crumbs (you should have about 1 1/2 cups).

2. Add the melted butter, and pulse to combine. Grease the bottom and sides of a 10-inch springform pan with butter and sprinkle the cookie crumbs inside. Shake the cake pan to distribute them evenly on the bottom, then use a fork to press them down evenly. Bake for 10 minutes.

FOR THE CHEESECAKE

1. Raise the oven temperature to 300°F. In the bowl of an electric mixer fitted with the paddle attachment, beat the cream cheese and sugar at medium speed until completely smooth, about 15 minutes. Stop the mixer occasionally to scrape down the sides of the bowl and the paddle with a spatula. Beat in the eggs one at a time until completely incorporated, scraping down the bowl and paddle before adding each egg.

2. Add the sour cream, lemon zest, and lemon juice and continue to beat until the mixture is uniformly smooth. Pour the batter over the cookie crumb crust and place on the center rack. Bake until the cake is just set, yet still wobbly in the center and will move slightly, in one piece, when the pan is gently shaken, about 60 minutes. Remove from the oven and place on a rack to cool, then refrigerate until completely chilled before serving, about 2 hours. To serve, run a thin knife or offset spatula around the sides of the pan, then release the sides, letting the cake remain on the pan's base. To slice the cake neatly, use a thin-bladed knife, and wipe it with a damp cloth in between cuts.

Mamie Eisenhower's Cheesecake, unbaked.   After baking.

Gingerbread Bundt with Freshly Ground Spices.

GINGERBREAD BUNDT
WITH FRESHLY GROUND SPICES

When I was working at the legendary Tavern on the Green in Central Park in the late 1980s, the extravagant owner, Warner LeRoy, and I spent a month trying gingerbreads until we arrived at our mutual ideal. LeRoy was one of those larger than life individuals—large in the physical sense (he weighed about 300 pounds), and large in his ideas and imagination. He used to wear garish multicolored sport coats every day, and never the same one twice. He was always looking for new ways to entertain and amuse his guests. He loved the circus tent atmosphere of Tavern on the Green, with its crystal chandeliers and Tiffany glass. He grew up as kind of a "Hollywood brat." His father was Mervyn LeRoy, a producer of *The Wizard of Oz*. In fact, he was given the dog who played Toto after the movie wrapped. Anyway, Warner wouldn't give up until he found the perfect gingerbread. For him, the search was part of his goal to bring a happy childhood memory to every guest who walked through his door. And that's how we finally hit upon this rich and fragrant recipe. Molasses makes this cake dark, intense, and moist, and freshly grated ginger gives it a real kick. I find that freshly ground whole spices give a huge boost to the cake's flavor.

In this recipe, I balance the ginger with extra cardamom and cinnamon. I add a touch of allspice and star anise to produce an intensely scented spice cake. Then I drizzle it with a sweet-tart orange glaze, which is really all it needs as embellishment, especially if you plan to give it as a gift or bring it to a holiday gathering.

Recipe continues

GINGERBREAD BUNDT
WITH FRESHLY GROUND SPICES

MAKES 1 BUNDT, 9-INCH ROUND, OR LOAF CAKE TO SERVE 8 TO 10

SPECIAL EQUIPMENT: GRATER, 6-CUP BUNDT, 9-INCH SPRINGFORM, OR 9-BY-5-INCH LOAF PAN,
SPICE GRINDER OR CLEAN ELECTRIC COFFEE GRINDER, SIFTER, ELECTRIC MIXER,
CAKE TESTER, OFFSET SPATULA

Unsalted butter, for the pan

All-purpose flour, for dusting

GINGERBREAD

3 green cardamom pods (see Sources, page 275)

3 allspice berries (see Sources, page 275)

1½ cinnamon sticks, broken into pieces

½ star anise (see Sources, page 276)

2 cups cake flour (8 ounces, 227 grams)

1 tablespoon baking powder (14.7 grams)

½ teaspoon baking soda (2.5 grams)

½ teaspoon salt (2.5 grams)

½ cup packed light brown sugar (4 ounces, 113 grams)

3 large eggs (5.1 ounces, 145 grams), at room temperature

12 tablespoons (1½ sticks) unsalted butter, melted and cooled (6 ounces, 170 grams)

½ cup half-and-half (4.25 ounces, 121 grams)

½ cup molasses (5.6 ounces, 161 grams)

1 tablespoon freshly grated fresh ginger (.6 ounce, 17 grams)

GLAZE

⅔ cup confectioners' sugar (2.7 ounces, 76.7 grams)

1 large egg white (1 ounce, 28 grams), at room temperature

1 tablespoon freshly squeezed orange juice (.5 ounce, 15 grams)

1 teaspoon finely grated orange zest (2 grams)

FOR THE CAKE

1. Position a rack in the center of the oven and preheat to 350°F. Butter generously and flour a 6-cup Bundt, 9-inch springform, or 9-by-5-inch loaf pan. In a spice grinder or clean electric coffee grinder, grind the cardamom, allspice, cinnamon, and star anise to a powder.

2. Sift the flour, baking powder, baking soda, and salt into the bowl of an electric mixer. Add the spices and brown sugar and mix with the paddle attachment at low speed to combine.

3. In a large bowl, whisk together the eggs, butter, half-and-half, molasses, and grated ginger until well combined. With the mixer at low speed, gradually pour the egg mixture into the flour mixture, then raise the speed to medium and mix until the batter is smoothly combined and pourable, about 2 minutes. Scrape the batter into the pan and bake on the center rack until a cake tester inserted into the middle of the cake comes out clean, 40 to 45 minutes. If the top browns too quickly, loosely cover it with aluminum foil and continue baking. Let the cake cool completely on a wire rack (at least 1 hour) before unmolding. When the cake is cool, slide a thin knife or offset spatula around the sides of the pan, then turn the pan over to unmold the cake onto a plate or serving platter.

FOR THE GLAZE

Whisk together the glaze ingredients until smooth. Drizzle the glaze over the cake and let set at room temperature for at least 3 hours.

Blackberry Buttermilk Bundt with Orange Glaze.

BLACKBERRY BUTTERMILK BUNDT
WITH ORANGE GLAZE

When working at Bouley Restaurant we were always thrilled to find a celebrity looking over our shoulder in the kitchen. It was just the nature of the place, I guess, and the nature of the irrepressible maître d', Dominique Simon, who delighted in telling the well-known celebrity that because of their elevated status they would be "allowed" into the kitchen. Most paid a visit to the kitchen, if only to stretch their legs between courses. One person in particular stands out, and I suppose I can talk about it now that it is more than ten years ago. The great actor Liam Neeson said something I will always remember: "I feel like my craft is like whittling wood, I want to remove all the excess until I find the perfect and smallest place to be, without anything extra." I think anyone who loves their work can relate to this, and I am always trying to find that perfect, unadorned dessert item, the one that has all it needs and nothing more, nothing less. One of the reasons I love the Blackberry Buttermilk Bundt is that it fits that bill, it has the taste of blackberries, a sweet and semiwild flavor, and the sour note of buttermilk to counteract the sugar, and finally the glaze to give it just a little edge. I put "buttermilk" in the title of this dessert because it does so much to change the flavor radically, and its sour kick is what sets this soft-textured yellow cake apart. The buttermilk tang, combined with the sweetness of the berries and richness of the butter, is what makes you want to reach for the next piece. Balance is the most important part of any dessert, or savory dish for that matter, and the blackberry/buttermilk duet here is in perfect harmony. Because of its simplicity, this cake is a good choice for a brunch.

Chef's Note I like to use a wooden spoon to fold berries into cake batter. The rough surface moves the fruit more efficiently than the smooth surface of a rubber spatula, incorporating the berries without crushing them.

MAKES 1 BUNDT CAKE TO SERVE 8 TO 10
SPECIAL EQUIPMENT: 2-QUART BUNDT PAN, ELECTRIC MIXER, CAKE TESTER, SKEWER

Recipe continues

2⅔ cups all-purpose flour (10.5 ounces, 300 grams)

1 tablespoon baking powder (14.7 grams)

½ teaspoon salt (3.35 grams)

½ teaspoon baking soda (2.5 grams)

½ pound unsalted butter (2 sticks), softened (8 ounces, 227 grams), plus additional for the pan

1¾ cups sugar (12.25 ounces, 350 grams)

4 large eggs (6.8 ounces, 193 grams), at room temperature

2 teaspoons vanilla extract (8 grams)

½ cup buttermilk (4.25 ounce, 121 grams)

2 pints blackberries (16 ounces, 454 grams)

ORANGE GLAZE

½ cup freshly squeezed orange juice (from about 1 medium orange) (4.25 ounces, 121 grams)

½ cup confectioners' sugar (2 ounces, 57 grams)

1. Preheat the oven to 350°F. Grease a 2-quart anti-adhesive Bundt pan with some butter, then spray lightly with nonstick cooking spray. You don't want this cake to stick! The new anti-adhesive cake pans prevent the bottom of the cake from sticking to the pan.

2. In a small bowl, whisk together the flour, baking powder, salt, and baking soda.

3. In the bowl of an electric mixer fitted with the paddle attachment, cream the butter and sugar on medium-high speed until light and fluffy. Beat in the eggs one at a time until incorporated. Beat in the vanilla. Reduce the speed to low and mix in half the flour mixture. Mix in the buttermilk, then the remaining flour mixture. Using a wooden spoon, gently fold in the blackberries.

4. Pour the batter into the prepared Bundt pan. Bake the cake until a cake tester inserted in the center comes out clean, about 1 hour. Let the cake cool in the pan for 10 minutes, then invert onto the serving platter.

FOR THE GLAZE

1. While the cake cools, combine the orange juice and sugar in a small saucepan and simmer over low heat until the sugar is dissolved.

2. Using a skewer or long thin knife, prick deep holes all over the surface of the cake. Pour half the glaze over the cake, letting it seep into the holes. Let the cake cool for 20 minutes more. Pour the remaining glaze over the cake and let set for 10 minutes. Slice and serve.

APPLE "CONVERSATION"

Yves Thuries, a French baker, published several volumes of important cookbooks on traditional and regional French desserts in the 1980s. This simple apple dessert from the Auvergne region is one of the best examples of why good food never goes out of style. Called a "conversation" in France (for reasons unknown to me), this is sure to inspire plenty of talk! I like a mix of Mutsu, Macoun, and McIntosh apples here, making for a complex interplay of flavors.

Somewhere between a cake and a tart, this unusual dessert is a showstopping alternative to traditional apple pie, and great for Thanksgiving. Royal icing, which is typically applied to desserts uncooked (usually piped onto cookies for decoration), is baked right onto the crust, creating a crackling brown lid on top of the bulging puff pastry—imagine a puffed tart with a sugared disk of brown royal icing tipped like the cap of a Parisian dandy. Inside, a filling of warm apples awaits the serving knife, ready to ooze forth in all its fragrant, fruity glory.

You can bake the "conversation" at home up to 12 hours ahead, transport it after it cools, and reheat it in a 350°F oven for 8 minutes before serving. Just be sure to serve it warm; the crust loses its flaky delicacy as it cools. (See photograph on page 106.)

MAKES 1 (8-INCH) TART TO SERVE 8
SPECIAL EQUIPMENT: ROLLING PIN, 8-INCH TART PAN, PASTRY BRUSH

APPLE TART

- 2 tablespoons (¼ stick) unsalted butter (1 ounce, 28 grams)

- 6 apples (about 3 pounds, 1.36 kilograms), ideally a mix of Mutsu, Macoun, and Macintosh, peeled, cored, and cut into ¼-inch slices (about 8 cups)

- ½ cup packed light brown sugar (4 ounces, 113 grams)

- ½ cup raisins (2.5 ounces, 71 grams)

- ½ cup Calvados, apple brandy, or rum (4.4 ounces, 125 grams), optional

- 1½ teaspoons ground cinnamon (6.5 grams)

- 1 pound puff pastry, either homemade (page 101) or packaged frozen all-butter pastry (such as Dufour) thawed according to package directions (16 ounces, 454 grams)

ROYAL ICING

- 1 cup confectioners' sugar (4 ounces, 113 grams)

- 1 large egg white (1 ounce, 28 grams), at room temperature

- Freshly squeezed juice of ½ lemon

Recipe continues

Apple "Conversation."

FOR THE TART

1. In a 12-inch skillet over medium heat, melt the butter. Add the apples, brown sugar, raisins, Calvados (or apple brandy or rum), if using, and cinnamon, and sauté until all the apples are soft, about 15 minutes. Transfer to a bowl and let cool before proceeding.

2. (If not using homemade pastry dough, roll out half the store-bought puff pastry to a round about 12 inches in diameter and 1/4 inch thick.) Carefully lower the round into the 8-inch tart pan, pressing it into the bottom and sides, working quickly so the dough remains cold and easy to handle.

3. Fill the tart with the cooled apple mixture and roll out a second sheet of puff pastry to a 12-inch round. Brush the edges with water, then flip the round over onto the tart. Pinch the edges of the two sheets of dough to seal and use scissors to cut off the excess dough. Place the tart in the freezer for at least 30 minutes and up to 2 days (if well wrapped) to make it firm and easier to handle. Poke three holes around the edge of the top crust to allow some steam to escape. When ready to bake, position the oven racks in the center and bottom of the oven and preheat to 375°F.

FOR THE ICING

In an electric mixer fitted with the whisk attachment mix together the confectioners' sugar, egg white, and lemon juice until thick and smooth, not runny. Reserve.

TO BAKE AND SERVE

Bake on the center rack until the lid is golden brown, 25 to 35 minutes. Remove the pan from the oven and then use an offset spatula to apply the royal icing to the top of the hot and semibaked tart. Return to the oven for another 20 minutes to set the icing. When the top is browned remove from the oven and let rest for 12 minutes before serving warm. Or let cool completely, and reheat within 12 hours of baking in a 350°F oven for 8 minutes before serving.

TIRAMISÙ SLICES WITH ESPRESSO CREAM

I love tiramisù—who doesn't? Even the DIY kind, when you dip ladyfingers in espresso, then in mascarpone cream, is to die for. This transportable version has just a little more panache—I've Frenchified it by molding the mixture in a loaf pan or terrine, then serving it in neat slices instead of piling everything up in a bowl. Gelatin lightens the mascarpone cream, and gives it more structure, but I retain the idea of separate elements by serving an espresso custard sauce on the side.

Chef's Notes The custard sauce recipe yields just under 1 1/2 cups, enough to serve with the tiramisù. If you prefer more sauce, or want to use the custard for other desserts (it's lovely with meringue cookies, drizzled over chocolate pudding, or as a sauce for ice cream), double the recipe.

The Savoiardi ladyfingers give this tiramisù a sturdy texture.

For added elegance, use a vegetable peeler to scrape some fresh chocolate shavings over the top of each serving and sprinkle on a few chocolate-covered coffee beans.

MAKES 1 (9-BY-5-INCH) LOAF TO SERVE 6
SPECIAL EQUIPMENT: ELECTRIC MIXER, 9-BY-5-INCH LOAF PAN, PASTRY BRUSH,
CANDY THERMOMETER, DOUBLE BOILER, SIFTER

MASCARPONE CREAM AND LADYFINGERS

- 2 teaspoons powdered gelatin (.25 ounce, 7 grams)
- ⅓ cup heavy cream (2.7 ounces, 77.3 grams)
- ⅔ cup mascarpone (see Sources, page 275) (5.3 ounces, 152.4 grams)
- 4 large egg whites (4 ounces, 113 grams), at room temperature

  Pinch of cream of tartar
- 5 teaspoons sugar (.7 ounce, 20.8 grams)
- 18 Savoiardi ladyfingers
- ½ cup strong, brewed espresso (4 ounces, 115 grams)

ESPRESSO CRÈME ANGLAISE

- 1 cup whole milk (8.5 ounces, 242 grams)
- 4 large egg yolks (2.4 ounces, 74.4 grams), at room temperature
- ¼ cup sugar (1.75 ounces, 50 grams)
- 2 tablespoons ground espresso beans (10 grams)
- 1 tablespoon rum or sambuca, optional (.5 ounce, 13.75 grams)
- ½ teaspoon vanilla extract (2 grams)

  Pinch of salt

- 3 tablespoons Dutch-processed unsweetened cocoa powder, for serving (.6 ounce, 17.25 grams)

FOR THE MASCARPONE CREAM

1. Place the gelatin in a small bowl and sprinkle 1 tablespoon water over it, to bloom.

2. In a saucepan over medium heat, bring the cream to a simmer. Whisk in the mascarpone until smooth, then add the gelatin.

3. In the clean dry bowl of an electric mixer fitted with the whisk attachment, beat the egg whites with the cream of tartar until they are very foamy, but do not yet hold peaks, about 2 minutes. With the mixer on medium speed, gradually sprinkle in the sugar a teaspoon at a time. Raise the mixer speed to high and beat until the whites hold soft peaks, about 5 more minutes. (See page 15 for more on meringues.)

4. Fold in the egg whites.

TO ASSEMBLE

Line a 9-by-5-inch loaf pan with plastic wrap. Dip the Savoiardi into the espresso and lay 6 of them crosswise, sponge side (bottom) up, in the base of the pan. Spread half of the mascarpone cream over the ladyfingers. Repeat with another layer of 6 ladyfingers, one-third of the espresso, and the remaining mascarpone cream. Finish with a final layer of ladyfingers and espresso, cover with plastic, and refrigerate overnight.

FOR THE ESPRESSO CRÈME ANGLAISE

1. Line a fine-mesh sieve with cheesecloth and set it over a bowl. Attach a candy thermometer to the side of a double boiler. In the top of the double boiler, whisk together the milk, egg yolks, sugar, and ground espresso beans. Stir over boiling water until this custard begins to thicken, about 4 minutes—it will be steaming, and thick enough to coat the back of a wooden spoon. The mixture should reach 170 to 180°F and should not come to a boil or reach more than 180°F.

2. Strain the custard into the bowl and add the rum or sambuca, if using, and the vanilla and salt. Let cool at room temperature, cover with plastic, then chill until ready to serve.

TO SERVE

Uncover the tiramisù and carefully invert it onto a platter. (To do this, place the platter upside down on top of the loaf pan. Holding both the plate and the pan securely, flip the platter over so that the terrine loaf pan rests upside down on top of the platter. Carefully remove the pan, and peel away the plastic wrap.) Sift the cocoa powder over the top. Serve in neat slices and pass the espresso crème anglaise, so the diners can help themselves to a good dollop.

PINE NUT TART WITH ROSEMARY

This very sturdy tart is ideal for bringing places—short of dropping it, there's nothing you can do to hurt it. Like a Mediterranean version of pecan pie, here whole pine nuts are suspended in a luscious caramel filling made of honey and brown sugar, flavored with the piney note of fresh rosemary. It's perfect served by itself, or with a dollop of fromage blanc or Greek-style yogurt.

MAKES 1 (9-INCH) TART TO SERVE 8

SPECIAL EQUIPMENT: RIMMED 11-BY-17-INCH BAKING SHEET

1 pâte sablée tart shell (see recipe opposite), pre-baked

FILLING

2 large eggs (3.4 ounces, 96 grams), at room temperature

½ cup Grade B maple syrup (5.75 ounces, 165 grams)

½ cup packed light brown sugar (4 ounces, 113 grams)

6 tablespoons unsalted butter, melted (3 ounces, 85 grams)

½ teaspoon finely chopped fresh rosemary (2 grams)

¼ teaspoon salt (1.25 grams)

1¼ cups pine nuts (5.6 ounces, 160 grams), roasted

1½ cups fromage blanc (see Sources, page 275) or plain Greek-style yogurt, for serving (12 ounces, 340 grams)

1 to 2 tablespoons medium-flavored honey such as orange blossom or clover, or to taste (.75 to 1.5 ounces, 22 to 43 grams)

FOR THE TART SHELL

Pre-bake the tart shell according to the box on page 135.

FOR THE FILLING

1. Whisk together all the filling ingredients in a bowl, except the pine nuts. Roast the pine nuts for 10 minutes on a sheet pan at 350°F, then fold them in.

2. Scrape the filling into the tart shell, place the tart pan on a rimmed 11-by-17-inch baking sheet (in case the filling leaks), and bake on the center rack until set—the filling should jiggle just slightly in the center—25 to 35 minutes. Remove from the oven to a cooling rack. Let cool in the pan.

TO SERVE

Whisk the fromage blanc or plain yogurt with honey to taste. Serve a dollop beside wedges of the tart.

HOW TO PRE-BAKE
A PÂTE SABLÉE TART SHELL

MAKES 1 (9-INCH) TART SHELL

SPECIAL EQUIPMENT: ELECTRIC MIXER, 9-INCH TART PAN, PIE WEIGHTS OR DRIED BEANS

10 tablespoons unsalted butter (5 ounces, 142 grams)

½ cup granulated sugar (3.5 ounces, 100 grams)

2 large eggs (3.4 ounces, 96 grams), at room temperature

2 cups all-purpose flour (8.5 ounces, 242 grams), plus additional for dusting

1 teaspoon salt (5 grams)

1. In the bowl of an electric mixer fitted with the paddle attachment, cream the butter and sugar. Add the eggs and mix until incorporated. Add the flour and salt and mix on low speed just until the dough comes together. Scrape the dough into a ball, then wrap in plastic wrap. Flatten into a disk and refrigerate for at least 1 hour or overnight (or up to 3 days).

2. Generously flour a work surface and roll out the dough 1/4 inch thick. Press it into a 9-inch tart pan, and trim the excess dough with a knife. Use the trimmed dough to patch any holes, and place the shell in the refrigerator or freezer until ready to bake (up to 1 hour).

3. When ready to bake, preheat the oven to 350°F. Line the tart shell with foil and fill with dried beans or pie weights. Bake for 30 minutes, then remove from the oven and take out the weights and foil. Return the tart shell to the oven and bake for an additional 10 minutes, until it colors slightly. Remove from the oven and transfer to a wire rack to cool.

Chocolate Caramel Tart with Sea Salt.

CHOCOLATE CARAMEL TART WITH SEA SALT

For this elegant tart, a crisp, cookie-like crust is first covered with a layer of caramel, then filled with a serious bittersweet ganache, which gets extra depth from a pinch of sea salt. The tart is chilled until firm, then served at room temperature, so it's ideal for transporting: Make it the day before you plan to serve it, then take it out of the fridge right before you leave, and it'll be at the right temperature by the time you're ready for dessert.

Chef's Note To create a shiny, smooth-textured ganache, carefully follow the directions for mixing, whisking gradually from the center and moving the whisk outward only as the center becomes fully combined. The result should be viscous and glossy and should hold a point when you remove the whisk.

MAKES 1 (9-INCH) TART TO SERVE 8
SPECIAL EQUIPMENT: CANDY THERMOMETER

1 pâte sablée tart shell (see recipe, page 135), pre-baked

CARAMEL LAYER

½ cup heavy cream (4.06 ounces, 116 grams)

1 cup sugar (7 ounces, 198 grams)

Pinch of Maldon sea salt

CHOCOLATE GANACHE FILLING

12 ounces bittersweet chocolate (preferably 60 to 66 cacao percent), coarsely chopped (about 2 cups, 340 grams)

Small pinch of Maldon sea salt

2 cups heavy cream (16.24 ounces, 464 grams)

FOR THE TART SHELL

Pre-bake the tart shell according to the box on page 135.

FOR THE CARAMEL

1. In a small saucepan, bring the 1/2 cup cream to a boil, then turn off the heat.

2. In a heavy saucepan fitted with a candy thermometer, combine the sugar with 5 tablespoons water and cook, stirring, over high heat until the sugar dissolves. Bring this caramel mixture to a boil and let cook, without stirring, for about 4 minutes, until it reaches a dark amber color (at about 374°F) and begins to smoke. Don't be afraid, the taste is worth it. Swirl the pan if the sugar is browning unevenly.

Recipe continues

3. Take the pan off the heat and slowly whisk the hot cream into the caramel, standing back as you pour since it will sputter. Stir until smooth. Add the salt. Put the pan over low heat if the caramel is not pourable, and warm it, swirling, until it can be poured.

4. Swirling the pan, pour the caramel into the tart shell, evenly covering the bottom. Let cool. It will become matte, rather than glossy, and will feel rubbery and no longer sticky. Refrigerate until ready to pour in the ganache.

FOR THE GANACHE

1. Place the chocolate and salt in a heatproof bowl. In a small saucepan over medium heat, bring the cream to a boil.

2. Pour the cream over the chocolate, let sit for 3 minutes, then whisk, beginning in the center and slowly working outward until the chocolate has been smoothly melted into the cream. Set aside.

TO ASSEMBLE

Scrape the ganache into the tart shell and give the pan a light rap on the counter to level the surface and remove any air bubbles. Allow the chocolate to set at room temperature for at least 3 hours and up to 12 hours. Sprinkle with the sea salt.

A slice of Chocolate Caramel Tart with Sea Salt.

LEMON TART BRÛLÉE

I first came up with this dessert after making the transition from being a restaurant pastry chef to learning the role of a bakery pastry chef at Bouley Bakery. One of my reservations about creating bakery desserts was that I thought people wouldn't experience the same visceral reaction that they get from a restaurant dessert that's been baked to order and delivered to the table warm. This dessert convinced me that such a reaction was possible. People would come up to me at the bakery and just rave about it. It was a pastry showstopper.

All that adulation can come to you too, because this dessert is simple to make and gorgeous to present. It uses an almond tart shell, which you fill with lemon curd. Since each step is done individually, you've got a lot of control, and you can prepare

the components in advance and assemble it at the last moment. Sprinkling a little Demerara or granulated sugar over the top and caramelizing it with the blowtorch leaves a beautiful burnished color on top of the lemon curd. That thin, sweet caramelized crust balances the tartness of the lemon curd itself, kind of like a lemon meringue pie but without the fluff! This is one for serious lemon-heads.

To brûlée in the oven: The tart crust may already be brown enough. If so, loosely cover the edges with foil and then place under a 500°F broiler until the sugar caramelizes.

MAKES 1 (10-INCH) TART TO SERVE 8 TO 10

SPECIAL EQUIPMENT: ZESTER, FOOD PROCESSOR, 10-INCH TART PAN, FINE-MESH SIEVE, CANDY THERMOMETER, IMMERSION BLENDER (OPTIONAL), BLOWTORCH OR CRÈME CARAMEL TORCH (OPTIONAL)

Recipe continues

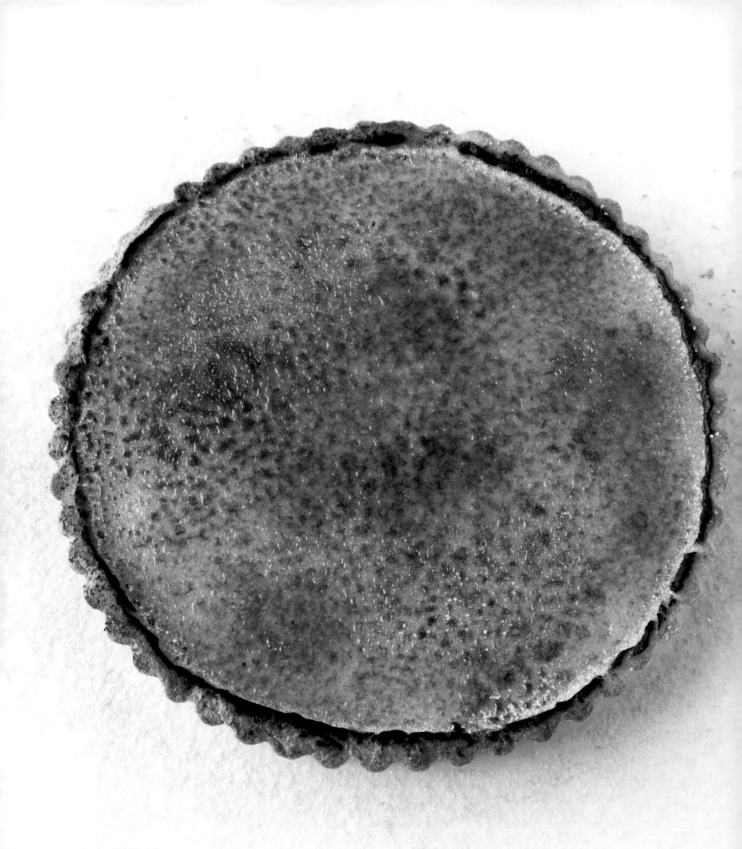

Lemon Tart Brûlée.

ALMOND TART SHELL

- 2 cups all-purpose flour (8 ounces, 240 grams), plus additional for dusting
- 1 cup confectioners' sugar (4 ounces, 113 grams)
- 1 cup almond flour (see Sources, page 275) or finely ground blanched almonds (3.7 ounces, 107 grams)
- 1 teaspoon fine sea salt (5 grams)
- 16 tablespoons (2 sticks) unsalted butter, chilled and cut into cubes (8 ounces, 226 grams)
- 2 large eggs (3.4 ounces, 96 grams), at room temperature

LEMON FILLING

- 1 cup plus 2 tablespoons granulated sugar (7.88 ounces, 225 grams)
- 4 large eggs (6.8 ounces, 193 grams), at room temperature
- ⅔ cup freshly squeezed lemon juice (from 3 to 4 lemons) (5.8 ounces, 166.6 grams)
- Finely grated zest of 3 lemons
- 21⅓ tablespoons unsalted butter, cubed and softened (10.67 ounces, 303 grams)
- Pinch of salt
- 1 (10-inch) almond tart shell, baked
- ½ cup Demarara or turbinado sugar, for serving, optional (4 ounces, 118 grams)

FOR THE ALMOND TART SHELL

1. Place the all-purpose flour, sugar, almond flour or ground almonds, and salt in a food processor and pulse to combine. Add the butter and pulse until the mixture resembles fine crumbs. Add the eggs and pulse until the dough just comes together.

2. Scrape the dough onto a piece of plastic wrap and pat it into a disk. Refrigerate until chilled, at least 2 hours or overnight (or up to 3 days).

3. When you are ready to bake the tart, position a rack in the center of the oven and preheat to 375°F. On a floured work surface, roll the dough out to 1/4 inch thick. Fit the dough into a 10-inch tart pan, trim it so that there is an inch of overhang all around, and fold the overhang in to build up the edge of the tart shell. Lightly prick the bottom of the tart shell with a fork to prevent bubbling. Freeze the tart shell for 1 hour.

4. Line the tart shell with aluminum foil, fill it with pie weights or dried beans, and bake on the center rack for 25 minutes. Gently lift the weighted aluminum foil off the shell, prick the crust a few more times with a fork, and bake for 5 more minutes until lightly browned. Let cool on a wire rack.

FOR THE LEMON FILLING

1. Have ready a clean bowl with a fine-mesh sieve set over it to strain the filling.

Recipe continues

2. In a bowl, beat together the sugar, eggs, lemon juice, and lemon zest until thoroughly combined. Pour into a heavy, nonreactive saucepan. Cook over medium heat, stirring constantly, until the mixture begins to bubble. Reduce the heat to low and continue to stir and cook until the lemon curd is as thick around the sides as mayonnaise, 12 minutes (about 196°F on a candy thermometer).

3. Pour the curd into the sieve and push through with a rubber spatula into the bowl. Let cool until it feels just warm to the touch, about 5 minutes.

4. Add the softened butter cubes and salt, and whisk until thoroughly combined. (Use an immersion blender to smoothly incorporate the butter).

5. Spread the curd evenly in the baked tart shell and refrigerate uncovered until firm, at least 3 hours and up to 1 day.

6. If you have a blowtorch or crème caramel torch, you can brûlée the top of the tart before serving by sprinkling an even layer of the Demarara or turbinado sugar over the top and browning it evenly. Or run it under the broiler, watching very carefully—depending on how far the pan is from the heat it can take anywhere from 30 seconds to 2 minutes, and you may need to move the tart around to caramelize the top evenly.

Almond Tart Shell for Lemon Tart Brûlée, before baking.

Caramelizing the top of Lemon Tart Brûlée with a blow torch.

YOGURT CAKE

This cake represents a major theme of this book; elegant simplicity. It will make a perfect finish to a lunch, coffee break, or dinner. By now you know I like natural fruit flavors in desserts. In my opinion, a well-balanced fruit dessert is the most difficult to achieve and satisfying to taste. Citrus is especially welcome in cakes because it adds a counterpoint to the sweetness. This cake pairs the bracing flavor of pink grapefruit zest with the tang of yogurt. Serve with a few pink grapefruit supremes if you are citrus fan, too.

MAKES 1 (9-OR-10-INCH) SINGLE LAYER CAKE TO SERVE 6

SPECIAL EQUIPMENT: 9- OR 10-INCH ROUND CAKE PAN, ZESTER, ELECTRIC MIXER, CAKE TESTER, SIFTER

1 large grapefruit, ideally pink (about 1 pound, 454 grams)

2 cups all-purpose flour (8.5 ounces, 240 grams)

1½ cups sugar (10.5 ounces, 300 grams)

1 teaspoon baking powder (4.9 grams)

½ teaspoon baking soda (2.5 grams)

Pinch of salt

1 cup plain yogurt (8 ounces, 228 grams), whole milk, not low fat

½ cup vegetable oil (4 ounces, 114 grams), plus some for the pan

2 large eggs (3.4 ounces, 96 grams)

Confectioners' sugar, for sifting

1. Finely grate the zest of the grapefruit and set aside. To "supreme" the grapefruit (see How to Supreme an Orange, page 8), use a serrated knife to cut off both ends. Stand the fruit upright on a board and slice away the rind, cutting with the curve of the fruit from top to bottom and leaving no pith. Hold the grapefruit over a bowl in one hand and slice the segments away from the membranes so that the fruit slides, whole, into the bowl. Squeeze any remaining juice into the bowl and discard any pits. Strain the juice, reserving the supremes for garnish.

2. In a large bowl, whisk together the flour, sugar, baking powder, baking soda, and salt.

3. Preheat the oven to 350° F. Grease a 9- to 10-inch cake pan and line with parchment paper.

Recipe continues

4. In the bowl of an electric mixer fitted with the paddle attachment, blend together the yogurt, oil, egg, grapefruit zest, and 1 tablespoon of the strained juice (reserve the rest for another use). Beat in the flour mixture until just combined.

5. Pour the batter into the prepared pan. Bake until a cake tester inserted in the center comes out clean, about 30 minutes. Let the cake cool in the pan for 10 minutes, then invert onto a wire rack to cool completely. Just before serving, sift confectioners' sugar over the top of the cake and garnish with the reserved grapefruit slices.

LEMON POUND CAKE SUPREME

When I first went to France to start training as a chef, I began to appreciate the way the French could elevate even the simplest dessert, like a pound cake, to the realm of the divine. At Au Vieux Four in Tours, I worked with master pastry chef Jacques Mahou, who made possibly one of the most awe-inspiring lemon pound cakes ever. To get another layer of lemon flavor into the cake, after baking, he submerged the warm cake in a lemon-flavored simple syrup. Then, very gently, he squeezed the cake with his hands as if it were a sponge to encourage it to absorb as much syrup as possible. The syrup moistened the interior of the cake, which improved the texture and helped it stay fresh for a week or more (when stored, well wrapped, in the refrigerator).

Over the years, I've stayed relatively true to Jacques' recipe, changing only one thing. To further intensify the citrus tang of the cake, I add lemon segments to the batter. While baking, the fruit evaporates away, leaving potent lemon-scented pockets. It's a cake for lemon-lovers only, but trust me, there's no better cake out there for them.

MAKES 1 (9-INCH) LOAF TO SERVE 8

SPECIAL EQUIPMENT: 9-BY-5-INCH LOAF PAN, ZESTER, SIFTER, ELECTRIC MIXER, CAKE TESTER, SIEVE, BAKING SHEET, OFFSET SPATULA

9 lemons (45 ounces, 1260 grams)

2¾ cups all-purpose flour (12.4 ounces, 357.5 grams)

1½ cups superfine sugar (10.5 ounces, 298 grams)

1½ teaspoons baking powder (7.35 grams)

¾ cup crème fraîche or heavy cream (6.09 ounces, 174 grams)

6 large eggs (10.2 ounces, 289 grams), at room temperature

11 tablespoons unsalted butter, melted (5.5 ounces, 156.1 grams), plus additional for the bottom and sides of the pan and the parchment paper

1½ cups granulated sugar (10.5 ounces, 298 grams)

½ cup confectioners' sugar (2 ounces, 57 grams)

1. Position a rack in the center of the oven and preheat to 350°F. Use butter to grease the bottom and sides of a 9-by-5-inch loaf pan, line the bottom with parchment or waxed paper, then grease the paper.

Recipe continues

Intense Chocolate Pound Cake (*left*);
Lemon Pound Cake Supreme (*right*).

2. Set 2 of the lemons aside. Grate the zest of 4 lemons and set those lemons and their zest aside also. Slice off the tops and bottoms of 3 unzested lemons. Stand each lemon on end on a cutting board and use a small knife to slice away the skin and white pith, leaving the flesh exposed. Working over a bowl, cut the segments away from the membranes (see How to Supreme an Orange, page 8) and let the fruit and juice fall into the bowl (remove any seeds). Using a fork, break the segments into 1-inch pieces.

3. Sift the flour, superfine sugar, and baking powder into the bowl of an electric mixer. Begin mixing on low speed, then add the crème fraîche or cream. Increase the speed to medium and beat in the eggs one at a time, the butter, and 3 tablespoons of the lemon zest. Gently fold the lemon segments and juices into the batter. Scrape the batter into the prepared pan and bake on the center rack for 15 minutes. Use a sharp knife to cut an incision lengthwise down the middle of the cake. This will prevent the cake from splitting on the side. Bake for 30 minutes longer. Lower the oven to 325°F and bake for 40 to 45 minutes longer, until a cake tester inserted in the center comes out clean.

4. Meanwhile, juice the 6 lemons you set aside in step 1 and strain the juice. Put the granulated sugar and the confectioners' sugar in a pot over high heat and add 1 1/2 cups water. Bring to a simmer and cook, stirring, until the sugar is dissolved. Stir in the lemon juice and remaining zest and let cool.

5. When the cake is done, transfer it to a wire rack to cool in the pan for 30 minutes. Raise the oven temperature to 350°F. Slide a thin knife or offset spatula around the sides of the pan and turn it over to unmold the cake onto a sheet pan, and carefully peel the parchment or waxed paper from the bottom of the cake. Pour the lemon syrup over the cake and very gently squeeze the cake to help it absorb the syrup. Carefully turn the cake over and squeeze a bit more until all the syrup is absorbed. It makes for messy hands, but is worth the effort. Transfer the cake to a clean cookie sheet and return it to the oven for 10 minutes to set the glaze. Cool on a rack.

Intense Chocolate Pound Cake with shiny dark chocolate glaze.

INTENSE CHOCOLATE POUND CAKE
WITH DARK CHOCOLATE GLAZE

Pound cakes are among the oldest cakes in existence, dating back to pre–Renaissance fifteenth-century Europe. French recipes for Quatre-Quatre call for equal weights of four ingredients: butter, sugar, flour, and eggs. I've found the formula works better if you lighten up some of the ingredients, say, favoring eggs over flour. Lightness is also achieved by whipping air into the butter and adding baking powder.

This dessert is the ideal portable frosted cake because the glaze sets to a smooth, nonsticky consistency. For both the glaze and the cake itself, I like to use a combination of cocoa, which adds a bitter, earthy background and a lot of good color, and bittersweet chocolate for that authentic chocolate taste and texture.

Because this is such a crowd pleaser, it's one of my first choices to put out at a buffet or any other large gathering. Unless there's a big plate of brownies on the table, this rich pound cake with its dark chocolate glaze is probably the first thing people will reach for and devour.

Chef's Note When buying chocolate, aim for a cacao percentage in the range of 55 to 70—anything above 70 percent I find overly bitter. Your basic bittersweet baking chocolate is about 58 percent, and most of the gourmet chocolates are 62 percent and up.

MAKES 1 (9-INCH) LOAF TO SERVE 8

SPECIAL EQUIPMENT: 9-BY-5-INCH LOAF PAN, ELECTRIC MIXER, OFFSET SPATULA, RIMMED
BAKING SHEET, FINE-MESH SIEVE

CHOCOLATE POUND CAKE

- 1½ cups all-purpose flour (6.75 ounces, 195 grams), plus additional for the pan

- 3 tablespoons Dutch-processed unsweetened cocoa powder (.6 ounce, 17.25 grams)

- ½ teaspoon baking powder (2.45 grams)

- ½ teaspoon baking soda (2.5 grams)

- ¼ teaspoon fine sea salt (1.25 grams)

- ¼ pound (1 stick) unsalted butter (4 ounces, 113 grams), plus additional for the pan

- ¾ cup confectioners' sugar (5.25 ounces, 150 grams)

- 4 large eggs (6.8 ounces, 193 grams), at room temperature

- ½ cup crème fraîche or sour cream (4.25 ounces, 121 grams)

- 3 ounces bittersweet chocolate (preferably 60 to 66 percent cacao content), melted (½ cup; 84 grams)

Recipe continues

DARK CHOCOLATE GLAZE

- 2 ounces bittersweet chocolate (preferably 60 to 66 percent cacao content), coarsely chopped (½ cup, 57 grams)
- ¼ cup light corn syrup (2.87 ounces, 82 grams)
- 3 tablespoons Dutched, unsweetened cocoa powder (.6 ounce, 17.25 grams)
- 1 tablespoon neutral vegetable oil such as canola or grapeseed (.5 ounce, 13.4 grams)
- ½ cup heavy cream (4.06 ounces, 116 grams)

FOR THE CAKE

1. Position a rack in the center of the oven and preheat to 350°F. Butter and flour a 9-by-5-inch loaf pan, line the bottom with parchment or waxed paper, then butter and flour the paper.

2. In a bowl, whisk together the flour, cocoa, baking powder, baking soda, and salt.

3. In the bowl of an electric mixer fitted with the whisk attachment, cream the butter with the sugar at medium speed until light and fluffy, about 5 minutes. Add the eggs one at a time, beating at medium speed to incorporate and scraping down the sides of the bowl after each addition. Set on a rack over a rimmed baking sheet.

4. On low speed, mix in a third of the flour mixture, then half of the crème fraîche or sour cream, and half the chocolate. Repeat, then end with the last third of the flour. Scrape down the bowl after each addition.

5. Scrape the batter into the prepared pan and bake on the center rack until a knife inserted into the center of the loaf comes out clean, about 1 hour. Transfer the pan to a wire rack to cool. When cool, run a thin knife or offset spatula around the sides of the pan and turn it over to gently unmold the cake onto the rack. Remove the parchment or waxed paper from the bottom of the cake and set the cake upright on the cake rack set over a rimmed baking sheet.

FOR THE GLAZE

1. In a bowl, combine the chocolate, corn syrup, cocoa, and oil.

2. In a heavy saucepan over medium-high heat, stirring frequently, bring the cream to a boil. Pour the cream over the ingredients in the bowl and whisk until the chocolate glaze becomes smooth. Use immediately.

TO SERVE

Pour the warm glaze through a fine-mesh sieve all over the top of the cake and let it drip down the sides. I like the look of the glaze drippings on the sides of the cake, but if you want a fully iced look, use a small offset spatula to scoop up the glaze that's pooled on the baking sheet after you've poured it, and use that to ice the sides completely. Refrigerate the cake for 1 hour to set the glaze before serving. If you like the effect of the shiny chocolate glaze in the photo, pass a hair dryer on medium heat over the surface of the glazed cake.

Orange-Glazed Olive Oil Cake with Fleur de Sel.

ORANGE-GLAZED OLIVE OIL CAKE
WITH FLEUR DE SEL

This is a variation on a Sicilian classic in which oranges are preserved by simmering with a small amount of sugar, then blended right into the cake batter. The candied oranges and olive oil make the cake particularly moist, and the flaky crystals of fleur de sel accentuate the intense citrus flavor. The orange glaze helps keep the cake moist for several days.

MAKES 1 (10-INCH) CAKE TO SERVE 8 TO 10

SPECIAL EQUIPMENT: 10-INCH ROUND CAKE PAN, SIFTER, FOOD PROCESSOR, ELECTRIC MIXER, CAKE TESTER, OFFSET SPATULA

Unsalted butter, for the pan

2 navel oranges or thin-skinned juice oranges, such as Valencia (about 11 ounces, 308 grams)

2⅓ cups sugar (16.3 ounces, 467 grams)

2½ cups all-purpose flour (11.25 ounces, 325 grams)

2 teaspoons baking powder (4.9 grams)

1 teaspoon baking soda (5 grams)

6 tablespoons extra-virgin olive oil (2.25 ounces, 65 grams)

4 large eggs (6.8 ounces, 193 grams), at room temperature

1 teaspoon vanilla extract (4 grams)

½ teaspoon fleur de sel (see Sources, page 275) (1.25 grams)

Orange glaze (see page 128)

1. In a large pot, bring 3 quarts water to a boil. Slice the bottoms and the tops off the oranges (where the rind is the thickest) and quarter the oranges. Plunge the orange, rind and all, into the water, allow the water to return to a boil, remove, and drain. Repeat the process two more times. This blanching will remove the bitterness from the orange rind.

2. Place the oranges in a pot filled with 1 quart fresh water and 1 cup of the sugar. Bring to a boil, stirring until the sugar has dissolved, then let simmer until the rind is softened and can be easily pierced with a fork, about 30 minutes. At this point, the oranges can be cooled and kept in a container, in the syrup, in the fridge for up to 3 weeks before you proceed with the recipe.

3. Position a rack in the center of the oven and preheat to 350°F. Grease a 10-inch round cake pan.

Recipe continues

4. Sift the flour, baking powder, and baking soda onto a piece of parchment or waxed paper and set aside.

5. Pull the prepared oranges from the syrup with a slotted spoon, and discard any remaining seeds in the cooked orange segments. Cut the oranges into chunks. Place them, rind and all, in the bowl of a food processor fitted with the blade attachment (discard the syrup), and pulse until the oranges form a puree. The puree will be slightly chunky and not perfectly smooth, and this is okay.

6. Add the eggs, the remaining 1 1/3 cups sugar, the flour mixture, and the vanilla extract to the food processor. Pulse until well blended.

7. Add the olive oil last and pulse until thoroughly blended.

8. Pour the batter into the prepared cake pan and bake on the center rack until a cake tester inserted in the center of the cake comes out clean and the top of the cake is golden brown, 40 to 50 minutes. Let cool in the pan for 10 minutes, then slide a thin knife or offset spatula around the sides of the pan and turn it over to unmold the cake onto a plate, then flip the cake onto a wire rack. Let cool thoroughly on the rack, at least 30 to 40 minutes more, and pour orange glaze over the cake when cool. Sprinkle the fleur de sel over the cake at the last minute.

A slice of Orange-Glazed Olive Oil Cake with Fleur de Sel.

HOW TO MAKE ORANGE-GLAZED OLIVE OIL CAKE WITH FLEUR DE SEL.

1. The oranges after boiling in water and sugar. Cut them into chunks.

2. Place the oranges in the bowl of a food processor fitted with the blade attachment.

3. Pulse the oranges to form a chunky puree.

4. Pulse in the eggs, sugar, flour mixture, and vanilla extract.

5. The mixture doubled in volume, fluffy and pale.

6. Top off the batter with olive oil and blend. Then pour the batter into a cake pan and bake on the center rack, 35 to 40 minutes. Sprinkle with fleur de sel.

RESTAURANT DESSERTS YOU CAN MAKE AT HOME

Whether you're hosting a dinner party for a group of friends or simply want to be more creative in the kitchen, focusing on presentation is an excellent way to take your baking to the next level. Designing a plated dessert is something most home cooks don't even think about doing, but in a professional kitchen, it's the norm because presentation is paramount to an extraordinary dining experience. Desserts like pies, cobblers, and crumbles have a certain homey charm to them, but when they collapse and spread out over an entire plate, they're not suitable for a restaurant—so they are presented in individual ramekins or molds, or some other clever way the pastry chef has imagined. Restaurants use all sorts of garnishes to make desserts look more attractive. Candied nuts, drizzled sauces, sugared flowers, and shaved chocolate are all good choices, but they must be added just before serving to make the dessert look its most appealing.

All the desserts in this chapter have been very popular in New York restaurants I've worked in, not just due to their marvelous flavors but also because of the original way in which they are assembled and presented. My goal is to have them please the eye with their clean and sharp design without being too architectural or overly conceived.

You can be playful with them, as I am with the jaunty Butterscotch–Dulce de Leche Pudding in Teacups (page 166) or the whimsical Floating Islands in Spiced Crème Anglaise (page 169). Think of the plate as a blank canvas and imagine you're assembling a collage with the ingredients you have at hand—this is where both the chef and artist in you get to shine!

Here's your chance to decorate your desserts with garnishes such as candied violets, caramelized nuts, or fruit compotes. Squeeze bottles are excellent tools for adding sauces and syrups to your dessert—you can "paint" Jackson Pollock–style or use the tip of the bottle to "draw" in flourishes around the edge of the plate.

If being artistic with sauces and garnishes is not your specialty, you can still make your desserts look fun and exciting by carefully choosing your serving medium. Find some interesting plates on which to serve your desserts—glass, glazed ceramics, or simply square-shaped plates are all easy ways to dress up a dessert. Or, if you don't mind hunting around a bit, purchase some funky teacups from a thrift shop or flea market. For desserts that involve fruit, you can use certain tropical leaves to make an exotic and unusual presentation. Banana leaves are sometimes available in Asian and Latin American markets and make terrific platters. Or do as the French do and serve orange, lemon, lime, or pineapple sorbet in the hollowed-out fruit shell. You needn't spend a lot of money to make your desserts stand out—look around your house for old serving sets and dishes and get creative!

OVEN-ROASTED PEACHES WITH GREEN TEA ELIXIR

Ripe, juicy peaches don't need much to make a spectacular finale, so with this summery dessert, I tread lightly. The peaches are halved and roasted until the juices condense slightly and the flesh warms through. Once they're roasted, I serve them simply, with a pale green froth made from Japanese matcha that's been blended with milk, sugar, and ice cubes. It's a stunning presentation that your guests are unlikely to have ever seen or eaten before. (See photograph on page 156).

Chef's Note Don't use anything in this recipe but matcha, the very high-quality, stone-ground powder of select, shade-grown Japanese green tea. Many studies claim health benefits from this antioxidant-rich tea, including increased mental clarity without the caffeine jitters. Use the ultra-high-quality ceremonial grade of matcha from Japan; Ito En is a good brand. Judge the tea powder by its color. If it is anything but bright, almost fluorescent green, don't use it. Stale green tea will take on a dull green color. See Sources on page 275 for green tea powder.

MAKES 6 ROASTED PEACHES TO SERVE 6
SPECIAL EQUIPMENT: BAKING SHEET, BLENDER

Unsalted butter, for the pan

3 large ripe peaches, unpeeled (about 15 ounces, 160 grams)

GREEN TEA ELIXIR

¼ cup whole milk (2.1 ounces, 60 grams)

2 tablespoons sugar (.9 ounce, 25 grams)

1 tablespoon good-quality matcha (green tea powder; see Sources, page 275) (5 grams)

1 cup ice cubes (4.75 ounces, 135 grams)

FOR THE PEACHES

1. Position a rack in the center of the oven and preheat to 350°F. Grease a baking sheet with unsalted butter.

2. Halve the peaches lengthwise and pit them. Don't peel yet. Place the peach halves, cut side up, on the baking sheet. Bake on the center rack until fork tender, about 15 minutes. When cool enough to handle, peel off the skins, and cut into 1-inch cubes.

FOR THE GREEN TEA ELIXIR

Place the milk, sugar, and green tea powder in a blender and blend to combine. Add the ice and continue to blend until smooth. Place the chopped peaches in a bowl or goblet. Pour the elixer over them and serve right away.

Sweet Basil Seed and
Tapioca Pudding.

SWEET BASIL SEED AND TAPIOCA PUDDING

This Southeast Asian–inspired dessert was always a best-seller in a Vietnamese restaurant I used to own in New York City. It's fantastic, flavorwise, with the rich, coconut-infused pudding accented with a piquant zing from pomegranate molasses. The mix of chewy tapioca and creamy pudding can be complemented by juicy, crunchy pomegranate seeds, as well as the pliant pearls of tapioca, and crunchy, gelatinous basil seeds. Sweet basil seeds are literally seeds that would grow into a basil plant. Texturally fascinating, they are a great vehicle for flavor, as they absorb flavored liquids while developing a gelatinous covering. This recipe requires an overnight rest, so plan accordingly. Both the pearl tapioca and the sweet basil seeds can be purchased online (see Sources, pages 275 and 276).

Chef's Note Sweet basil seed is an exotic ingredient that is very usual in appearance but that can be used to transmit flavors without adding extra fat. Although fat is the best transmitter of flavors, the basil seed absorbs the flavors surrounding it and allows them to linger on the tongue for prolonged enjoyment. The silky texture is refreshing, and the seeds can be stored in the fridge for weeks in a closed container with citrus rinds, vanilla beans, and herbs.

MAKES ABOUT 3 CUPS PUDDING TO SERVE 6
SPECIAL EQUIPMENT: ZESTER, 6 SHALLOW BOWLS, FOR SERVING

BASIL SEED GARNISH

- 1 tablespoon sweet basil seeds (see Sources, page 276) (9 grams)
- ⅓ cup water (preferably uncarbonated mineral water) (2.8 ounces, 78.7 grams)
- Finely grated zest of 1 orange
- 1½ teaspoons medium-flavored honey such as orange blossom or clover (10.8 grams)

COCONUT TAPIOCA

- 1 cup pearl tapioca (see Sources, page 275) (6 ounces, 170 grams)

- 1 (15-ounce) can cream of coconut (see Sources, page 275) (427 grams)
- 1 (13.5-ounce) can sweetened coconut milk (384 grams)
- ⅔ cup sugar (5 ounces, 143 grams)
- 1 vanilla bean, split lengthwise, seeds scraped and reserved, or 1 teaspoon vanilla extract (4 grams)
- Large pinch of salt

OPTIONAL

Pomegranate molasses, for serving (see Sources, page 275)

Pomegranate seeds, for serving

Recipe continues

FOR THE GARNISH

Place the basil seeds in a bowl. In a saucepan, bring the mineral water to a boil. Add the orange zest and honey, stir to melt the honey, and pour over the basil seeds. Cover and refrigerate overnight.

FOR THE TAPIOCA

1. Place the pearls in a large bowl with water to cover. Cover and refrigerate overnight.

2. The next day, drain the tapioca. In a medium-size heavy-bottomed saucepan, combine the soaked pearls with the coconut cream and milk, sugar, vanilla bean seeds and pod, and salt. Bring to a boil, reduce heat, stirring constantly, and simmer for 4 minutes. Let cool, then transfer to a bowl, cover, and refrigerate until chilled, about 2 hours.

TO SERVE

Serve the tapioca in shallow bowls. Scatter a ring of basil seeds along the outside edge of each bowl. Garnish with banana slices and pistachios. Drizzle with a little pomegranate molasses and garnish with pomegranate seeds, if desired.

WARM MOLTEN VANILLA CAKES

My contribution to the molten cake genre is an ideal vehicle for floral vanilla beans and buttery white chocolate. It was originally conceived of as part of a plated presentation, with vanilla gelée, vanilla ice cream, a vanilla tuile, and a candied vanilla bean. It was a surprise success at the Citarella restaurant in New York City, where it quickly became the most requested dessert. Although gelée, tuiles, and candied vanilla beans aren't necessary for the pleasure of the cake, I highly recommend adding a cool, fragrant scoop of vanilla ice cream to set off the warm cake and flowing white chocolate center. The experience is as much about the delightful perfume of vanilla as it is about its flavor, so inhale deeply as you dig in.

MAKES 12 INDIVIDUAL CAKES IN A MUFFIN TIN OR 16 CAKES IN RAMEKINS
SPECIAL EQUIPMENT: SIFTER, DOUBLE BOILER, ELECTRIC MIXER,
12-CUP STANDARD-SIZE MUFFIN TIN OR 16 (4-OUNCE) RAMEKINS, OFFSET SPATULA

⅓ cup all-purpose flour (1.4 ounces, 40.3 grams)

16 ounces coarsely chopped white chocolate (about 4½ cups, 454 grams)

7 tablespoons unsalted butter, plus additional for the muffin tin (3.5 ounces, 99 grams)

5 large eggs (8.5 ounces, 241 grams), separated, at room temperature

3 vanilla beans, split lengthwise, seeds scraped and reserved, or 1 teaspoon vanilla extract (4 grams)

Pinch of cream of tartar

⅓ cup sugar (2.3 ounces, 67 grams)

1. Have your serving plates or platter ready to receive the upended cakes. Sift the flour onto a piece of parchment or waxed paper and set aside. Set aside 8 ounces (half) of the white chocolate, cut or broken into twelve 1-inch cubes (16 cubes if using ramekins) for the cake centers.

2. In a double boiler over steaming—but not boiling—water, melt the butter with the remaining 8 ounces of white chocolate, stirring occasionally. (Alternatively, melt them in the microwave at 50 percent power, stirring every minute.) Stir until smooth, then whisk in the egg yolks and the seeds of the vanilla beans or vanilla extract. Sprinkle the flour over this mixture and whisk until smooth.

3. In the bowl of an electric mixer fitted with the whisk attachment, beat the egg whites and cream of tartar on medium speed until very foamy. Gradually add the sugar, then raise the speed to high and beat until the meringue forms soft, glossy

Recipe continues

Warm Molten Vanilla Cakes with vanilla ice cream.

peaks. Fold the meringue into the white chocolate mixture until smooth. Cover the bowl with plastic wrap and refrigerate overnight.

4. Position a rack in the center of the oven and preheat to 375°F. Generously butter a 12-cup muffin tin or 16 ramekins. Cut small parchment paper rounds (or cut the bases from paper muffin liners) and fit them into the bottom of each muffin cup or ramekin. Divide the batter evenly among the cups. Push a square of the reserved 3 ounces of white chocolate cubes down into the center of each cake.

5. Bake on the center rack until the tops of the cakes give resistance, about 18 minutes. When pushed with a finger, they should feel like a filled balloon (no need to use a cake tester, since the centers are melted white chocolate!). Remove from the oven. Slide a thin knife or offset spatula around the sides of the muffin cups or ramekins, cutting away one cake at a time. Invert the tin over a baking sheet large enough to accommodate all twelve. Unmold and, working quickly, carefully transfer the cakes to the reserved plates or platter one at a time. Carefully remove the parchment paper circles from the bottoms of the cakes and serve right away, with softened vanilla ice cream. When your guests cut into them, the cakes will ooze white chocolate.

BUTTERSCOTCH–DULCE DE LECHE PUDDING IN TEACUPS

Adding dulce de leche, that caramelized milk sauce used in Latin American desserts, to butterscotch pudding intensifies its caramel taste. This recipe will still yield a fine traditional butterscotch flavor if you leave it out. I serve the nutty, brown sugar–rich butterscotch pudding in sturdy teacups or ramekins, then top the puddings with whipped cream and spoon over some dulce de leche.

MAKES 8 SINGLE-SERVING PUDDINGS
SPECIAL EQUIPMENT: CANDY THERMOMETER, 8 (6-OUNCE) TEACUPS OR RAMEKINS.

BUTTERSCOTCH PUDDING

1½ cups packed dark brown sugar (12.6 ounces, 358.5 grams)

4 large egg yolks (2 ounces, 57 grams), at room temperature

½ cup cornstarch (1.4 ounces, 50 grams)

4 cups whole milk (34 ounces, 968 grams)

1 vanilla bean, split lengthwise, seeds scraped and reserved, or 1 teaspoon vanilla extract (4 grams)

½ teaspoon salt (2.5 grams)

4 tablespoons dulce de leche (see Sources, page 275) or commercial butterscotch sauce, optional (1 ounce, 40 grams), plus more for garnish

4 tablespoons (½ stick) unsalted butter (2 ounces, 57 grams)

Whipped cream, for garnish

FOR THE PUDDING

1. In a heavy-bottomed saucepan, whisk together the brown sugar, eggs, and cornstarch. Set aside. In another saucepan, over medium-high heat, bring the milk, vanilla bean or vanilla extract, and salt to a boil.

2. Take the milk mixture off the heat and slowly whisk the mixture into the sugar-egg mixture, and continue to whisk until it has been fully incorporated. Whisk in the dulce de leche or butterscotch sauce, if using.

3. Attach a candy thermometer to the side of the pan. Transfer the pan to the heat and bring to a simmer, stirring constantly with a heatproof rubber spatula or wooden spoon, taking care to scrape the inside of the pan. Do not let the mixture come to a boil or reach more than 180°F, or it will curdle.

4. When the pudding has thickened slightly (at 160 to 170°F), remove from the heat and stir in the butter. Divide the pudding among eight 6-ounce teacups or ramekins, allow to cool, and cover each with plastic. Refrigerate until chilled, about 2 hours.

TO SERVE

Serve the chilled puddings with whipped cream and dulce de leche, resting on top.

Butterscotch-Dulce de Leche Pudding in Teacups.

Floating Islands in Spiced Crème Anglaise.

FLOATING ISLANDS IN SPICED CRÈME ANGLAISE

This French classic—a combination of soft meringue clouds floating on a pool of vanilla-flavored crème anglaise—should be in every baker's repertoire because everybody loves it. I learned how to make it at Perigord Park restaurant in New York, where it was plated to order from a very old-school dessert cart wheeled around the dining room. It was equally popular with the set that used to come in for brunch to nurse the effects of dancing all night at Studio 54, and our more mature and stately regulars, Laurence Olivier, Claudette Colbert, and Douglas Fairbanks Jr. among them, who said the dessert reminded them of haute cuisine dinners in France.

My innovation here is to infuse the custard sauce with cardamom and star anise for an earthier, more intense flavor, which is an interesting and unexpected contrast to the ethereal meringue.

MAKES ABOUT 2¼ CUPS OF CRÈME ANGLAISE AND 12 MERINGUES TO SERVE 6

SPECIAL EQUIPMENT: SIFTER, DOUBLE BOILER, FINE-MESH SIEVE, CANDY THERMOMETER, RIMMED 11-BY-17-INCH BAKING SHEET, NONSTICK LINER (OPTIONAL), ELECTRIC MIXER, 9-BY-13-INCH BAKING PAN, 6 SHALLOW, WIDE DESSERT BOWLS, FOR SERVING

SPICED CRÈME ANGLAISE

- 2 cups whole milk (17 ounces, 484 grams)

- 1 teaspoon green cardamom pods, lightly crushed (see Sources, page 275) (.25 ounce, 7 grams)

- 2 whole star anise (see Sources, page 276)

- 5 large egg yolks (3 ounces, 85 grams), at room temperature

- 5 tablespoons sugar (2.5 ounces, 71 grams)

- Pinch of salt

CARAMEL SAUCE

- ⅓ cup granulated sugar (2.3 ounces, 67 grams)

FLOATING ISLANDS (ÎLES FLOTTANTES)

- 1 cup whole milk (8.5 ounces, 242 grams), for poaching liquid

- 4 egg whites (4 ounces, 113 grams), at room temperature

- ¼ teaspoon cream of tartar (.77 gram)

- 1 cup confectioners' sugar, sifted (4 ounces, 113 grams), plus additional for sprinkling

- 1 pint whole raspberries or sliced strawberries, for serving

Recipe continues

FOR THE CRÈME ANGLAISE

1. In a saucepan over medium heat combine the milk, cardamom pods, and star anise, and bring to a simmer. Simmer for 2 minutes, then turn off the heat and let the spices infuse for 5 minutes.

2. Bring an inch of water to a simmer in the base of a double boiler (or in a saucepan over which you will be able to suspend a metal bowl).

3. In the top bowl of the double boiler (or metal bowl), whisk the egg yolks with the sugar and salt. Return the milk mixture to a simmer and strain it through a fine-mesh sieve into the yolks, while whisking constantly (discard the whole spices). Attach a candy thermometer to the side of the double boiler (or metal bowl). Transfer this custard to the top of the double boiler (or the bowl) and cook, stirring constantly, until it thickens and coats the back of a wooden spoon (at 160 to 170°F), 3 to 5 minutes. Transfer to a bowl and let cool to room temperature.

FOR THE CARAMEL SAUCE

Have ready 1/4 cup hot water. Pour the sugar into a heavy saucepan and add 2 tablespoons cold water. Cook over high heat, stirring, until the sugar dissolves. Let the mixture bubble, swirling the pan occasionally if it colors unevenly, until it forms a dark amber caramel (at about 374°F), about 10 minutes. Take the pan off the heat and carefully whisk the hot water into the caramel (it may sputter). Return the pan to the heat and stir until smooth. Set aside, covered.

FOR THE FLOATING ISLANDS

1. In a saucepan over medium heat, prepare the poaching liquid. Combine the milk with 1 cup water and bring to a simmer, then turn off the heat.

2. In the bowl of an electric mixer fitted with the whisk attachment, beat the whites with the cream of tartar on medium speed until foamy, about 8 minutes. Gradually add the sifted confectioners' sugar. When all the sugar has been added, raise the speed to high, and beat until the meringue forms firm, glossy peaks, about 8 more minutes, which will give the meringue the strength it needs.

3. Fill a glass with very hot tap water. Dip two serving spoons into the water, then scoop an egg-size amount of meringue into one of the wet spoons. Rotate the "egg" of meringue, transferring it from spoon to spoon, to get a smooth, ovoid shape, then slide it onto the lined baking sheet. Repeat with the rest of the meringue (you should have twelve "islands").

4. Position a rack in the center of the oven and preheat to 350°F. Line a rimmed 11-by-17-inch baking sheet with parchment paper or a nonstick liner.

5. Bring the milk-and-water mixture back to a simmer and pour it into the 9-by-13-inch baking pan. Use a wet spatula to transfer the meringue "eggs" to the pan. Sift 2 or 3 tablespoons of confectioners' sugar over the tops of the meringues. Bake on the center rack until set, about 10 minutes. Use the spatula to transfer the meringues to a parchment-lined baking sheet once they are cooked. Allow the meringues to cool to room temperature. They last for 2 hours uncovered, no longer.

TO SERVE

Ladle in 1/3 cup of the crème anglaise onto each of six shallow, wide bowls. Place two meringues on top of each pool, drizzle them with caramel sauce, and scatter with raspberries or strawberries.

Serving options: Floating Islands in Spiced Crème Anglaise can be served unadorned (*left*) or with a drizzle of caramel sauce (*right*).

CRÊPES SUZETTE
WITH DARK RUM AND ORANGES

I always picture this romantic classic being flambéed tableside by a tuxedoed waiter in an old-school French restaurant, but it is also an exciting and vaguely retro dish for a special dinner at home. In my version, the delicately thin, tender crêpes—spiked with orange zest, dark rum, and walnut oil—are enveloped by warm, buttery orange sauce studded with glistening sections of the sweet-tart fruit. A scoop of ice cream adds a cold contrast, particularly if you plan to flambé the crêpes.

Keep in mind that the French say the first crêpe belongs to the dog. It's the trial run, when the pan may still be coming up to temperature and you're getting the hang of the swirl, so don't lose heart if your first few crêpes aren't perfectly even and tissue thin; the recipe makes plenty and you'll get the hang of it after a bit. If you don't have crêpe pans, one or two slope-sided nonstick pans will do the trick. Two or more pans are used in professional kitchens—the second pan adds a little element of challenge to crêpe making, but it's twice as fast. You can be pouring one crêpe while the second is cooking, and eventually you get a very quick rhythm going.

Chef's Note If you have the luxury of making the crêpe batter earlier in the day or even the night before, that not only saves time later but also allows the batter to fully absorb the flour, resulting in a thinner and more even crepe.

You can also cook the crêpes in advance if you like. Stack them up with sugar sprinkled between the layers to prevent sticking, then wrap in plastic and refrigerate for up to a day. The next day, just reheat them in the sauce they're to be served in. You can also freeze the stack. Defrost at room temperature and then reheat in the sauce.

The older the rum, the more intense the flavor. Look for the word "anejo," which means aged, on the label. Venezuelan aged rum is the gold standard of aged rum. Mellow, smoky, earthy, and oaky, it is the tops.

MAKES 24 TO 27 CRÊPES TO SERVE 8 TO 10
SPECIAL EQUIPMENT: ONE OR TWO 10-INCH NONSTICK, SLOPE-SIDED PANS, LADLE

1 cup all-purpose flour (6.75 ounces, 195 grams)

¾ cup sugar (5.25 ounces, 150 grams), plus additional for sprinkling

Finely grated zest of 1 orange

¼ teaspoon salt (1.25 grams)

3 large eggs (5.1 ounces, 145 grams), at room temperature

2 tablespoons walnut oil (see Sources, page 276) or vegetable oil (.95 ounce, 26.87 grams)

2 tablespoons dark rum (see Chef's Note) (.95 ounce, 27.5 grams)

1 teaspoon vanilla extract (4 grams)

2 cups whole milk (17 ounces, 484 grams)

Canola oil or butter, for cooking

2 navel oranges (7 ounces, 198 grams)

½ cup freshly squeezed orange juice (4.25 ounces, 121 grams)

2 tablespoons unsalted butter

Freshly squeezed juice of 1 lemon

Vanilla ice cream, for serving (optional)

1. If possible, make the crêpe batter the night before. At a minimum, you should let it sit for 20 minutes. In a large bowl, whisk together the flour, 1/2 cup of the sugar, the orange zest, and the salt. Whisk in the eggs, walnut or vegetable oil, rum, and vanilla. Gradually whisk in the milk. Let rest for 20 minutes or cover and refrigerate for up to a day.

2. Heat one or two 10-inch nonstick, slope-sided pans over medium heat and coat them with a very small amount of oil or butter. Starting in the center of the pan, ladle an ounce of batter in a very thin layer, swirling the batter to the edges of the pan. The key here is to use a kind of swirling motion with the pan as soon as you put the batter into it, which I recommend doing by holding a ladle over the middle of the pan, slowly pouring it, and with the last few drops from the ladle, filling any last-minute holes that appear. The goal is to create the thinnest possible crêpe that still holds together. Cook over medium heat until the top is dry and the edges are beginning to brown and curl. The top should not be shiny or moist; it should be opaque, white, and dry. When you peek underneath, you should see a good browning of the bottom of the crêpe. Flip it over at the last minute, just to finish cooking the surface of the crêpe, until it is golden, 10 to 15 seconds. Even if you're using a nonstick pan, slide an offset spatula gently under the crêpe and flip it over onto the plate. This will save your fingers from possible burns. Adjust the heat slightly if the crêpes are browning too fast. As they are finished, pile them on a plate, sprinkling sugar between each layer. Once cooled, the crêpes may be wrapped in plastic and refrigerated or frozen, if desired.

Recipe continues

3. To supreme the oranges (see How to Supreme an Orange on page 8), use a sharp knife to cut the top and bottom off each orange. Stand one of the oranges up on a cutting board and cut the peel and white pith away from the fruit, following the curve with your knife, so that the segments are exposed. Hold the peeled fruit over a bowl and cut out the segments, letting them fall into a separate bowl along with the juice; discard the seeds. Repeat with the second orange.

4. Place the orange segments and orange juice, butter, and lemon juice in a pan with the remaining 1/4 cup of sugar and heat the liquid, stirring until the sugar dissolves. Lay each crêpe over the juices in the pan to heat it, then fold it in quarters and serve with vanilla ice cream if desired.

CRÊPES SUZETTE FLAMBÉ

While flambéing the crêpes really won't add much to their flavor, it will provide a lovely bit of theatricality to an already dramatic dessert. Be sure to call your guests into the kitchen to witness this fleeting-but-fun spectacle!

¼ cup orange liqueur, such as Grand Marnier (2 ounces, 55 grams)

Before heating the crêpes in the sauce, fold them into triangles. Working in batches of 4 to 6, place the crêpes in the pan with the sauce and heat briefly. Take the pan off the heat and add the liqueur to flambé. When the Grand Marnier is warm, bring a match or lighter to the edge of the pan and stand back. When the flame dies out, transfer the crêpes to a serving platter with a spatula. Pour the sauce over them. Add ice cream, if desired, and serve immediately.

BOULEY BANANA CHOCOLATE TART

When I was the pastry chef at Bouley Restaurant in New York City, it was a formative and inspiring time in my life, and likewise in the food world. David Bouley really changed the way Americans thought about food. Dinner itself became an event. Something special was happening and diners became adventurous. New combinations of flavors were embraced with a leap of faith. This banana tart was a creation that came out of that experience. Citrus was not a flavor usually paired with chocolate but its acidity nicely contrasts with the richness of chocolate. That unfamiliar combo is tempered by the caramelized bananas, which bring to mind the American classic Bananas Foster. The silky ganache made by mixing hot cream with chopped chocolate creates a lush finish to this dessert.

MAKES 1 (9-INCH) TART TO SERVE 8
SPECIAL EQUIPMENT: WOODEN SPOON, CANDY THERMOMETER, HEATPROOF SPATULA

Pâte Sablée Tart Shell (see page 135)

BANANA-CARAMEL FILLING

Freshly squeezed juice of 2 limes (2.5 ounces, 70 grams)

3 tablespoons granulated sugar (1.5 ounces, 40 grams)

2 tablespoons unsalted butter (1 ounce, 30 grams)

1 tablespoon light brown sugar, packed (.75 ounce, 20 grams)

2 semiripe bananas, sliced into ½-inch rounds (11.5 ounces, 330 grams)

CHOCOLATE GANACHE

4.5 ounces bittersweet chocolate (preferably 60 to 66 percent cacao content), coarsely chopped into ¼-inch pieces or larger (¾ cup, 125 grams)

2 tablespoons unsalted butter, cubed (1 ounce, 28 grams)

½ cup heavy cream (4.06 ounces, 116 grams)

2 teaspoons honey (.75 ounce, 20 grams)

FOR THE BANANA-CARAMEL FILLING

1. In a skillet over medium heat, stir to combine the lime juice and granulated sugar. Cook, stirring occasionally with a wooden spoon, until the sugar is completely dissolved. Boil over medium heat until the caramel turns a light golden brown color and reads 350°F on a candy thermometer.

2. Add the butter and brown sugar and stir on the heat until the butter melts and no lumps of brown sugar remain in the caramel.

Recipe continues

3. Add the sliced bananas, stirring to coat with the caramel. Cook just until the bananas start to fall apart. Set aside.

FOR THE GANACHE

1. Place the chocolate and butter in a medium bowl.

2. In a small saucepan over medium heat, warm the cream and honey just until it boils. Pour the hot cream mixture over the chocolate and butter and whisk until smooth.

ASSEMBLY

1. Spread the banana-caramel filling into the tart shell.

2. Pour the ganache over the banana-caramel filling and smooth with a spatula. Gently tap the side of the tart mold to release any air bubbles in the ganache.

3. Allow the tart to set for 1 hour and serve at room temperature.

BITTERSWEET CHOCOLATE HALVAH MARJOLAINE WITH SESAME HALVAH CREAM

The Middle Eastern sesame candy sold here as halvah (which is also the generic term for sweets in the Middle East) is one of my favorite flavors, and makes a perfect close to a formal dinner or holiday meal. Halvah's texture is crunchy, caramelized, and chewy, like praline or nougatine, and it has one of those subtle but penetrating flavors that lasts a long time on the palate, offering up a faint yet persistent aroma as you eat it. Its rich, musky sesame flavor blends well with dairy, fruit, chocolate, and nuts.

This recipe is my sesame version of a marjolaine, a classic French dessert created by the great Fernand Point of La Pyramide in Vienne, France, a legendary 3-star restaurant. The crisp almond meringue layers, the buttercream, and the tahini (sesame paste) in the halvah cream lend nuanced contrast to layers of fudgy ganache. The multiple layers make each bite feel light on your palate. It's a magnificent, unusual cake that will impress even your most sophisticated guests while introducing them to a flavor combination they might never have tasted before, but will likely think about again and again.

MAKES 1 (9-INCH) MARJOLAINE TO SERVE 8
SPECIAL EQUIPMENT: TWO BAKING SHEETS, MARKER, ELECTRIC MIXER, PASTRY BAG FITTED WITH A LARGE PLAIN TIP OR A LARGE PLASTIC FREEZER BAG, CANDY THERMOMETER, 9-INCH SPRINGFORM PAN, KITCHEN SHEARS, OFFSET SPATULA

COCOA MERINGUE

1½ cups confectioners' sugar (6 ounces, 170 grams), plus additional for dusting

⅓ cup plus 1 tablespoon Dutch-processed unsweetened cocoa powder (1.3 ounces, 36.4 grams)

6 large egg whites (6 ounces, 170 grams), at room temperature

¾ cup plus 2 tablespoons granulated sugar (6 ounces, 170 grams)

⅛ teaspoon cream of tartar (.4 gram)

BITTERSWEET CHOCOLATE GANACHE

8 ounces bittersweet chocolate (preferably 60 to 66 percent cacao content), coarsely chopped (1⅓ cup, 224 grams)

1 cup heavy cream (8.12 ounces, 232 grams)

HALVAH CREAM

1 cup whole milk (8.5 ounces, 242 grams)

3 tablespoons medium-flavored honey such as orange blossom or clover (2.6 ounces, 75 grams)

¼ cup tahini (sesame paste) (see Sources, page 276) (3 ounces, 85 grams)

¼ cup plus 1 tablespoon cornstarch (.7 ounces, 20 grams)

1 large egg yolk (.6 ounce, 17 grams), at room temperature

¾ cup crumbled plain halvah (see Sources, page 275) (5 ounces, 140 grams)

¾ cup heavy cream (6 ounces, 171 grams)

Recipe continues

FOR THE MERINGUE

1. Position a rack in the center of the oven. Line two baking sheets with parchment paper and use a marker to trace three 9-inch circles onto the paper. Turn the marked side of the paper down.

2. Sift the confectioners' sugar and cocoa powder into a large bowl and set aside.

3. In the bowl of an electric mixer fitted with the whisk attachment, whip the egg whites at medium-high speed until foamy. Add a tablespoon of the granulated sugar and all the cream of tartar and continue to whip until soft peaks form, about 8 minutes. With the mixer running, gradually pour in the rest of the granulated sugar and whip until stiff peaks form, about 10 minutes. Stop the machine and, using a spatula, fold a third of the egg white into the confectioners' sugar and cocoa mixture. Then add the rest of the egg white and incorporate.

4. Preheat the oven to 250°F. Transfer the mixture to a pastry bag fitted with a large plain tip or to a gallon-size resealable plastic bag with one of the corners cut off. Starting just within the circles marked on the parchment paper, pipe spiral rounds of batter, working inward, so that you have three disks, each just a little smaller than 9 inches. Bake on the center rack for 2 hours, until the meringue feels dry to the touch, then turn off the oven and let dry until the oven has cooled completely, at least 4 hours longer, to ensure the meringue will stay crisp. For baking ahead, wrap the meringue in plastic and store in a cool, dry place for up to 2 days.

FOR THE GANACHE

Place the chocolate in a bowl. In a saucepan over medium heat, bring the cream to a boil. Pour it over the chocolate and let sit for 3 minutes. Starting in the center, whisk well, moving the whisk slowly outward as the center is smoothly combined. Cover and refrigerate until thickened, 1 to 2 hours.

FOR THE HALVAH CREAM

1. Attach a candy thermometer to the side of a saucepan, place the pan over medium heat, and bring the milk to a simmer. Meanwhile, in a large heatproof bowl, whisk together the honey, tahini, cornstarch, and egg yolks. Whisking constantly, pour a little of the hot milk into the tahini mixture. Continue to whisk while adding the rest of the milk to the bowl. Pour the mixture back into the saucepan and bring to a simmer over medium heat, whisking constantly. Simmer, whisking, until very thick and custard-like (at about 180°F), 2 to 3 minutes. Transfer to a bowl and whisk in half of the crumbled halvah. Cover the surface of the mixture with plastic wrap, let cool slightly, then refrigerate until chilled, at least 1 hour.

2. Whip the heavy cream just until it is thick enough to hold soft peaks. Gently fold the cream and the remaining crumbled halvah into the chilled tahini mixture.

TO ASSEMBLE AND SERVE

1. Save the flattest, most intact meringue disk for the top layer. Place one of the meringue layers in the bottom of a 9-inch springform pan (use kitchen shears to trim the sides of the meringue if necessary for fit). Spread half of the halvah cream over the meringue. Place another round of meringue over the halvah cream. Spread the ganache onto the meringue in an even layer. Allow to cool in the fridge 30 minutes, uncovered. Cover the ganache with the remaining halvah cream. Top with the third round of meringue and wrap the cake in plastic. Freeze for a minimum of 3 hours or overnight.

2. Before serving, thaw for 15 minutes, then run a thin knife or offset spatula around the inner edge of the pan and remove the sides. Sift a thin layer of confectioners' sugar over the top. To slice, use a serrated knife dipped in hot water and wiped dry between cuts, or an electric knife, which yields cleaner slices.

BIRTHDAY AND CELEBRATION CAKES

To a baker, there may be no greater pride than that you feel when you present a beautifully made cake to someone for their birthday or a dinner party. Just imagine: a lofty, moist lemon cake layered with silky lemon cream and topped with a tangy glaze as in the Small Lemon Chiffon Layer Cake (page 193). Or a dreamy, intense chocolate mousse sandwiched between crisp, candy-like shards of chocolate meringue that provide a pleasant crunch against the melting texture of the mousse as in The Concorde (page 187).

An immense amount of effort, care, and thought goes into creating desserts of such proportions. And all of it is perfectly within the grasp of the careful and patient home baker. When you accomplish these cakes, you've really

achieved something. And even the relatively simple-to-make desserts, like the Red Eye Devil's Food Cake (page 183) and Deluxe Diner Yellow Cake with Seven-Minute Frosting (page 203), will look magnificent when you bring them to the table.

In terms of appearance, the cakes in this chapter will have the greatest impact of any of the desserts you make from this book. Nothing can match the look of a towering layer cake spread with rich icing. It's an iconic vision that deserves to be served on an elegant platter. Since these cakes are so impressive in their own right, they don't need lots of fancy touches and garnishes—the Classic Sachertorte (page 189) features a shiny chocolate glaze on top—it's just a matter of paying attention to how you ice and decorate them. Take the time necessary to make your dessert beautiful, because a neatly iced cake is much more spectacular than bringing a big bouquet of flowers; it could even be the centerpiece of a party. As always, feel free to deviate from my suggestions if you so desire. There's a lot of fun in the presentation of cakes, and, just as before, I encourage you to be creative with the final touches you add to a dessert.

Here, more than ever, what I have recommended elsewhere in the book applies. That is, weigh or measure all the ingredients first, keep a clean work surface, and make sure you aren't distracted. To have a really good experience making these cakes you will need commitment and concentration. If you clean up as you go along, the whole process will be more enjoyable—especially by the end! Having dirty dishes piled around you will not only distract you visually but will also take away valuable counter space that you need to keep things in order. And, perhaps most important, don't be afraid. If you're feeling overwhelmed by a particular aspect of the cake, leave it alone and come back to it later. Sometimes it helps to partially assemble a cake and put all the parts in the fridge—both for the sake of convenience and state of mind. Then you can finish the cake just before serving. Professional pastry chefs will tell you that most cakes taste better the second day. The melding of flavors and softening of textures is a good thing in cakes, provided the cake is well covered in the fridge so it does not absorb unwanted flavors. Preparing separate elements; i.e., cake and frosting, and assembling later can work too, provided you follow instructions for preparation.

Grand cakes illustrate that baking is about being precise and having confidence. If you follow these recipes carefully, take your time, and keep in mind that nothing is as hard as it seems, your cakes will come out perfectly divine.

RED EYE DEVIL'S FOOD CAKE

This is my updated version of an American classic. The name refers to the coffee in the batter, like the Red Eye coffee drink in espresso bars that's punched up with an extra shot of espresso. Here, coffee gives the cake a lightly bitter edge that cuts the sweetness of the chocolate, and the coffee-enhanced cocoa layers sandwich a surfeit of fudgy, bittersweet ganache. If this is not the ultimate birthday cake, I can't imagine what is.

For a change of pace, you might consider icing the cake with the Milk Chocolate Ganache on pages 214–15. Since that is whipped, it has a more buoyant texture, which is a nice contrast to the buttery cake. (See photograph on page 180.)

MAKES 1 (9-INCH, 2-LAYER) CAKE TO SERVE 10

SPECIAL EQUIPMENT: TWO 9-INCH ROUND CAKE PANS, SIFTER, ELECTRIC MIXER, CAKE TESTER, OFFSET SPATULA, CAKE STAND OR SERVING PLATTER

CAKE

- 3 cups all-purpose flour (12.75 ounces, 363 grams)
- 2 teaspoons baking soda (10 grams)
- ½ teaspoon baking powder (2.45 grams)
- ½ teaspoon salt (2.5 grams)
- 1 cup Dutch-processed unsweetened cocoa powder (3.2 ounces, 92 grams)
- 2 cups strong brewed coffee (8 ounces, 230 grams)
- ½ pound (2 sticks) unsalted butter, softened (8 ounces, 227 grams), plus additional for the pans
- 3 cups granulated sugar (21 ounces, 600 grams)
- 4 large eggs (6.8 ounces, 193 grams), at room temperature

CHOCOLATE GANACHE

- 14 ounces coarsely chopped extra-bitter chocolate (minimum 70 percent cacao content) (397 grams)
- 3 cups heavy cream (24.36 ounces, 696 grams)

About ½ pound block of bittersweet chocolate for chocolate curls for decorating (see page 110), optional

Whipped cream, for serving, optional

Fresh berries, for serving, optional

FOR THE CAKE

1. Position a rack in the center of the oven. Grease two 9-inch round cake pans with unsalted butter and line the bottoms with parchment or waxed paper rounds. Grease the rounds.

Recipe continues

Red Eye Devil's Food Cake.

2. Sift the flour, baking soda, baking powder, and salt onto a piece of parchment or waxed paper and set aside.

3. Place the cocoa in a small bowl and whisk in the coffee a little at a time until smooth.

4. In the bowl of an electric mixer fitted with the paddle attachment, cream the butter, then beat in the sugar. Beat on high speed until very light and fluffy, 6 to 8 minutes.

5. Preheat the oven to 350°F. Add half the flour mixture to the butter mixture and mix on low speed until just incorporated. Add the eggs one at a time, beating to incorporate after each addition. Add the cocoa-coffee mixture and beat to incorporate. Add the remaining flour mixture and mix until just incorporated.

6. Divide the batter evenly between the two pans and bake on the center rack, turning the pans from back to front during the baking, until a cake tester inserted into the middle of the cakes comes out completely clean, about 45 minutes. Let cool in the pans on racks for about 30 minutes, then slide a thin knife or offset spatula around the sides of the pans and turn them over to unmold the cakes onto the racks. Carefully peel the parchment or waxed paper rounds from the bottoms of the cakes and allow to cool completely, at least 30 to 40 minutes more, then cover and refrigerate the layers. This will make the cake less crumbly and easier to slice when cutting the layers. Make the ganache icing while the cake cools.

FOR THE GANACHE

Place the chocolate in a heatproof bowl. In a medium saucepan over medium-high heat, bring the cream to a boil. Pour the hot cream over the chocolate, and let it sit for 3 minutes. Whisk until thoroughly combined and slightly cooled, then cover tightly with plastic wrap and refrigerate for at least 4 hours. Once the ganache is chilled, whisk until just fluffy.

TO ASSEMBLE AND SERVE

Using a long, serrated knife, cut the cake into thin layers horizontally. Place one hand flat on top of the cake. Starting at the edge, slice into the cake about 1/2 inch from the top and using a sawing motion move the knife into the cake about 1 inch. Then, still slicing back and forth, turn the cake (counterclockwise if you are right-handed, clockwise if you are left-handed) on the table, going around the circumference of the cake. After the first full circle is completed, holding the knife level, dig into the cake

Recipe continues

another inch and turn the cake again in the same direction. Repeat until you have sliced all the way through the cake, then remove this top layer and repeat three more times to obtain 4 layers from each of the two cakes. Place the bottom cake layer on the serving platter you wish to use and spread a thin layer of ganache over it. Repeat with the other 7 layers. Use the remaining ganache to cover ("mask") the outside of the cake. First give it a thin coat; this is called the "crumb coat" because it sets the ganache over the outside crumbs, preventing them from appearing on the outside of the cake. Refrigerate for an hour after this "crumb coat," then ice the cake a second time with the remaining ganache. Finish with chocolate curls.

Interior of Red Eye Devil's Food Cake.

THE CONCORDE

This unusual dessert is composed of crunchy, cocoa-tinted meringue layers enveloped in a creamy chocolate mousse. In a way, it resembles a traditional French dacquoise in that both desserts consist of layers of filled and frosted baked meringue disks. But instead of using a dense buttercream to hold the nut-studded disks together as you find in a dacquoise, these lighter, nutless meringues are enveloped in a fluffy chocolate mousse, resulting in an airy treat that melts in the mouth once you crunch through the crisp disks. It's a marvelous interplay of textures, anchored with the intensity of bittersweet cocoa and dark chocolate. This cake, made famous by Gaston Lenôtre, the legendary pastry chef, has fascinated me for years. Although the French adore well-designed Cartesian perfection, this meringue, crumbling into mousse, is also a favorite. I like to adorn the sides of the cake with abstract strips of meringue to give the finished dessert a uniquely sculptural, modernist look. It makes a stunning presentation that is thrilling to serve: the second you cut into the gorgeous whole, the meringue shatters into an asymmetric pile of delicious crisp chips suspended in the dark chocolate mousse. Serve it at the table with all your guests gathered round, and let them watch the dramatic first cut.

MAKES 1 (8 INCH, TWO-LAYER) CAKE TO SERVE 8

SPECIAL EQUIPMENT: TWO 11-BY-17-INCH BAKING SHEETS, NONSTICK LINER (OPTIONAL), SIFTER, ELECTRIC MIXER, PASTRY BAG FITTED WITH A PLAIN TIP OR A LARGE PLASTIC FREEZER BAG

CHOCOLATE MOUSSE

- 8 ounces bittersweet chocolate (preferably 60 to 66 percent cacao content), coarsely chopped (about 1½ cups, 227 grams)

- 9 tablespoons unsalted butter (4.5 ounces, 127.7 grams)

- 4 large eggs (6.8 ounces, 193 grams), separated, at room temperature

- 2 egg whites (2 ounces, 57 grams), at room temperature

- ½ teaspoon cream of tartar (1.5 grams)

- 5 tablespoons granulated sugar (2.2 ounces, 62.5 grams)

CRISP COCOA MERINGUE

- 1½ cups confectioners' sugar (6 ounces, 170 grams), plus additional for sifting

- ¼ cup plus 2 tablespoons Dutch-processed unsweetened cocoa powder (1.2 ounces, 34.5 grams), plus additional for sifting

- 6 large egg whites (6 ounces, 170 grams), at room temperature

- ½ teaspoon cream of tartar (1.5 grams)

- ¾ cup plus 2 tablespoons granulated sugar (6 ounces, 170 grams)

FOR THE MOUSSE

1. In a saucepan over low heat (or in the microwave), melt the chocolate and butter, whisking until smooth. Let cool.

Recipe continues

2. In the bowl of an electric mixer fitted with the whisk attachment, beat the 6 egg whites with the cream of tartar on medium speed until frothy. Continuing to beat at medium speed, gradually add the granulated sugar, then raise the speed to high and beat until the meringue forms stiff, glossy peaks, 5 more minutes.

3. Whisk the 4 egg yolks into the chocolate-butter mixture, then gently fold some meringue into the chocolate mixture. Add the rest of the meringue and fold until thoroughly combined. Cover the bowl and refrigerate for at least 4 hours to set the mousse. You can leave it in the refrigerator for 4 days if you want to work ahead.

FOR THE BAKED MERINGUE

1. Position the racks in the top and bottom thirds of the oven and preheat to 250°F. Line two 11-by-17-inch baking sheets with parchment paper or nonstick liners.

2. Sift the confectioners' sugar and cocoa powder onto a piece of parchment or waxed paper and set aside.

3. In a clean bowl of an electric mixer fitted with the whisk attachment, beat the egg whites with the cream of tartar on medium speed until frothy. Beating at medium speed, gradually add the granulated sugar a tablespoon at a time, then raise the speed and beat until the meringue forms stiff, glossy peaks, 5 more minutes.

4. Sprinkle the sugar-cocoa mixture over the meringue and fold it in using a rubber spatula. Spread some of the meringue with a spoon or spatula onto one of the prepared baking sheets into two 8-inch circles. On the second baking sheet, using a pastry bag fitted with a plain tip or a resealable plastic bag with one corner snipped off, pipe out 9-inch-long strips of meringue in straight lines, about finger thickness, leaving about 1 1/2 inches between each strip. Bake both sheets until the circles and strips of the meringues are thoroughly dried, 1 1/2 to 2 hours (they will be crisp, but will not change color). Let cool, then peel the parchment off the circles and strips. Set aside.

TO ASSEMBLE AND SERVE

Spread a little mousse in the center of a serving plate, then place one meringue circle over it. Spread about half of the mousse over the meringue, dolloping it evenly so that you can spread it without working it more than necessary. Top with the second meringue circle, then spread the rest of the mousse all over the outside of the cake. Break the meringue strips into random-size sticks and apply them all around the sides of the cake at zigzag angles. Refrigerate the cake until chilled, at least 3 hours and up to 12 hours. Sift confectioners' sugar or cocoa powder over the cake before serving.

CLASSIC SACHERTORTE

Along with Napoleons, cannoli, éclairs, and macaroons, Sachertortes are among the most famous bakery desserts in the world. The one and only official Sachertorte—a dense chocolate-almond cake split and filled with apricot preserves, then covered with dark chocolate glaze—is made in Vienna at the Hotel Sacher (as was declared by Austria's highest court after a lengthy lawsuit). But my somewhat lighter version is just as good, if not better. And, if you make your own, it's bound to be fresher than having one shipped all the way from Vienna!

The principal booby trap when making a Sachertorte is lumpy batter, but that is easily avoided. The secret to creating smooth batter is to make sure you integrate the eggs gradually into the thick almond paste, scraping down the sides of the bowl as you go. In time, the batter will become quite fluffy, since the almond paste can capture air and expand its volume as it absorbs the eggs. This, along with the meringue folded into the batter, helps keep the cake on the airy side.

The authentic Sachertorte uses a glaze that is deliberately crystallized—anathema to French pastry chefs. They always strive for that smooth, silky, melt-on-your-tongue texture. But here the crystallization in the glaze works very well, lending a contrasting, pleasantly gritty crunch to the tender cake. This is a perfect example of pastry that really distinguishes Eastern from Western Europe.

MAKES 1 (9-INCH, 2-LAYER) CAKE TO SERVE 8
SPECIAL EQUIPMENT: 9-INCH SPRINGFORM PAN, SIFTER, ELECTRIC MIXER, CAKE TESTER,
CANDY THERMOMETER, 11-BY-17-INCH SHEET PAN, OFFSET SPATULA

CHOCOLATE-ALMOND CAKE

Unsalted butter, for the pan

¾ cup Dutch-processed unsweetened cocoa powder (2.4 ounces, 69 grams)

½ cup all-purpose flour (2 ounces, 57 grams)

1 cup almond paste (see Sources, page 275) (10 ounces, 283 grams)

¾ cup confectioners' sugar (3 ounces, 85 grams)

7 large eggs (12.25 ounces, 250 grams) (2 whole and 5 separated), at room temperature

2 large egg whites (2 ounces, 57 grams), at room temperature

6 tablespoons granulated sugar (3.25 ounces, 95 grams)

1 teaspoon cream of tartar (3.1 grams)

6 tablespoons unsalted butter, melted (3 ounces, 85 grams)

GLAZE AND FILLING

2½ cups granulated sugar (17.5 ounces, 500 grams)

14¾ ounces bittersweet chocolate (preferably 60 to 66 percent cacao content), coarsely chopped (about 2¾ cups, 418 grams)

1 cup apricot preserves, strained (9 ounces, 255 grams)

Recipe continues

FOR THE CHOCOLATE-ALMOND CAKE

1. Sift the cocoa powder and flour onto a piece of parchment or waxed paper and set aside.

2. In the bowl of an electric mixer fitted with the paddle attachment, beat the almond paste and confectioners' sugar at medium speed until thoroughly combined. Add 2 whole eggs and beat until perfectly smooth. Be sure to scrape down the sides of the bowl frequently. Separate 5 eggs, reserving the whites. Once the mixture is smooth, add the 5 yolks one at a time, beating very well between each addition. Scrape down the sides of the bowl frequently to avoid lumps. Beat the mixture at medium-high speed until it is fluffy and lump-free and climbs up the sides of the bowl, 10 to 15 minutes. Fold the cocoa-flour mixture into the almond mixture with a rubber spatula.

3. Position a rack in the center of the oven and preheat to 350°F. Grease a 9-inch springform pan with unsalted butter.

4. Transfer the 7 egg whites to a clean bowl of an electric mixer fitted with the whisk attachment. Add 2 tablespoons of the granulated sugar and the cream of tartar and beat on medium speed until foamy. Increase the speed to high and add the remaining 4 tablespoons of sugar. Beat until the meringue reaches firm peaks, about 3 minutes, then gently fold the whites into the batter. Whisk in 2 tablespoons of the melted butter, then gently fold in the remaining 4 tablespoons butter.

5. Transfer the batter to the prepared pan and smooth the top evenly with a spatula. Bake on the center rack until a cake tester comes out clean, 30 to 40 minutes. Transfer to a wire rack and let cool completely in the pan, at least 1 hour.

FOR THE GLAZE

1. Fill a large metal bowl halfway with ice water. Set aside. Attach a candy thermometer to the side of a medium saucepan. In the saucepan, over medium-high heat, combine the sugar with 3/4 cup water. Bring the mixture to a boil and cook until the sugar has dissolved. Stir in the chocolate and continue to cook, stirring, until the glaze registers 230°F on the candy thermometer. Immediately set the pot in the ice water bath to stop the cooking.

2. Strain the glaze through a sieve into a bowl. Working on pastry marble or a clean 11-by-17-inch sheet pan, pour out half the glaze onto the work surface. Using two metal spatulas, spread the glaze over the work surface, scrape up, and repeat several times, until the glaze becomes matte, loses its shine, and has thickened slightly. Return the glaze to the bowl and stir to combine with the unthickened glaze.

Repeat pouring out and moving half the glaze on the surface, then returning it to the bowl three or four times, until the glaze begins to crystallize and turn grainy. You will see small specks form in the glaze. Let cool in the bowl until the glaze has completely crystallized.

FOR FILLING AND ASSEMBLY

When the cake is cool, slide a thin knife or offset spatula around the sides of the pan and remove the sides, then carefully turn the cake over onto a plate and remove the bottom of the pan. Slice the cake into two layers. Spread the apricot preserves on the bottom layer, cut side up, and cover with the top layer, cut side down. Place the cake on an 11-by-17-inch sheet pan fitted with a cooling rack. Return the glaze to the pot and heat, stirring, to soften—or quickly warm it in the microwave until soft enough to pour. Pour the glaze over the cake, using an offset spatula to guide the glaze to and around the edges. You will have to move swiftly to get the glaze where you want it; once it is set there is no going back! Let the glaze set for at least 4 hours. This cake will keep for 4 days, refrigerated.

Small Lemon Chiffon Layer Cake.

SMALL LEMON CHIFFON LAYER CAKE

Light and tender, this cake has a tart, airy lemon cream filling. It would make a charming birthday cake any time of year. It comes together very quickly, and you can substitute orange marmalade or raspberry preserves for the lemon cream to make your work even easier.

MAKES 1 (9-INCH, 2-LAYER) CAKE TO SERVE 6 TO 8

SPECIAL EQUIPMENT: ZESTER, SIFTER, ELECTRIC MIXER, 8-INCH SPRINGFORM PAN, CAKE TESTER, CANDY THERMOMETER, IMMERSION BLENDER (OPTIONAL)

Unsalted butter, for the pan

All-purpose flour, for the pan

CAKE

1 cup cake flour (4.25 ounces, 120 grams)

1½ teaspoons baking powder (7.35 grams)

¼ teaspoon salt (1.25 grams)

4 large eggs (6.8 ounces, 192 grams), separated, at room temperature

¾ cup granulated sugar (5.3 ounces, 150 grams)

¼ cup safflower or corn oil (1.87 ounces, 53.75 grams)

Finely grated zest and freshly squeezed juice of ½ lemon

Seeds scraped and reserved from ½ vanilla bean or ½ teaspoon vanilla extract (2 grams)

LEMON CREAM

½ cup plus 2 tablespoons granulated sugar (4.4 ounces, 125 grams)

2 large eggs (3.4 ounces, 96 grams), at room temperature

¾ teaspoon finely grated lemon zest (1.5 grams)

5 tablespoons freshly squeezed lemon juice (about 2 lemons, 2.7 ounces, 78 grams)

11 tablespoons unsalted butter, cut into pieces and softened (5.5 ounces, 156 grams)

Pinch of salt

½ cup heavy cream (4.06 ounces, 116 grams)

LEMON GLAZE

Freshly squeezed juice of 1½ lemons

½ cup confectioners' sugar (2 ounces, 57 grams)

Recipe continues

FOR THE CAKE

1. Position a rack in the center of the oven. Butter and flour an 8-inch springform pan.

2. Sift the flour, baking powder, and salt onto a piece of parchment or waxed paper and set aside.

3. In the bowl of an electric mixer fitted with the whisk attachment, beat 4 eggs on medium speed until foamy. Gradually add the sugar, then raise the speed to high and beat until the meringue forms cloudlike peaks, about 8 to 10 minutes.

4. Preheat the oven to 350°F. In a medium bowl, whisk together the oil, lemon zest and juice, and vanilla with 1/4 cup water. Remove the bowl from the mixer, sprinkle the flour mixture over the egg mixture in 3 additions, and fold together with a rubber spatula. (See page 15 for more on meringues.) Fold in the oil-lemon mixture.

5. Scrape the batter into the prepared pan and bake on the center rack until a cake tester inserted into the center of the cake comes out clean and the top of the cake springs back when pressed, 35 to 45 minutes. Cool completely in the pan on a wire rack, at least 1 hour.

FOR THE LEMON CREAM

1. Attach a candy thermometer to the side of a saucepan. Over medium heat, whisk together the sugar, eggs, lemon zest, and lemon juice. Cook, stirring constantly and adjusting the heat as necessary to avoid curdling the eggs, until the mixture is as thick as custard (at about 196°F), about 3 minutes—it should stay just below a simmer. Transfer the lemon curd to a bowl and let cool until the mixture feels just warm to the touch, about 20 minutes.

2. Whisk in the butter and salt until the mixture is well combined (alternatively, for the smoothest consistency, you can blend in the butter using an immersion blender or a stand mixer). Refrigerate until thickened to spreading consistency, at least 1 hour and up to 3 days, covered.

3. Whip the heavy cream to soft peaks and fold into the cool lemon curd. Refrigerate until you're ready to assemble the cake.

TO ASSEMBLE

When the cake is cool, slide a thin knife or offset spatula around the sides of the pan and remove the sides. Gently turn the cake over onto a flat plate or board and carefully remove the pan bottom. Use a long, serrated knife to slice the cake into two even layers (see pages 185–86). Place a layer on your serving plate and spread it with the lemon cream, leaving 1/4 inch base around the edge of the cake. Cover the outside of the cake with the glaze, pouring the glaze over the top and letting it drip down the sides. Refrigerate for at least 1 hour. Sprinkle with confectioners' sugar just before serving.

FOR THE GLAZE

Prepare the glaze right before you are ready to assemble the cake: Place the lemon juice in a bowl and sift the confectioners' sugar over it. Whisk until smooth and use immediately.

Small Lemon Chiffon Layer Cake with wild strawberries and black raspberries.

Walnut Layer Cake.

WALNUT LAYER CAKE WITH APPLE-CARAMEL FILLING AND CALVADOS CREAM CHEESE ICING

This grand cake is the ultimate homemade expression of old-fashioned baker's pride and is bound to impress. It also happens to be very sturdy and will maintain its shape during transport, staying moist thanks to the caramel-apple filling and cream cheese icing that covers the tender, nutty layers. You can make the cake up to 3 days ahead and store it in the refrigerator. If you'd rather not use Calvados, you can substitute another liquor, such as brandy or rum, or just leave it out.

Chef's Note Apples are still the favorite dessert ingredient for Americans, and there are hundreds of varieties for the home baker to choose from. As a general rule, the prettier and shinier they look, the worse they bake. For baking my choices remain: Macoun, McIntosh, Golden, Granny Smith, Mutsu, Honeycrisp, and, if you are lucky, Newtown Pippin. Thomas Jefferson wrote from Paris that, "They have no apples here to compare with our Newtown Pippin." Queen Victoria liked them so much she lifted the tax on imported apples.

MAKES 1 (8-INCH, 2-LAYER) CAKE TO SERVE 8 TO 10

SPECIAL EQUIPMENT: FOOD PROCESSOR (FOR GROUND ALMONDS, OPTIONAL), 8-INCH SPRINGFORM PAN, SIFTER, ELECTRIC MIXER, CAKE TESTER, CANDY THERMOMETER, OFFSET SPATULA, CARDBOARD CAKE CIRCLE OR SERVING PLATTER, PIE PLATE

WALNUT CAKE

Unsalted butter, for the pan

1¼ cups confectioners' sugar (5 ounces, 142)

¾ cup almond flour (see Sources, page 275) or finely ground blanched almonds (2.77 ounces, 80.25 grams)

¾ cup all-purpose flour (3 ounces, 142 grams)

Pinch of salt

8 large egg whites (10 ounces, 280 grams), at room temperature

Pinch of cream of tartar

1 tablespoon granulated sugar (.4 ounce, 12.5 grams)

½ cup packed light brown sugar (4 ounces, 113 grams)

1 cup finely chopped walnuts (about 2.85 ounces, 84 grams)

APPLE-CARAMEL FILLING

1 cup granulated sugar (7 ounces, 198 grams)

Freshly squeezed juice of 1 lemon

1 cup heavy cream (8.12 ounces, 232 grams)

3 small Golden Delicious apples, peeled, cored, and diced into cubes (about 2.25 cups, 1.5 pounds, 680 grams)

Pinch of salt

Recipe continues

CALVADOS CREAM CHEESE ICING

  2 packages cream cheese (16 ounces, 454 grams)

  ½ cup confectioners' sugar (2 ounces, 57 grams)

  ¼ cup heavy cream (2 ounces, 57 grams)

1½ tablespoons Calvados, optional (.4 ounce, 11.87 grams)

  ½ teaspoon vanilla extract (2 grams)

    Candied or finely chopped walnuts, for garnish, optional (see recipe below)

FOR THE CAKE

1. Position a rack in the center of the oven and preheat to 350°F. Grease an 8-inch springform pan with unsalted butter. If you plan to make the candied walnut garnish (see recipe below), do so now.

2. Sift the confectioners' sugar, almond flour or ground almonds, all-purpose flour, and salt onto a piece of parchment or waxed paper and set aside.

3. In the bowl of an electric mixer fitted with the whisk attachment, beat the egg whites with the cream of tartar and granulated sugar on medium speed until foamy and cloudlike. Gradually add the brown sugar, then raise the speed to high and beat until the meringue forms stiff, glossy peaks, about 10 minutes. This meringue must be super strong.

4. Sprinkle the sugar-flour mixture over the meringue and fold in until partially incorporated. Add the walnuts and fold just until the nuts are distributed—do not overmix. Scrape the batter into the pan and smooth out level. Bake on the center rack until a cake tester inserted into the center of the cake comes out clean, 50 to 70 minutes. Cool completely in the pan on a wire rack, at least 1 hour.

FOR THE FILLING

Attach a candy thermometer to the side of a medium-size heavy saucepan. Over medium heat, melt the sugar with the lemon juice until it is a clear liquid, swirling the pan a few times to help it along, but do not stir. Make sure the cream is nearby and at the ready. Let the sugar syrup simmer, stirring occasionally, until the mixture is a dark golden-brown caramel (about 374°F), about 7 minutes. Drizzle in the cream, stirring, until it is smoothly incorporated. (Do not pour it in too fast or the caramel will foam up and spatter.) Add the apples and reduce the heat to keep the liquid at a gentle simmer until the apples are completely soft and golden in color, about 15 minutes. Stir in the salt and let cool.

FOR THE ICING

In the bowl of an electric mixer fitted with the paddle attachment, beat the cream cheese until softened. Add the confectioners' sugar and beat until completely smooth, about 10 minutes. With the mixer running slowly, drizzle in the cream, Calvados, if using, and vanilla, scraping down the sides of the bowl. Beat for 5 minutes more to achieve a soft, spreadable consistency.

TO ASSEMBLE

Slide a thin knife or offset spatula around the sides of the pan and release the sides. Turn the cake over onto a flat surface and carefully remove the bottom of the pan. Using a long, serrated knife, slice the cake in half horizontally (see pages 185–86), and place the bottom half directly onto the serving platter. Use a slotted spoon to lift out the apples, shaking gently to remove as much caramel as possible. Scatter the apples evenly over the bottom layer of the cake. Replace the top cake layer and spread a third of the cream cheese icing over the whole cake to seal in the crumbs. This "crumb coat" is the first layer of icing, preventing the crumbs from migrating to the outside of the cake. Refrigerate for an hour to firm up the icing. When cool, apply the second layer of icing. Decorate with candied walnuts, or sprinkle with finely chopped walnuts.

CANDIED WALNUTS	3 tablespoons granulated sugar (1.3 ounces, 37 grams)
12 perfect walnut halves	

Position a rack in the center of the oven and preheat to 350°F. Place the walnuts in a pie plate and sprinkle with the sugar and 2 tablespoons water. Toast on the center rack, basting occasionally, for 20 minutes. Use a slotted spoon to take the walnuts out of the syrup and let them dry on a plate.

Interior of Walnut Layer Cake.

CARROT CAKE WITH MANDARIN ORANGES AND CREAM CHEESE ICING

Nearly everyone adores this classic American dessert, which makes it an excellent choice for a birthday cake. My subtly spiced version uses mandarin oranges in the batter and scattered between the layers; they add a juicy little twist to an old favorite and pull double duty by keeping the cake extra moist. The silky smooth cream cheese icing is quick to whip up, especially if the cream cheese and butter are at room temperature before you beat them together. All this cake needs is a circle of chopped walnuts for crunchy decoration, add a birthday candle, and voilà!

MAKES 1 (8-INCH, 2-LAYER) CAKE TO SERVE 8
SPECIAL EQUIPMENT: TWO 8-INCH ROUND CAKE PANS, SPATULA, WIRE RACK

CARROT CAKE

- 3 cups light brown sugar, packed (16 ounces, 454 grams)
- 1½ cups vegetable oil (10.75 ounces, 305 grams)
- 2¼ cups all-purpose flour (12 ounces, 340 grams)
- 1½ teaspoons baking soda (.25 ounce, 10 grams)
- 1 teaspoon cinnamon (5 grams)
- ½ teaspoon salt
- 3 large eggs (5.5 ounces, 155 grams)
- 1 teaspoon vanilla extract (.25 ounce, 5 grams)
- 2 cups grated carrots (7 ounces, 200 grams)
- 2 (11-ounce) cans mandarin oranges, drained (312 grams)
- 1¼ cups chopped walnuts, lightly toasted (4.75 ounces, 132 grams)

CREAM CHEESE ICING

- 1 cup cream cheese, room temperature (8 ounces, 227 grams)
- ¼ pound unsalted butter (1 stick), room temperature (4 ounces, 113 grams)
- ½ cup confectioners' sugar, sifted (2 ounces, 60 grams)
- 1 tablespoon freshly squeezed orange juice (½ ounce, 10 grams)
- 1 teaspoon vanilla extract (.25 ounce, 5 grams)

FOR THE CAKE

1. Place a rack in the center of the oven. Grease two 8-inch round cake pans and line the bottoms with parchment paper.

2. In the bowl of an electric mixer, beat together the brown sugar and oil until light and fluffy, about 5 minutes.

3. In a medium bowl, sift together the flour, baking soda, cinnamon, and salt. With the mixer set on low speed, beat in half of the dry mixture just to combine.

4. Scrape down the sides of the bowl and beat in the eggs one at a time, scraping after each addition. Add the vanilla and beat to combine.

5. Beat in the remaining half of the dry mixture, just to combine.

6. Preheat the oven to 350°F. Using a spatula, fold in the carrots, 1 cup (8 ounces, 225 grams) of the mandarin oranges, and 1 cup (3.75 ounces, 105 grams) of the walnuts. Scrape the batter into the cake pans, and bake for 60 to 70 minutes or until a tester inserted into the center of the layers comes out clean.

7. Allow the cake layers to cool in the pans for 10 minutes, then invert them onto a wire rack, peeling off the parchment rounds, to cool completely.

FOR THE ICING

1. In the bowl of an electric mixer, beat together the cream cheese and butter until no lumps remain, about 5 minutes.

2. Add the confectioners' sugar, orange juice, and vanilla and beat until the sugar is completely absorbed and the icing thickens, another 5 minutes.

TO ASSEMBLE

1. When the cake has completely cooled, spread the top of one layer with 1/3 of the cream cheese icing. Scatter the remaining mandarin oranges over the icing.

2. Sandwich with the remaining cake layer and frost the top and the sides. Place the remaining 1/4 cup of walnuts (1 ounce, 27 grams) in a circle around the top of the cake.

Deluxe Diner Yellow Cake with Seven-Minute Frosting.

DELUXE DINER YELLOW CAKE WITH SEVEN-MINUTE FROSTING

Reminiscent of a lemon meringue pie with its sour citrus note, and complemented by a billowing topping of glossy meringue, this cake is a beauty to behold. It is an iconic staple dessert that appears in American diners. Their version is lemon coconut. I give a zingy lime curd filling instead. If you want the classic, replace the 3/4 cup of lime juice with lemon juice and sprinkle a cup of unsweetened shredded coconut over the cake.

You can make the cake and lime curd 4 to 5 days ahead of time, saving the preparation of the frosting and the assembly for the day you want to serve it.

MAKES 1 (8-INCH, 4-LAYER) CAKE TO SERVE 8 TO 10

SPECIAL EQUIPMENT: CANDY THERMOMETER, ELECTRIC MIXER, TWO 8-BY-2-INCH ROUND CAKE PANS, SIFTER, CAKE TESTER, OFFSET SPATULA, SPATULA OR PASTRY BAG FITTED WITH A PLAIN TIP, BLOWTORCH (OPTIONAL)

LIME CURD

8 large eggs (13.6 ounces, 386 grams), at room temperature

1 cup sugar (7 ounces, 198 grams)

¾ cup freshly squeezed lime juice (about 5 limes, 6.5 ounces, 187.5 grams)

¼ cup freshly squeezed lemon juice (about 2 lemons, 2.17 ounces, 62.5 grams)

10 tablespoons unsalted butter, cubed and chilled (5 ounces, 142 grams)

CAKE

Unsalted butter, for the pan

2 cups all-purpose flour (8.5 ounces, 242 grams)

1½ cups sugar (10.5 ounces, 300 grams)

⅔ cup almond paste (see Sources, page 275) (6.66 ounces, 190 grams)

8 large eggs (13.6 ounces, 386 grams), at room temperature

6 large egg yolks (3.9 ounces, 116 grams), at room temperature

8 tablespoons (1 stick) unsalted butter, melted and cooled (4 ounces, 114 grams)

SEVEN-MINUTE FROSTING

7 large egg whites (8.75 ounces, 250 grams)

4 cups confectioners' sugar (1 pound, 454 grams)

2 teaspoons freshly squeezed lime juice (.25 ounce. 5 grams)

FOR THE LIME CURD

1. Suspend a large bowl over (not in) a medium saucepan of simmering water. Have ready a candy thermometer to test the temperature of the curd. In the bowl, whisk

Recipe continues

together the eggs, sugar, and citrus juices. Cook, whisking, until thick (at about 196°F), 15 to 20 minutes.

2. Transfer the curd to the bowl of an electric mixer fitted with the whisk attachment. Let cool for a few minutes, until the mixture is warm but no longer hot. Whisking on low speed, add the butter piece by piece until it is all incorporated. Raise the speed to medium and whisk until fluffy. Refrigerate overnight; this curd will be a soft consistency like yogurt.

FOR THE CAKE

1. Position a rack in the center of the oven and preheat to 350°F. Use the butter to grease two 8-by-2-inch round cake pans.

2. Sift the flour onto a piece of parchment or waxed paper and set aside.

3. In the bowl of an electric mixer fitted with the paddle attachment, mix the sugar and almond paste together on low speed until the almond paste has completely broken up and the mixture resembles cracker crumbs, about 5 minutes.

4. Switch to the whisk attachment and add the eggs one at a time, scraping down the bowl and beating on medium speed until each egg is smoothly incorporated before adding the next. Add the yolks one by one in the same manner and beat until thoroughly combined and smooth. (As with the cream cheese in Mamie Eisenhower's Cheesecake, if lumps form now, you won't be able to get rid of them.)

5. Once the eggs and yolks are incorporated, run the mixer on medium speed for 10 to 15 minutes to aerate the mixture. You want to achieve a mousselike, ivory-colored batter.

6. Remove the bowl from the mixer. Sprinkle the flour over the batter in three additions and fold it in by hand. Lastly, fold in the melted butter.

7. Scrape the batter into the prepared pan and bake until the top is golden brown and a cake tester inserted in the center of the cake comes out clean, about 45 minutes. Let cool in the pan for 15 minutes, then slide a thin knife or offset spatula around the sides of the pan to loosen the cake, and turn the pan over to unmold the cake onto a rack to cool completely, at least 1 hour.

Recipe continues

HOW TO DECORATE YELLOW CAKE WITH SEVEN-MINUTE FROSTING.

1. Place filled layers on a cake turntable.

2. Fill the pastry bag 3/4 full with seven-minute frosting. Snip the end.

3. Zigzag a line of frosting around the sides.

4. Pipe over the empty spots.

5. Use a wet spatula to smooth around the edges.

6. Pipe frosting onto the top of the cake.

7. Make peaks in the frosting with the spatula.

8. With a swirling motion, smooth out the frosting.

9. Voilà! The finished cake.

TO ASSEMBLE

Use a serrated knife to cut the cooled cake into 4 even layers (see pages 185–86). Place the bottom cake layer on a serving platter and spread about 1/4 cup of the lime curd, stopping about 1/2 inch short around the edge of the layer. Place the second layer atop the first and repeat with more lime curd. Repeat with the remaining layers. Spread a thin layer of lime curd over the top and outside of the cake. Chill while preparing the frosting.

FOR THE SEVEN-MINUTE FROSTING

1. Put 2 inches of water in a medium saucepan over medium heat and bring to a boil, then reduce the heat to low. In the bowl of an electric mixer place the egg whites, confectioners' sugar, and lime juice and whisk by hand to combine. Attach a candy thermometer to the side of the bowl.

2. Suspend the bowl with the egg whites over the water and stir until the sugar dissolves. Heat until the temperature reads 120°F (hot but not burning to the touch), stirring constantly to prevent the whites from cooking on the side of the bowl.

3. After the desired temperature is reached, transfer the bowl to the electric mixer and, using the whisk attachment, mix until the frosting has thickened and cooled, 10 to 15 minutes. The frosting should be used immediately, and the mixer kept running while using.

4. Use a pastry bag fitted with a large round tip or a spatula to apply the seven-minute frosting to the lime-curd-covered cake and smooth it out with a spatula. (See photographs on page 205.) If the spatula becomes too sticky, dip it into hot water to clean it off and continue. Once the frosting has been applied to the cake, it will begin to set and cannot be moved (only covered with more frosting), so make the first application a good one. If you want to brown the cake to make it look more like a lemon meringue pie, you can use a blowtorch to singe the surface.

BIRTHDAY SHORTCAKE
WITH FRESH STRAWBERRIES AND CREAM

My choice for the best birthday cake stars fruit, and this cake is definitely worthy of an elegant, cut-crystal cake stand. Juicy strawberries are paired with a moist almond cake. This lush dessert overflows with billowy whipped cream.

Since this dessert is really all about showcasing ripe seasonal strawberries, make it when you can get your hands on some really good ones. Your best bet is to make a connection with a local farmer or shop the farmers' market. I've been buying organic strawberries from my own strawberry guru, Franca Tantillo of Berried Treasures, at the Union Square market in New York City for over two decades now, and they still amaze me every year. Because she has such a green thumb, some years Franca has strawberries available until the end of November, and I've even been able to make strawberry shortcake as an appropriate, if unexpected, Thanksgiving dessert.

MAKES ONE (8-INCH) ROUND CAKE, ENOUGH FOR 8 SERVINGS
SPECIAL EQUIPMENT: ONE (8-INCH) ROUND CAKE PAN,
PARCHMENT PAPER, CAKE TESTER, SIFTER

SHORTCAKE

- 1 cup all-purpose flour (4.25 ounces, 121 grams)
- ¾ cup confectioner's sugar (5.25 ounces, 150 grams)
- ⅓ cup almond paste (see Sources, page 275) (3.3 ounces, 95 grams)
- 4 large eggs (6.8 ounces, 193 grams), at room temperature
- 3 large egg yolks (1.95 ounces, 55.8 grams), at room temperature
- 4 tablespoons (½ stick) unsalted butter, melted and cooled (2 ounces, 57 grams)

WHIPPED CREAM

- 1 pint heavy cream (20 ounces, 567 grams)
- 3 tablespoons granulated sugar (1.6 ounces, 37.5 grams)
- 1 teaspoon vanilla extract (.25 ounce, 5 grams)

TOPPING AND FILLING

- 2 pints fresh strawberries, green hulls cut off (5 cups, 830 grams)
- Superfine sugar to taste

FOR THE SHORTCAKE

1. Use butter to grease an 8-inch round cake pan, line the bottom with a parchment circle cut to size, and spray lightly with nonstick food spray. Preheat the oven to 350°F.

Recipe continues

Birthday Shortcake with Fresh Strawberries and Cream.

2. Sift the flour onto a piece of parchment or waxed paper and set aside.

3. In the bowl of an electric mixer fitted with the paddle attachment, mix the confectioner's sugar and almond paste together on low speed until the mixture becomes smooth.

4. Add the eggs one at a time, scraping down the sides of the bowl between each addition. Make sure each egg is incorporated before adding the next. Add the yolks in the same manner, and beat for 10 to 15 minutes until thoroughly combined, well aerated, and smooth. Sprinkle the flour over the batter and fold it in gently by hand. Fold in the melted butter.

5. Scrape the batter into the prepared pan and bake on the center rack until the top is golden brown and a cake tester inserted in the center of the cake comes out clean, 45 to 50 minutes.

6. Remove from the oven and cool on a cake rack for 15 minutes before unmolding. Remove the parchment paper from the bottom and allow the cake to cool completely.

FOR THE WHIPPED CREAM

1. When the cake is cool, remove it from the mold and slice it in half horizontally. Place the cake layer cut side up on the cake plate or serving platter.

2. Whip the heavy cream with the granulated sugar and vanilla extract to stiff peaks.

TO ASSEMBLE AND SERVE

1. Spoon half the whipped cream onto the bottom layer of the cake. Place half the hulled strawberries, tightly spaced, over the cream.

2. Place the other cake half, cut side up again, on top of the strawberries, making sure the sides are well aligned, and press down very gently.

3. Spoon the remaining whipped cream onto this layer and top with the rest of the strawberries and a dusting of superfine sugar. Refrigerate for at least 2 hours; serve directly from the refrigerator.

Fresh Coconut Cupcakes with Orange and Rum.

FRESH COCONUT CUPCAKES
WITH ORANGE AND RUM

This is Melissa's favorite recipe in the whole book! She's certain that these are the best coconut cupcakes you'll ever taste. The lovely orange and vanilla–scented cakes become particularly moist, thanks to a rum-and-orange-flavored soaking syrup, and the rich coconut buttercream that is sandwiched in the middle of each cupcake and slathered on top is so good you might want to consider it for other cakes as well. These cupcakes are out of the ordinary yet universally appealing—a go-to recipe for picnics and birthday parties.

Chef's Notes The secret to transporting iced cupcakes is to put them back in the (clean) muffin tin after you've decorated them. They won't move around as much and are very conveniently carried.

If you're feeling adventurous, make a spectacular garnish by cracking a fresh coconut open with the back of a heavy cleaver or a hammer (catch the coconut water in a bowl and enjoy!) and scraping out thin, half-dollar-size "coins" from the white coconut meat by moving a vegetable peeler in a circular motion. Toast the coconut coins on a baking sheet in a 350°F oven until nicely golden (about 12 minutes), and stick one of these coins into the icing of each cupcake at a jaunty angle. Peel the brown skin from the rest of the coconut meat and grate the meat for the icing.

To toast dry unsweetened coconut flakes, or fresh shredded coconut, heat in a dry skillet over medium heat until golden, stirring constantly so the flakes or shreds cook evenly, then transfer immediately to a plate and let cool. This will take 2 to 3 minutes for dried coconut, a few minutes longer for fresh.

MAKES 1 DOZEN STANDARD-SIZE CUPCAKES
SPECIAL EQUIPMENT: 12-CUP STANDARD-SIZE MUFFIN TIN, ELECTRIC MIXER, CAKE TESTER, CANDY THERMOMETER, FINE-MESH SIEVE, PASTRY BRUSH

CUPCAKES

1½ cups all-purpose flour (6.4 ounces, 181.5 grams)

¾ teaspoon baking powder (3.7 grams)

¼ teaspoon baking soda (1.25 grams)

¼ teaspoon salt (1.25 grams)

10 tablespoons unsalted butter, softened (5 ounces, 142 grams), plus additional for the muffin tin

1½ cups granulated sugar (10.5 ounces, 300 grams)

Finely grated zest of 1 orange

½ vanilla bean, split lengthwise, seeds scraped and reserved, or ½ teaspoon (2 grams) vanilla extract

3 large eggs (5.1 ounces, 145 grams), at room temperature

⅔ cup sour cream (5.7 ounces, 161.3 grams)

Recipe continues

¼ cup granulated sugar (1.75 ounces, 50 grams)

Freshly squeezed juice of 1 orange (about ½ cup, 4.25 ounces, 121 grams)

2½ tablespoons Malibu rum (1.2 ounces, 35 grams)

COCONUT BUTTERCREAM

3 large egg yolks (1.8 ounces, 55.8 grams), at room temperature

6 tablespoons cream of coconut (see Sources, page 275) (4.5 ounces, 130 grams)

6 tablespoons unsweetened coconut milk (see Sources, page 276) (3.25 ounces, 95 grams)

Pinch of fine sea salt

8 tablespoons (2 sticks) unsalted butter, softened (8 ounces, 227 grams)

6 tablespoons confectioners' sugar, sifted if lumpy (1.5 ounces, 43 grams)

1 tablespoon dark rum (.5 ounce, 13.75 grams)

¾ teaspoon vanilla extract (3 grams)

1½ cups grated unsweetened coconut, preferably fresh, toasted (see Chef's Notes) or store-bought dry coconut flakes (4 ounces, 113 grams)

FOR THE CUPCAKES

1. Position a rack in the center of the oven and preheat to 325°F. Grease a 12-cup muffin tin with unsalted butter or line it with paper liners. In a bowl, whisk together the flour, baking powder, baking soda, and salt.

2. In the bowl of an electric mixer fitted with the paddle attachment, cream the butter, granulated sugar, orange zest, and vanilla until light and fluffy (about 5 minutes), scraping down the bowl occasionally. Beat the eggs in one at a time, scraping down the bowl after each addition. To the bowl, add one-third of the flour mixture, followed by one-third of the sour cream. Beat on low speed until just combined. Repeat twice.

3. Using a spoon, divide the batter evenly among the muffin tins. Bake on the center rack until the cakes are golden and the tops bounce back when pressed, and a cake tester inserted into the center comes out clean, about 30 minutes. Let cool in the tins on a cooling rack.

FOR THE SOAKING SYRUP

In a small saucepan over medium heat, combine the granulated sugar with 1/4 cup water and cook, stirring, until the sugar dissolves. Take the pan off the heat and stir in the orange juice and rum.

FOR THE BUTTERCREAM

1. Place the egg yolks in a bowl. Attach a candy thermometer to the side of a small saucepan. In the pan, stir together the coconut cream and coconut milk and heat over medium heat until it just reaches a simmer (one bubble is enough!). Drizzle this mixture slowly over the yolks, whisking constantly. Return the coconut-yolk mixture to the pan and stir constantly over low heat until it is slightly thickened and a spoon leaves a trail, 1 to 2 minutes. The mixture should reach at least 160°F but should not go over 180°F, or the eggs will curdle. Using a fine-mesh sieve, strain the mixture into a clean bowl to stop the cooking and stir in the salt. Refrigerate, covered, until thoroughly chilled.

2. In an electric mixer fitted with the paddle attachment, beat the butter with the confectioners' sugar on medium speed until very light and fluffy. Beat in the rum and vanilla extract. With the mixer on low speed, gradually beat in the cold coconut-yolk mixture until thoroughly incorporated. Fold in the shredded coconut.

TO ASSEMBLE

Halve the cupcakes horizontally and brush both cut sides with the soaking syrup. Spread layers of buttercream on the bottom halves and replace the top halves to make "sandwiches." Spread the tops of the cupcakes with about 2 tablespoons buttercream. Follow the directions in the Chef's Notes on page 211 if you want to make a fresh coconut garnish with the "coins."

CHESTNUT CAKE WITH MILK CHOCOLATE GANACHE AND SINGLE-MALT SCOTCH SYRUP

With its airy, brown sugar–almond layers soaked in Scotch syrup, satiny, milk chocolate buttercream icing, and a filling of candied chestnuts, this cake has pretty much everything you'd want in a showstopper. It is a perfect dessert to make for a wintry European or Japanese-themed dinner because those are the two places in the world where chestnut is really revered as a flavor.

There are a lot of steps necessary to create this beauty, but all of them can be done a day or two ahead. In fact, the cake can even be assembled a few days ahead and refrigerated. Just bring it to room temperature before serving.

Whiskey, espresso, or latte are all excellent beverage pairings.

MAKES 1 (8-INCH, THREE-LAYER CAKE) TO SERVE 8

SPECIAL EQUIPMENT: THREE 8-INCH ROUND CAKE PANS, FOOD PROCESSOR (IF USING GROUND ALMONDS), SIFTER, ELECTRIC MIXER, OFFSET SPATULA, 8- OR 9-INCH ROUND OF CARDBOARD OR SPRINGFORM PAN BOTTOM OF THE SAME SIZE

Unsalted butter, for the pans

All-purpose flour, for dusting

CHESTNUT CAKE

1 cup confectioners' sugar (4 ounces, 113 grams), plus more for serving

1 cup almond flour (see Sources, page 275) or finely ground blanched almonds (3.7 ounces, 107 grams)

1 cup all-purpose flour (4.25 ounces, 121 grams)

8 large egg whites (8 ounces, 227 grams), at room temperature

1 cup lightly packed light brown sugar, sifted (7.6 ounces, 217 grams)

Pinch of cream of tartar

WHISKEY SYRUP

½ cup granulated sugar (3.5 ounces, 99 grams)

¼ cup aged, single-malt Scotch whiskey (1.95 ounces, 56 grams)

MILK CHOCOLATE GANACHE

14 ounces milk chocolate, coarsely chopped (397 grams)

3 cups heavy cream (24.36 ounces, 696 grams)

FILLING AND ASSEMBLY

1 jar chestnuts, packed in syrup, drained (see Sources, page 275) (15 ounces, 425 grams), Sabaton brand

Cocoa powder, optional

FOR THE CAKE

1. Position 2 racks in the oven, upper and lower, and preheat to 375°F. Grease three 8-inch round cake pans with unsalted butter and dust with flour. Line the bottoms with waxed or parchment paper. Grease the paper.

2. Sift the confectioners' sugar, almond flour or ground almonds, and all-purpose flour onto a piece of parchment or waxed paper and set aside.

3. In the bowl of an electric mixer fitted with the whisk attachment, whip the egg whites until foamy. Add 1 tablespoon of the brown sugar and the cream of tartar and beat until soft peaks form. Gradually add the remaining brown sugar and whip until very stiff and glossy.

4. Using a spatula, gently fold the sugar-flour mixture into the meringue in three additions folding gently from the bottom. Divide the batter among the three pans and use a spatula to smooth the tops. Place the cakes onto the upper and lower racks of the oven; rotate the cakes halfway through the baking time. Bake until the tops are brown and spring back when lightly pressed, 17 to 20 minutes. Transfer to wire racks and let cool in the pans for 15 minutes. Remove the parchment paper from the bottom of each cake and cool completely.

FOR THE SYRUP

In a small saucepan over high heat, combine the granulated sugar with 1/2 cup water and bring to a boil, stirring until the sugar dissolves. Let cool, then stir the Scotch into the syrup.

FOR THE GANACHE

Place the chocolate in a heatproof bowl. In a medium saucepan over medium-high heat, bring the cream to a boil. Pour the hot cream over the chocolate, and let it sit for 3 minutes. Whisk until thoroughly combined and slightly cooled, then cover tightly with plastic wrap and refrigerate for at least 4 hours or overnight.

TO ASSEMBLE AND SERVE

1. Transfer the ganache from the refrigerator to the bowl of an electric mixer fitted with the whisk attachment and whip on medium-low speed, just until it holds firm peaks. Do not overwhip. It will look like chocolate whipped cream, spreadable, but it will hold its shape.

Recipe continues

2. Coarsely chop all but 4 of the chestnuts. Run a thin knife or offset spatula around the sides of each cake pan and gently turn over to unmold the cakes onto plates. Peel away the parchment or waxed paper rounds from the bottoms of the cakes.

3. For the bottom layer, place one cake on the platter you will use for serving and brush the top with a generous amount of Scotch syrup. Spread about 3/4 cup ganache on top and sprinkle with half of the chopped chestnuts. Lay another cake on top to make the second layer and brush the top with more syrup. Spread another coat of ganache on top and sprinkle with the remaining chopped chestnuts. Repeat with a final layer of cake, more syrup, and more ganache. Using a metal spatula, spread a thin coat of ganache over the sides of the cake. Refrigerate the cake for 1 hour to firm up the ganache. Remove from the refrigerator. Spread the remaining ganache over the top and sides of the cake, smoothing it well. Arrange the reserved whole candied chestnuts on top. Serve immediately, or refrigerate the cake for up to 3 days (covered lightly with plastic wrap). Sprinkle around the edge with cocoa powder, if desired, just before serving.

You may also decorate the top of the cake with chocolate curls by using a vegetable peeler to grate a chocolate block (see photograph on page 110).

DEVIL DOGLETS FOR GROWN-UPS

Whenever I revisit childhood favorites like Circus Peanuts, Devil Dogs, and Hostess CupCakes, I'm surprised that I was able to like them quite as much as I did. They don't taste that good to the adult me, yet the memory of happily devouring those treats is still alive in my mind. I've had great fun revisiting these retro desserts in my kitchen, trying to make the sweet as satisfying as the memory. This recipe has been the most successful—it's inspired by the Devil Dog, a chocolate cake with a white cream filling. My version is deeper and moister, with a rich, buttery cake made from almond flour sandwiching a sumptuous white chocolate mousse flavored with peanut butter.

When you're mixing the cake batter, it's important to combine the chocolate and cream very smoothly, whisking from the center out, so that when you add it to the other ingredients (in this case, egg whites, flour, almond flour, and butter), the batter will retain a kind of elasticity. This prevents any oil from escaping as the cakes bake and gives the finished product a longer life and better texture.

I developed this recipe using hot dog–shaped molds (available at baking supply stores or online), but here I've adapted it to cupcake molds. If you do want to use a more Devil Dog–like, elongated mold, reduce the baking time by 5 to 10 minutes.

MAKES 1 DOZEN STANDARD-SIZE CUPCAKES

SPECIAL EQUIPMENT: FOOD PROCESSOR (IF USING GROUND ALMONDS), ELECTRIC MIXER, SIFTER, 12-CUP STANDARD-SIZE MUFFIN TIN, PASTRY BAG FITTED WITH A PLAIN TIP OR A LARGE PLASTIC FREEZER BAG, CAKE TESTER, OFFSET SPATULA, FINE-MESH SIEVE (FOR VARIATION, OPTIONAL)

PEANUT BUTTER–WHITE CHOCOLATE MOUSSE

1½ teaspoons gelatin (.12 ounce, 3.5 grams)

1 cup heavy cream (8 ounces, 228 grams)

1 tablespoon creamy peanut butter (1 ounce, 28 grams)

3 large egg yolks (1.8 ounces, 50 grams), at room temperature

¼ cup confectioners' sugar (1 ounce, 28 grams)

Pinch of salt

5 ounces white chocolate (preferably 18 to 20 percent cacao content) (about 1 cup, 140 grams)

Recipe continues

Devil Doglets for Grown-ups.

CHOCOLATE CUPCAKES

- 1 cup confectioners' sugar (4 ounces, 113 grams)

- ½ cup plus 1 tablespoon all-purpose flour (2.4 ounces, 68 grams)

- 1 teaspoon baking powder (4.9 grams)

- ¾ cup almond flour (see Sources, page 275) or finely ground blanched almonds (2.8 ounces, 80.25 grams)

- 4 large egg whites, lightly beaten (4 ounces, 113 grams), at room temperature

- 8 ounces bittersweet chocolate (preferably 60 to 66 percent cacao content), coarsely chopped (1½ cups, 227 grams)

- 1½ cups heavy cream (12.2 ounces, 348 grams)

- 8 tablespoons (1 stick) unsalted butter, melted and warmed to about 100°F (4 ounces, 113 grams)

- Unsalted butter, for the muffin tin

FOR THE MOUSSE

1. Fill a medium pot with 2 inches of water and bring to a gentle simmer. Fill a small bowl with 1/4 cup cold water, and sprinkle the gelatin over the water. Let sit for 10 minutes. It will not dissolve completely.

2. In a heavy-bottomed saucepan over medium heat, combine 3/4 cup of the cream with the peanut butter and stir to combine. Bring to a boil, and immediately remove from the heat.

3. In a large mixing bowl, whisk together the yolks, confectioners' sugar, and salt. Whisking constantly, slowly pour the hot cream into the yolk mixture.

4. Set a medium bowl over the pot of gently simmering water (the bottom of the bowl should not touch the water). Add the white chocolate to the bowl, and melt, stirring constantly, until smooth. Remove the bowl from the heat. Whisking constantly, pour the cream-yolk mixture over the chocolate until smoothly combined. Add the gelatin-water mixture, and stir until the gelatin completely dissolves, 3 to 5 minutes. Let the mixture cool completely to room temperature.

5. When the mixture has cooled, whip the remaining 1 1/2 cups cream in the bowl of an electric mixer fitted with the whisk attachment. Fold the cream into the cooled chocolate mixture. Cover with plastic wrap and refrigerate for several hours or overnight.

FOR THE CUPCAKES

1. Sift the confectioners' sugar, flour, and baking powder into a large mixing bowl. Add the almond flour or ground almonds. Stir in the egg whites, forming a loose batter.

Recipe continues

2. To make the ganache, place the chocolate in a dry, heatproof bowl. In a medium saucepan over medium-high heat, bring the cream to a boil. Slowly pour the hot cream over the chocolate, let sit for 3 minutes, then whisk, mixing from the center and slowly moving the whisk outward once the center is fully combined, until the ganache has a thick, smooth consistency.

3. Slowly pour the ganache over the batter. Whisk in the melted butter until everything is well combined. Cover the bowl and store in the fridge for 4 hours.

4. Position a rack in the center of the oven and preheat to 350°F. Grease a 12-cup muffin tin or the custom-made mini hot dog tins available at N.Y. Cake & Baking (see Sources, page 275) with unsalted butter.

5. Transfer the chilled batter to a pastry bag fitted with a plain tip or a resealable plastic bag with the corner snipped off. Squeeze the batter into the muffin cups, filling each cup about two-thirds full. (Alternatively, a spoon works nearly as well.)

6. Bake the cupcakes on the center rack until a cake tester inserted in the center comes out clean, 30 to 40 minutes. Let cool slightly in the pan, then invert the pan onto a baking sheet, remove the pan, and transfer the cupcakes to a wire rack to cool completely, 30 to 40 minutes more.

TO ASSEMBLE

Using a serrated knife, halve each cupcake horizontally. Using an offset spatula or a spoon, spread about 3 tablespoons of the white chocolate mousse on the bottom half of the cupcake. Replace the top half, forming a sandwich, and serve with a dollop of whipped cream.

PARTY CUPCAKE TREE

The cupcake is a perfect vehicle for your imagination to run wild. The original individual dessert, cupcakes are popular with all ages, convenient to transport and serve, and require minimal cleanup. People always worry about cutting and portioning a cake; that is another advantage of the august cupcake. It is a complete portion (and a reasonable one at that) that doesn't have to be shared—it's all yours!

There are plenty of whimsically shaped cupcake pans and special cupcake decorations at baking supply stores (see Sources page 275), or you could go to the candy counter if you want to doll up your cupcake; lemon drops, Red Hots, jimmies, or chocolate-dipped raisins are all fair game. The prize for the most famous cupcake decoration has to go to the Milford Baking Company in Milford Township, Michigan. When the FBI came to their small town in 2006 to look for the remains of Jimmy Hoffa, the bakery created a cupcake with chocolate cake crumbs on the top to resemble soil and a green plastic hand sticking up out of the dirt! Ghoulish, but they sold thousands.

In my version of the cupcake tree, I have given a minimalist canvas that is pretty in its simplicity, but the buttercream is sturdy enough to hold small decorations that fit the theme of your party.

MAKES 24 CUPCAKES

SPECIAL EQUIPMENT: MUFFIN TINS, ICE CREAM SCOOP, ST. HONORÉ TIP #6 (A ROUND TIP WITH A "V" CUT INTO THE SIDE), CUPCAKE PAPERS (SEE SOURCES, PAGE 275), CAKE TESTER

3 cups all-purpose flour (12.75 ounces, 363 grams)

2 teaspoons baking soda (10 grams)

½ teaspoon baking powder (2.45 grams)

½ teaspoon salt (2.5 grams)

1 cup Dutch-processed unsweetened cocoa powder (3.2 ounces, 92 grams)

2 cups hot water (8 ounces, 230 grams)

½ pound (2 sticks) unsalted butter, softened (8 ounces, 227 grams), plus additional for the pans

3 cups sugar (21 ounces, 600 grams)

6 large eggs (10.2 ounces, 288 grams), at room temperature

1. Position a rack in the center of the oven. Line two standard muffin tins with cupcake papers.

2. Sift the flour, baking soda, baking powder, and salt onto a piece of parchment or waxed paper and set aside.

Recipe continues

Party Cupcake.

3. Place the cocoa in a bowl and whisk in the hot water a little at a time until smooth.

4. In the bowl of an electric mixer fitted with the paddle attachment, cream the butter, then beat in the sugar. Beat on high speed until very light and fluffy, 6 to 8 minutes. Preheat the oven to 350°F.

5. Add half the flour mixture to the butter-sugar mixture and mix on low speed until just incorporated. Add the eggs one at a time, beating to incorporate after each addition. Add the cocoa-water mixture and beat to incorporate. Add the remaining flour mixture and mix until just incorporated.

6. Using an ice cream scoop, fill each of the cups in the lined muffin tins 2/3 of the way. Bake at 350°F for 30 minutes or until a cake tester comes out clean. Transfer the muffin tins to a baking rack to cool. When ready to decorate, place a #5 or #6 St. Honoré pastry tip in a pastry bag and fill with the softened butter cream. You may also use a standard star tip.

VANILLA BEAN BUTTERCREAM

This buttercream uses a base of crème anglais to make it a bit sturdier than the average icing, and is just the thing for a tiered cupcake tree that may need to be transported or sit out for a few hours sans refrigeration.

SPECIAL EQUIPMENT: MEDIUM SAUCEPAN, WOODEN SPOON, FINE-MESH SIEVE, ICE BATH, SMALL SAUCEPAN, CANDY THERMOMETER, ELECTRIC MIXER

CRÈME ANGLAISE

- ½ vanilla bean split lengthwise, seeds scraped and reserved
- 1 cup milk (8 ounces, 225 grams)
- 6 large egg yolks (4.5 ounces, 125 grams)
- 1¼ cups sugar (8.75 ounces, 250 grams)

ITALIAN MERINGUE BUTTERCREAM

- 1¼ cups plus 2 tablespoons sugar (9.75 ounces, 285 grams)
- 6 large egg whites (7.75 ounces, 200 grams)
- 1 teaspoon cream of tartar (.25 ounce, 5 grams)
- 2 pounds (8 sticks) unsalted butter, cubed, at room temperature (2 pounds, 908 grams)

Recipe continues

Special baking papers.

FOR THE CRÈME ANGLAISE

1. Using the amounts appropriate for the full or half batch, put the vanilla seeds and the pod in a medium saucepan and add the milk, stirring to combine.

2. Have a bowl of ice nearby. Place the saucepan over a medium flame. In a medium heatproof bowl, whisk together the egg yolks and sugar until the mixture is thick and pale yellow.

3. When the milk comes to a boil, take it off the heat. Pour one-third of the milk into the egg yolk mixture and whisk vigorously to combine. Pour the egg yolk–milk mixture back into the remaining milk in the saucepan and return to the heat.

4. Stirring constantly with a wooden spoon, cook the custard for 3 to 5 minutes, until it thickens enough to coat the back of the wooden spoon.

5. Using a fine-mesh sieve, strain the custard into a heatproof bowl over the bowl of ice. Discard the vanilla bean pod and allow the custard to cool to room temperature. The crème anglaise can be made up to 2 days in advance and stored, covered, in the refrigerator.

FOR THE ITALIAN MERINGUE BUTTERCREAM

1. In a small saucepan over medium-low heat, add 11/4 cups sugar and 1/3 cup water (2.25 ounces, 60 grams). Using a wet pastry brush, wash down the sides of the saucepan to remove any sugar crystals. In a mixer fitted with the whisk attachment, whip the egg whites. While the whites are whipping, cook the sugar-water mixture to 220°F.

2. When the eggs are foamy, sprinkle in the cream of tartar and the remaining sugar and continue whipping.

3. When the sugar reaches 220°F, take it off the heat, reduce the speed of the electric mixer to low, and slowly pour the sugar into the whipping whites. Continue whipping until stiff peaks form.

4. When the meringue has cooled to room temperature whip in the butter, one cube at a time, until fully incorporated.

Recipe continues

5. Gradually whip in the crème anglaise. The buttercream may be used immediately or covered and refrigerated for up to 3 days. To use it later, re-whip it in the mixer for 10 to 15 minutes on medium speed until smooth. When you first start mixing the cold buttercream out of the refrigerator, it will appear broken and crumbly like cottage cheese. After whipping it for several minutes it will become smooth and shiny.

ASSEMBLING THE TREE

1. Fit a large pastry bag with a St. Honoré tip.

2. Fill the pastry bag 1/3 full with the softened buttercream. Squeeze gently from the back of the bag to pipe three parallel "S" shapes on the top of each cupcake. Arrange the decorated cakes on the cake stand tiers.

Party Cupcake Tree.

HOLIDAY DESSERTS

For a baker or dessert maker, the holiday season is the time of year when restraint has been put in abeyance and you can be sure that your family and guests will happily devour your creations with the same zeal with which you made them.

Many of the recipes in this chapter are inspired by American classics. Their flavors will resonate with people who either grew up here in the United States, or who have adopted an American palate. The Painted Cookies (page 250) are reminiscent of the sugared or frosted butter and sugar cookies that Grandma would have made (or did make). Spiced Orange Doughnuts (page 247) are definitely a throwback to an earlier time, when people weren't quite so averse to deep-frying foods, and actually had the time to make fresh doughnuts for breakfast on the weekend.

While I'm sure you're not complaining, you may be wondering why I use so much chocolate in this particular chapter. The answer is simple: Chocolate is a sure-fire crowd pleaser, no matter what age your audience is, and is an ingredient well suited for special occasions. Plus the holidays are a time of extravagance, and what expresses that more than chocolate? Chocolate is also a flavor that, in my mind, has wintry connotations, which is apropos to much of the holiday season. Chocolate's rich, somewhat toasted nuttiness seems perfect after a dinner of roasted meat and root vegetables. When buying chocolate, bear in mind that there are many varieties out there today, ranging from bitter to smooth to smoky to sweet. My own chocolate experiments have led me to favor Valrhona chocolate; I love its pudding-like texture when it melts, and of course its incomparable flavor. I suggest you audition several different brands to find your own favorite—the most delicious research assignment I can think of.

I know you will find these very enjoyable recipes to make (and eat) because they're based on homey desserts that have been vetted by generations of children and adults. I promise that making any one of them will provide a delightful end to any holiday meal.

INDIVIDUAL FLOURLESS CHOCOLATE CAKES FOR PASSOVER

This is my take on the flourless chocolate cake. My Jewish friends were constantly asking me to come up with a light version to serve after an extravagant seder dinner.

The key to these feathery little cakes is to take your time beating the eggs until they form a thick, stable foam. They'll look fluffy and bubbly right away, but you need to keep going! You'll know they're ready if, when you stop the machine, the foam holds up, rather than collapsing, and you don't see bubbles bursting—you want to incorporate all this air so that even after you lose some—which is inevitable no matter how gently you fold the chocolate in—there will still be enough to encourage the cakes to rise evenly in the oven and hold their shape. Since I can never leave well enough alone, I give these smooth cakes a creamy chocolate glaze, which pushes chocoholics over the edge.

MAKES 8 INDIVIDUAL CAKES OR 1 (9-INCH) CAKE

SPECIAL EQUIPMENT: EIGHT 6-OUNCE RAMEKINS OR 9-INCH ROUND CAKE PAN, ROASTING PAN, ELECTRIC MIXER, OFFSET SPATULA

FLOURLESS CHOCOLATE CAKES

Dutch-processed unsweetened cocoa powder, for dusting

½ pound plus 4 tablespoons (2½ sticks) unsalted butter (10 ounces, 283 grams), plus additional for the ramekins

¼ teaspoon instant coffee (1 gram)

8 ounces bittersweet chocolate (preferably 60 to 66 percent cacao content), chopped (2 cups, 227 grams)

2½ ounces unsweetened chocolate, coarsely chopped (½ cup plus 2 tablespoons, 70.87 grams)

Pinch of fine sea salt

5 large eggs (8.5 ounces, 241 grams), at room temperature

1 cup lightly packed light brown sugar (8 ounces, 226 grams)

GLAZE (OPTIONAL)

2 tablespoons heavy cream (1 ounce, 28 grams)

1 tablespoon granulated sugar (.4 ounce, 12.5 grams)

1 tablespoon light corn syrup (.7 ounce, 20.5 grams)

5 ounces bittersweet chocolate (preferably 60 to 66 percent cacao content), coarsely chopped (see Sources, page 275) (1¼ cups, 140 grams)

1 tablespoon unsalted butter (.5 ounce, 14.2 grams)

Recipe continues

FOR THE CAKES OR CAKE

1. Position a rack in the center of the oven. Butter eight 6-ounce ramekins and line the bottoms with parchment or waxed-paper rounds. Butter the paper, then dust the bottoms and sides of the ramekins with cocoa powder, shaking out the excess cocoa. Place the ramekins in a roasting pan.

2. In a saucepan over medium heat, melt the butter with 1/2 cup water and the instant coffee. Take the pan off the heat, and stir in both chocolates and the salt until smooth.

3. Preheat the oven to 325°F. In the bowl of an electric mixer fitted with the whisk attachment, beat the eggs with the brown sugar at medium-high speed until light in color, with a thick, mousselike texture and a glossy sheen that resembles mayonnaise, 10 to 15 minutes.

4. Off the machine, fold the chocolate mixture into the egg mixture, then divide the batter among the ramekins (or pour into the 9-inch cake pan). Place the roasting pan on the center oven rack and pour very hot tap water into the roasting pan to come half to two-thirds of the way up the ramekins, and bake until the cakes are puffed and springy in the centers, 35 to 40 minutes (60 minutes if using the 9-inch cake pan).

5. Transfer the roasting pan to a wire rack and let the ramekins cool, surrounded by the warm water in the pan, for 20 to 30 minutes before serving. Make the glaze while the cakes cool.

FOR THE OPTIONAL GLAZE

In a small saucepan over medium heat, combine the cream, sugar, and corn syrup with 1/4 cup water and bring to a boil. Take the pan off the heat and stir in the chocolate. Stir until smooth, then whisk in the butter.

TO SERVE

Dip the bottoms of the ramekins in hot water for 30 seconds, run a thin knife or offset spatula around the sides to loosen the cakes, invert each ramekin onto a dessert plate, then carefully peel the parchment or waxed paper rounds from the bottoms of the cakes.

If using the glaze, pour and spread warm chocolate glaze over the top of each cake, letting it fall over and down the sides (you should be able to use all the glaze). Serve immediately.

CARDAMOM NUT BUTTERBALLS

So many cultures lay claim to these cookies—a buttery, nutty shortbread ball that's coated with confectioners' sugar—and for good reason. They are melt-in-the-mouth

delicious and absolutely addictive. But whether you call them pecan butterballs, Mexican or Greek wedding cookies, or Russian teacakes, it all adds up to the same wonderful taste experience. Here, I've given the basic idea a Turkish slant by spicing them with cardamom.

Chef's Note Ground cardamom loses flavor as it sits, so I prefer to grind fresh cardamom right before I use it. To do this, use the side of a knife or the bottom of a glass to crush 4 whole green cardamom pods, then place in a coffee grinder and grind to a powder.

MAKES ABOUT 6 DOZEN (1-INCH) COOKIES
SPECIAL EQUIPMENT: TWO RIMMED 11-BY-17-INCH BAKING SHEETS, ELECTRIC MIXER, SIFTER

½ pound (2 sticks) unsalted butter (8 ounces, 227 grams), plus additional for the pan

½ cup confectioners' sugar (2 ounces, 57 grams), plus additional for rolling

2 cups all-purpose flour (8.5 ounces, 242 grams)

1 cup coarsely chopped nuts, preferably a mix of pecans, walnuts, almonds, and hazelnuts (about 4 ounces, 114 grams)

4 green cardamom pods (2.5 grams) (see Chef's Note)

1 teaspoon vanilla extract (4 grams)

¼ teaspoon salt (1.25 grams)

1. Position the oven racks in the top and bottom thirds of the oven and preheat to 350°F. Grease two 11-by-17-inch baking sheets with butter.

2. In an electric mixer fitted with the paddle attachment, cream the butter until light, then blend in the confectioners' sugar. Add the flour, nuts, cardamom, vanilla, and salt, and continue mixing until just combined.

3. Fill a wide bowl with confectioners' sugar and set aside. Roll the cookie dough into 1-inch balls and place them on the prepared cookie sheets. Bake the cookies, turning the baking sheets from back to front and switching them between the top rack and the bottom halfway through, until they begin to firm up, about 12 minutes.

Recipe continues

4. Immediately transfer the warm cookies to the bowl of confectioners' sugar and spoon sugar over them to coat. Gently transfer to wire racks to cool.

5. Sift additional confectioners' sugar over the cookies before serving. Store in an airtight tin for up to 1 week.

Cardamom Nut Butterballs in a tin.

CHERRY, ALMOND, AND PISTACHIO BISCOTTI

I'm a fan of these biscotti because, packed with a cup of fruit, they maintain that chewy/crunchy balance for a long time. I use dried cherries here, but feel free to add your own touch with a variety of dried fruit, whatever strikes your fancy: apricots, pears, cranberries, blueberries, papaya, or even a mixture. Go wild! Store them in an airtight container and they'll keep for at least a week. Even better, if you have the freezer space, double wrap in plastic and freeze the once-baked logs, then slice and re-bake whenever you want them. Dip them in your afternoon espresso, if you're a traditionalist. Though I admit I love them as a special treat with lemonade.

MAKES 2 1/2 DOZEN COOKIES

SPECIAL EQUIPMENT: ELECTRIC MIXER, PLASTIC WRAP, RIMMED BAKING SHEET,
SMALL OFFSET SPATULA

- 1 cup whole-wheat flour (4 ounces, 125 grams)
- 1 cup all-purpose flour (4 ounces, 125 grams)
- ⅓ cup light brown sugar (2 ounces, 60 grams)
- 1 teaspoon baking powder (5 grams)
- Pinch salt
- 2 large eggs (3.4 ounces, 96 grams), lightly beaten

- ⅓ cup milk (2 ounces, 60 grams)
- 3½ tablespoons macadamia or canola oil (2 ounces, 60 grams)
- 2 tablespoons honey (1 ounce, 35 grams)
- ½ teaspoon almond extract (3 grams)
- 1 cup dried cherries (4 ounces, 125 grams)
- ⅓ cup shelled pistachios (1 ounce, 30 grams)

1. Preheat the oven to 350°F. In the bowl of an electric mixer fitted with the paddle attachment, slowly beat to combine the flours, brown sugar, baking powder, and salt. In a separate bowl, whisk together the eggs, milk, oil, honey, and almond extract. Add the wet mixture to the dry all at once and beat just enough to bring the dough together. Using a wooden spoon or spatula, fold in the dried fruit and nuts.

2. Scrape the dough onto a long piece of plastic wrap. Bring one side of the plastic wrap over the dough and roll it into a log 12 inches long and 2 to 3 inches in diameter. Chill the dough until firm enough to slice, at least 4 hours and up to 2 days.

Recipe continues

3. Carefully unwrap the dough and transfer the log to a parchment-lined baking sheet. Bake until golden brown, 30 to 35 minutes. Turn off the oven and slide the log onto a wire rack to cool to room temperature.

4. When the log has cooled, preheat the oven to 325°F. Using a serrated knife, slice the log on a slight diagonal into slices 1/8 to 1/4 inch thick. Arrange the slices close together on the parchment-lined baking sheet and bake for 15 minutes.

5. Remove the baking sheet from the oven and, using a small offset spatula, flip the slices over. Return the baking sheet to the oven and bake until the slices are golden brown on each side, about another 15 minutes. Transfer the biscotti to a wire rack to cool. Store in an airtight container for up to 1 week.

SANDY PECAN PRALINES

Even if you have never been to New Orleans, you've probably tasted these cookie-like candies, or candy-like cookies, depending upon your perspective. In a city known for naughty, they may be one of the naughtiest pleasures around—really, an excuse to consume large quantities of pure sugar, butter, and nuts. This recipe is from a neighbor of ours in Toledo, Ohio, a transplanted Southerner who used to give them to our family for Christmas.

There are two different kinds of praline, the chewy, caramelesque ones and the sandy, crisp, yet creamy, ones with a crystallized sugar crunch around the edges. These are the sandy ones. Be sure to stir the pecans well once they are added to the mixture. This is what develops the unique texture. (See photograph on next page.)

MAKES ABOUT 2 DOZEN (1½-INCH) PRALINES
SPECIAL EQUIPMENT: THREE RIMMED 11-BY-17-INCH BAKING SHEETS, CANDY THERMOMETER

1 cup pecan halves (3.5 ounces, 99 grams)

1 cup packed dark brown sugar (8.4 ounces, 239 grams)

½ cup sour cream (4.25 ounces, 121 grams)

4 tablespoons (½ stick) unsalted butter (2 ounces, 57 grams)

1 vanilla bean, split lengthwise, and seeds scraped and reserved, or 1 teaspoon vanilla extract (4 grams)

1. Position a rack in the center of the oven and preheat to 325°F. Line two rimmed 11-by-17-inch baking sheets with parchment or waxed paper. Spread the pecans out on a third rimmed 11-by-17-inch baking sheet and toast them on the center rack for about 10 minutes, tossing halfway through, until lightly browned and fragrant. Transfer to a rack to cool.

2. In a heavy saucepan with a candy thermometer attached to the side, melt together the brown sugar, sour cream, and butter, stirring, over medium heat. Raise the heat and bring the mixture to a boil. Boil, without stirring, until the thermometer registers 236°F (soft-ball stage), about 15 minutes. Take the pan off the heat and let cool for 2 minutes.

3. Stir in the pecans and vanilla seeds or extract, taking care not to splash the molten mixture. Continue to stir until the pecan mixture is thick and creamy, 1 to 2 minutes. Immediately pick up some of the mixture with two tablespoons and, working quickly, drop 1 1/2-inch pralines onto waxed or parchment paper. If the batter gets too firm, place the saucepan back on medium heat to loosen it up, and continue scooping the pralines. Let them cool and set.

Sandy Pecan Pralines in a tin.

I love caramel. The flavor of semi-burnt sugar is intoxicating to me—I think because its sugary-sweetness is tempered by cooking. It is important to know how to cook caramel. Here are a few suggestions:

Start with dry sugar in a heavy saucepan on medium heat and a few drops of lemon juice. Stand over it and watch closely because it goes from just hot sugar to combustion very quickly. In order to mix the sugar and the semi-burnt caramel, swirl the pot around to move the liquid/solids together, overstirring can cause the caramel to crystallize or "block" into a stiff lump.

In some recipes you are required to "deglaze," or to stop the cooking by adding a liquid to the hot sugar. If you are adding water, make sure it is very hot and pour it slowly, and at arm's length (with your arm covered in a sleeve or a towel) so when it spatters it does not burn you. If you are adding butter or cream the spattering is not so bad, but still exercise caution.

In all cases, pour the liquid slowly and let the caramel absorb and mix with the liquid before adding more. Again, swirling the pan is your best approach.

Coffee Toffee.

COFFEE TOFFEE

Though I love munching on amber shards of your basic sweet, buttery toffee, I am always on the lookout for a more interesting version. This recipe definitely fits the bill. The assertive espresso cuts the toffee's richness and lends an unexpected intensity, while the pecans provide an elegant grace note. This candy, which I love to serve at Christmas, is also perfect for that late afternoon pick-me-up or for passing around post-meal at your next dinner party, instead of or alongside coffee.

MAKES ABOUT 1 POUND OF TOFFEE PIECES

SPECIAL EQUIPMENT: ONE 11-BY-17-INCH RIMMED BAKING SHEET,
NONSTICK LINER (OPTIONAL), HEAT-RESISTANT SPATULA, CANDY THERMOMETER,
OFFSET SPATULA, DOUBLE BOILER (OPTIONAL)

12 tablespoons (1½ sticks) unsalted butter (6 ounces, 168 grams), plus some for the foil

1¾ cups granulated sugar (12.25 ounces, 350 grams)

2 tablespoons sweetened condensed milk (1.375 ounces, 27 grams)

1 tablespoon corn syrup (.7 ounce, 20.5 grams)

1 tablespoon vanilla extract (12 grams)

1 teaspoon instant espresso powder (see Sources, page 275)

Pinch of salt

¼ teaspoon baking soda (1.25 grams)

1 cup toasted pecans, finely chopped (about 4 ounces, 114 grams)

1. Line an 11-by-17-inch rimmed baking sheet with a buttered sheet of aluminum foil or a nonstick liner.

2. In a medium, heavy-bottomed saucepan over medium heat, combine the butter, sugar, condensed milk, corn syrup, vanilla, espresso powder, salt, and baking soda. Cook, stirring frequently, until the ingredients are incorporated (this prevents the butter solids from burning on the bottom of the pan). Continue to cook, stirring occasionally with a heat-resistant spatula (too much stirring encourages crystallization), until a candy thermometer reads 300°F, about 15 minutes. Add the pecans and stir again.

3. Pour the toffee onto the baking sheet. Working quickly, use a greased, offset spatula to spread the toffee into a 1/4-inch-thick layer that fills the sheet. Let cool completely.

4. Using a knife or your hands, break the toffee into irregular pieces. Store in an airtight container at room temperature.

Mexican Almond Toffee.

MEXICAN ALMOND TOFFEE

What's Mexican about this recipe for a rich almond toffee? Well, I add smoky ancho chile powder and ground cinnamon. Made with less sugar than most, this toffee contains spices that add another dimension and give the candy a slightly savory feel, which is fashionable these days in the pastry kitchen. You can substitute other nuts, such as walnuts or pecans, for the almonds. Olé!

MAKES 1 POUND TOFFEE

SPECIAL EQUIPMENT: ONE RIMMED 11-BY-17-INCH BAKING SHEET, CANDY THERMOMETER, PASTRY BRUSH

½ cup slivered, blanched almonds (2.1 ounces, 60 grams)

2 cups sugar (14 ounces, 397 grams)

10 tablespoons unsalted butter (5.3 ounces, 151.3 grams), plus additional for the pan

1 tablespoon white vinegar (.5 ounce, 15 grams)

1 tablespoon light corn syrup (.72 ounce, 20.5 grams)

1 teaspoon vanilla extract (4 grams)

½ teaspoon ancho chile powder (see Sources, page 275) (1.66 grams)

¼ teaspoon ground cinnamon (.5 gram)

Large pinch of salt

1. Position a rack in the center of the oven and preheat to 350°F. Place the almonds on a rimmed 11-by-17-inch baking sheet and bake on the center rack for about 10 minutes, tossing halfway through, until deep golden brown. Set aside in a bowl.

2. Line the baking sheet with parchment paper, butter the paper, and place the sheet on a wire cooling rack. In a heavy saucepan combine the sugar, butter, vinegar, corn syrup, vanilla, chile powder, and cinnamon with 1/4 cup water and bring to a boil, stirring, until the butter and sugar are dissolved. Attach a candy thermometer to the side of the pan and let the mixture simmer. If the toffee cooks unevenly, swirl the pan. If sugar begins to crystallize on the sides of the pan, brush the crystals down with a clean pastry brush dipped in water. Avoid stirring because that will make the toffee sticky. Simmer until the mixture reaches 300°F, about 15 minutes. It will be a golden brown color.

3. Take the pan off the heat, stir in the almonds and salt, and immediately pour the toffee out onto the prepared baking sheet. Let cool partially (until warm, but not scalding), then score if you want to be able to break the toffee into regular shapes. Otherwise, let cool completely, then break the toffee into irregular pieces. Store in an airtight container for up to 2 weeks.

Homemade Marshmallows

HOMEMADE MARSHMALLOWS

These delectable little confections are a fragrant and sophisticated version of a favorite childhood candy. Homemade marshmallows are softer and more cloudlike than commercial ones, which have been usually hanging around the supermarket for months before you buy them. And everyone will be impressed that you made these, even though they aren't at all difficult.

The one thing to keep in mind about the marshmallow flavorings, whether you choose the orange blossom water, vanilla extract, almond extract, bergamot oil, rose water, or grapefruit oil, is to use them with great discretion. Too much could overwhelm the palate. Start out by adding the flavoring slowly, drop by drop, tasting the mixture as you go to gauge how much is just enough. It should be full flavored and just a touch stronger than you'd like the resulting candy to be, since the flavor will lessen in intensity as it sits.

If you're using an essential oil, be sure to get food-grade oils and not anything called "absolute"—that is for perfumes. I recommend buying from Mandy Aftel (see Sources, page 275), who has a mail-order business selling high quality food-grade essential oils.

MAKES ABOUT 3 DOZEN (1½-INCH) MARSHMALLOWS
SPECIAL EQUIPMENT: 9-BY-13-INCH BAKING PAN, ELECTRIC MIXER, CANDY THERMOMETER,
OFFSET SPATULA, KITCHEN SHEARS, SIEVE

½ cup confectioners' sugar, for dusting (2 ounces, 57 grams)

½ cup cornstarch, for dusting (2.1 ounces, 60 grams)

1 envelope gelatin (.25 ounces, 7 grams)

4 egg whites (4 ounces, 113 grams), at room temperature

2 cups granulated sugar (14 ounces, 397 grams)

½ teaspoon cream of tartar (1.5 grams)

¼ cup light corn syrup (3 ounces, 85 grams)

Flavoring, to taste (orange blossom extract, vanilla extract, almond extract, bergamot oil, rose water, or grapefruit oil), optional (see Sources, page 275)

1 to 2 drops food coloring, optional

1. Line a 9-by-13-inch baking pan with aluminum foil. Whisk together the confectioners' sugar and the cornstarch, and sift half of this over the pan to coat the bottom generously.

2. Place 1 tablespoon of water in a large glass measuring cup or other heatproof bowl. Sprinkle the gelatin over the water.

Recipe continues

3. In the clean bowl of an electric mixer fitted with the whisk attachment, combine the egg whites with 1 tablespoon of the granulated sugar and the cream of tartar. Beat the egg whites on medium speed until they form firm peaks.

4. In a saucepan, combine the remaining granulated sugar and 1/2 cup water with the corn syrup. Bring to a boil, stirring until the sugar dissolves.

5. While the whites are beating, boil the sugar mixture until it reaches 260°F on a candy thermometer (the hard-ball stage), about 10 minutes. Transfer the syrup to the glass measuring cup or bowl with the gelatin in it and whisk to incorporate the gelatin.

6. With the mixer running, carefully pour the sugar syrup down the side of the bowl into the egg whites in a thin stream, avoiding the beaters. Beat on high speed until the bowl is cool enough to touch but still warm, about 5 minutes. If using a handheld mixer, similarly pour the hot syrup down the sides of the bowl into the whites, being careful to avoid getting syrup on the beaters (and thus splashing it out of the bowl). Beat in the flavoring, starting with 1/8 teaspoon and adding more to taste. Flavor the mixture a little more strongly than you'd like, since it will mellow with time, but avoid adding too much at once—you can always add another drop. Add the food coloring, if using.

7. Using an offset spatula, spread the mixture onto the prepared pan, smoothing it toward the edges of the pan. Sift the remaining sugar-cornstarch mixture over the pan. Let set for at least 3 hours at room temperature.

8. Use kitchen shears or a knife to cut the marshmallows into 1 1/2-inch squares, then toss them in the sugar-cornstarch mix remains in the pan. Transfer the marshmallows (and the confectioners' sugar mix) to an airtight container and store for up to 1 week. Dust the excess powder off the marshmallows or shake them in a sieve before serving.

SPICED ORANGE DOUGHNUTS

Sweet, sugary doughnuts are truly a Hanukkah dessert, since the holiday is all about the gift of oil. Hanukkah is celebrated by lighting a candle every night for eight consecutive nights to celebrate the miracle that occurred when the Maccabees reclaimed the Temple in Jerusalem from the Greeks and lit an oil lamp to rededicate the temple. There was only enough oil to burn for one night, yet the light burnt for eight nights until more oil was procured. To celebrate this, traditional Hanukkah foods are fried in oil, like potato latkes or these doughnuts.

But really, doughnuts are welcome any time of year, breakfast, lunch, dessert—truly, there's never an inappropriate time to serve them.

These doughnuts are surprisingly light and delicately perfumed with orange zest and juice and spices, then rolled in cinnamon sugar for a slight crunch. To fry them, you can use any oil, such as vegetable, peanut, or sunflower, but I recommend pure olive oil for the most fabulous taste. (See photographs on page 228 and on the following page.)

MAKES ABOUT 12 DOZEN (4-INCH) DOUGHNUTS TO SERVE 18

SPECIAL EQUIPMENT: ZESTER, ELECTRIC MIXER, 11-BY-17-INCH BAKING SHEET, 3-QUART SAUCEPAN, CANDY THERMOMETER, SKIMMER

FOR THE CINNAMON SUGAR

- ½ cup sugar (3.5 ounces, 99 grams)
- 1 tablespoon ground cinnamon (10 grams)

FOR THE DOUGHNUTS

- ⅓ cup warm whole milk (2.8 ounces, 80.67 grams)
- 1 envelope (2 teaspoons) active dry yeast (about .25 ounce, 7 grams)
- 2¾ cups all-purpose flour (12.4 ounces, 357.5 grams), plus additional for dusting, if necessary

  Finely grated zest and freshly squeezed juice of 2 oranges

- 1 large egg (1.7 ounces, 50 grams), at room temperature
- 2 tablespoons sugar (.87 ounce, 25 grams)
- ½ teaspoon salt (2.5 grams)

  Pinch of ground cinnamon

  Pinch of freshly ground nutmeg

  Pinch of ground mace

- 2 tablespoons (¼ stick) unsalted butter, melted (1 ounce, 28.4 grams)

- 2 quarts pure olive or vegetable oil, for frying

Recipe continues

Spiced Orange Doughnuts

FOR THE CINNAMON SUGAR

In a small bowl combine the sugar and cinnamon and set aside.

FOR THE DOUGHNUTS

1. Place the milk and yeast in the bowl of an electric mixer fitted with the paddle attachment. Cover the mixture with the flour and let sit for 10 minutes. Add the orange zest and juice, egg, sugar, salt, and spices, and mix on medium-low speed until the dough pulls away from the sides of the bowl, about 10 minutes.

2. Pour in the melted butter and continue to mix until completely incorporated, about 5 minutes more. Cover the bowl with plastic wrap and leave at room temperature for 20 minutes. Transfer the dough to the refrigerator to chill for 2 hours. It will be denser than bread dough, yet slightly springy.

3. Cut the dough into 1-ounce cubes (about 2 inches across in size) and roll the cubes into balls, dusting the dough with flour if it is too sticky to handle. Place them on an 11-by-17-inch cookie sheet 3 inches apart. Cover the tray with a damp kitchen towel and let sit in a warm place, about 85°F to 95°F, until the dough has doubled in size, about 2 hours.

TO FRY AND SERVE

Have ready a paper towel–lined plate and the bowl of cinnamon sugar. In a 3-quart saucepan, heat the oil to 350°F (use a clip-on thermometer to measure the heat). Carefully lower 4 doughnuts at a time into the oil with a spoon, turning frequently until golden brown, 1 to 2 minutes. Skim the broken pieces of dough off the surface of the oil periodically. Before adding the next 4 doughnuts, wait for the temperature to return to 350°F. Transfer the doughnuts with a slotted spoon to the towel-lined plate. Roll the doughnuts in the cinnamon sugar while they are still warm. Serve immediately.

PAINTED COOKIES

Classic holiday cookies are fun to look at, but invariably tough and doughy, with an overly sweet icing. My recipe yields tender, buttery and crisp cookies with a thin layer of vibrantly colored decoration; as sensational to eat as they are stunning to admire. The dough, my variation of French sablé cookie dough, has a rich flavor that's not cloying, and a wonderfully flaky texture. The secret is adding the flour in two stages, and incorporating it without overmixing. It will be a little sticky to work with, but that can be controlled by keeping everything very cold and well floured.

Of course as good as the cookies themselves are, the really exciting thing about this recipe is the decoration. Instead of painting gobs of royal icing onto baked cookies, I decorate the raw dough with an edible, egg-based icing that is baked on, creating a gorgeous, stained glasslike finish. (It's similar to the egg tempera used by Byzantine and Medieval painters.) I did a lot of experimenting to develop the technique of painting onto greased parchment or a Silpat mat. The cookie dough

is pressed onto the egg icing, letting the color set in the oven. This decorating technique takes a little practice, but once you determine the right amount of pressure to apply to the dough, you'll turn over the finished cookies to reveal gorgeous results with a lovely matte finish. Decorated free-form, the cookies have a loose, painterly style, while using a stencil will give more precision to your patterns.

MAKES 3 DOZEN (2½-INCH) COOKIES

SPECIAL EQUIPMENT: FOOD PROCESSOR (FOR GROUND ALMONDS, OPTIONAL), ELECTRIC MIXER, BAKING SHEETS, CONTAINERS FOR PAINT, PAINTBRUSHES, MAT KNIFE AND STENCILS (OPTIONAL), ROLLING PIN, PASTRY BRUSH, SKEWER (OPTIONAL)

COOKIES

12 tablespoons (1½ sticks) unsalted butter (6 ounces, 170 grams)

¾ cup confectioners' sugar (3 ounces, 85 grams)

1 large egg (1.7 ounces, 48 grams), at room temperature

1 tablespoon vanilla extract (12 grams)

1¾ cups all-purpose flour (7.9 ounces, 224 grams), plus additional for rolling

1 cup almond flour (see Sources, page 275) or finely ground blanched almonds (3.7 ounces, 107 grams)

Nonstick cooking spray, for the cookie sheets

Granulated sugar, for sprinkling

COOKIE PAINT

1 cup all-purpose flour (4.5 ounces, 130 grams)

4 large eggs (6.8 ounces, 193 grams), at room temperature

2 tablespoons corn syrup (1.4 ounces, 41 grams)

Food coloring

FOR THE COOKIES

1. In the bowl of an electric mixer fitted with the paddle attachment, cream the butter and confectioners' sugar on low speed. Add the egg and vanilla, and beat until combined.

2. In another bowl, whisk the flour together with the almond flour or ground almonds. With the mixer on low speed, gradually add half the flour mixture to the butter mixture. Beat until combined. Add the remaining flour mixture and mix, scraping down the bowl as necessary. Scrape the dough onto a piece of plastic wrap, pat it into a disk, and wrap it tightly. Refrigerate for at least 4 hours or overnight.

FOR THE COOKIE PAINT

1. In the bowl of an electric mixer fitted with the whisk attachment, combine the flour, eggs, and corn syrup and beat until smooth. Allow the mixture to rest, covered, at room temperature for 1 hour.

2. Divide the paint among several containers, using one container for each desired color. Stir drops of food coloring into the containers to achieve the desired colors.

Recipe continues

Painted Cookies.

TO PAINT AND BAKE

1. Position the oven racks in the top and bottom thirds of the oven. Line several baking sheets with Silpat nonstick sheets or parchment paper. Lightly spray the parchment with cooking spray, and blot with a paper towel. Using the cookie paint and paintbrushes, fingers, or a small knife, paint designs on the parchment paper. Be sure to paint in a single thin layer. Only the paint touching the parchment paper will show up on the baked cookie. For best results, paint designs that are smaller than the cookies. Alternatively, make a stencil: use a mat knife to cut stencils from heavy-duty plastic notebook dividers or plastic can lids. Paint a background color on the parchment, then stencil over in a contrasting color, or just stencil directly onto the parchment. For a more precise look, use an art brush to paint directly on each cookie and bake with the painted side up.

2. Preheat the oven to 325°F. Lightly flour a work surface and a rolling pin, and roll out the dough 1/8 inch thick. Cut out cookies using cookie cutters. Lift the cookies with a spatula and dust the tops with a clean pastry brush to remove any excess flour. Place the cookies, dusted side down, onto the paint. Use a rolling pin or your palm to press the cookies gently and evenly into the paint, taking care not to slide or move them. If you plan to use the cookie as a tree ornament, use a skewer to form a hole slightly larger than you want it to be when baked.

3. Reassemble the scraps of dough into a ball, and push it back together. Flatten it between two sheets of plastic film and refrigerate again for 20 minutes. Then re-roll the dough out and cut more cookies. If you are rolling to 1/8 of an inch you will have enough dough for 36 cookies.

4. Sprinkle the cookies with granulated sugar. Bake for 9 to 12 minutes, until the cookies are firm and barely golden at the edge. Cool the cookie sheets on a wire rack before removing the cookies from the parchment.

Chef's Note Decorating tip: With the last of the paint make swirled decorations like the endpapers of a book.

DAMSON PLUM CAKE

This cake is far more refined than the bricks of candied cherry–studded cakes one usually encounters during the holidays. More like a French pain d'epices, this cake is laced with warm spices, tart dried cranberries, and luscious plum jam that melts into sticky pockets during baking. Tiny nuggets of walnut add a nice crunch.

I created this as a cake version of the popular English dessert Sticky Toffee Pudding. The brown sugar and butter pudding is a staple of English desserts, and here it is in simple cake form.

MAKES 1 (9-BY-5-INCH) LOAF TO SERVE 8
SPECIAL EQUIPMENT: 9-BY-5-INCH LOAF PAN, CAKE TESTER

2 cups all-purpose flour (8.5 ounces, 242 grams)

½ teaspoon baking powder (2.5 grams)

½ teaspoon baking soda (2.5 grams)

1 teaspoon freshly grated nutmeg (1.25 grams)

1 teaspoon ground allspice (1.25 grams)

1 teaspoon ground cinnamon (2 grams)

1 teaspoon salt (5 grams)

2 large eggs, lightly beaten (3.4 ounces, 96 grams), at room temperature

1 cup granulated sugar (7 ounces, 198 grams)

⅓ cup canola oil (2.5 ounces, 72 grams), plus some for the pan

½ cup buttermilk (4.25 ounce, 121 grams)

1 cup dried cranberries (3.9 ounces, 120 grams)

1 cup chopped walnuts (2.85 ounces, 84 grams)

1 cup damson plum jam (10.4 ounces, 150 grams)

1. Position a rack in the center of the oven and preheat to 350° F. Grease a 9-by-5-inch loaf pan with some canola oil.

2. In a large bowl, whisk together the flour, baking powder, baking soda, nutmeg, allspice, cinnamon, and salt.

3. In a separate large bowl, or using an electric mixer fitted with the paddle attachment, beat together the eggs and sugar until combined. Beat in the oil. Slowly beat in the flour mixture. Stir in the buttermilk. Using a spatula, fold in the cranberries and walnuts. Swirl in the jam in three to four strokes.

4. Pour the batter into the prepared pan and bake for 45 to 50 minutes, until a cake tester inserted in the center comes out clean. Let cool in the pan for 25 minutes, then slide a thin knife or offset spatula around the sides of the pan and turn it over to unmold the cake onto a wire rack. Allow the loaf to cool on the rack for about 5 minutes, then serve warm. This cake lasts a week well covered.

Christmas Tart.

CHRISTMAS TART

Perhaps it's a bit corny of me, but I like to make this recipe around the holidays because of its red and green colors—it's just so festive! Flavorwise, the tartness of the raspberries really lifts the sweetness of the pastry cream, preventing it from being cloying. In terms of texture, the buttery, cookie-like crust lends a crisp contrast against all the creaminess and juiciness of the filling. Although you can make the components of this dessert several days ahead, it's best not to bake it until the day you plan to serve it. That keeps the crust at its most crisp and delectable.

MAKES 1 (9-INCH) TART TO SERVE 6 TO 8
SPECIAL EQUIPMENT: FOOD PROCESSOR (FOR GROUND PISTACHIOS, OPTIONAL),
FINE-MESH SIEVE

1 pâte sablée tart shell (see recipe page 135), pre-baked

PASTRY CREAM

6 tablespoons sugar (2.6 ounces, 74 grams)

4 tablespoons cornstarch (1 ounce, 30 grams)

1 cup whole milk (8.5 ounces, 242 grams)

1 teaspoon vanilla extract (4 grams)

2 large eggs, beaten (3.4 ounces, 96 grams), at room temperature

ASSEMBLY

½ cup seedless raspberry jam (5.2 ounces, 150 grams)

2 cups fresh raspberries (9 ounces, 255 grams)

Finely chopped unsalted pistachios, for garnish, optional

FOR THE TART SHELL

Pre-bake the tart shell according to the box on page 135.

FOR THE PASTRY CREAM

1. Fill a large bowl with water and ice. Place a medium bowl in the ice water, and set a fine-mesh sieve over it. In a small bowl whisk together the sugar and cornstarch. In a small saucepan over medium heat, bring the milk and the vanilla extract to a boil. Working quickly, add the cornstarch mixture and the egg to the milk mixture and whisk vigorously until the mixture thickens, about 30 seconds. Pour the mixture through the sieve into the medium bowl and cover the pastry cream by laying a piece of plastic wrap directly on its surface (so it cannot form a skin). Let the strained

Recipe continues

pastry cream cool in the ice bath. (The pastry cream can be made up to 3 days ahead; store covered in the refrigerator.)

TO ASSEMBLE AND SERVE

1. Place the pre-baked tart shell on a baking sheet. Spread the seedless raspberry jam over the bottom of the cooled baked tart shell. Cover the jam with the pastry cream and bake in a 350°F oven until lightly browned. Remove from the oven and allow to cool 20 minutes on a wire rack.

2. Top with fresh raspberries and sprinkle with chopped pistachios.

Chef's Note Optionally, you may fill the tart shell with the pastry cream, and cover with the fresh raspberries, omitting the baking step, for a softer, creamier version.

HALVAH SESAME SUNDAE

The recipe makes the most out of a single ingredient by using four different sesame products: halvah, tahini paste, toasted sesame oil, and toasted sesame seeds. Melissa and I are both halvah lovers, and this sundae is the harmonious marriage of halvah, sesame ice cream, and caramel. The tan and golden color palette and range of textures and temperatures are reminiscent of a butterscotch sundae, but the flavors are so much more intense, complex, and unexpected. So be adventurous, excite your dinner guests, try this combination!

If you want a shortcut, you can use good-quality, purchased vanilla ice cream instead of making the sesame ice cream.

MAKES ABOUT 1 QUART OF ICE CREAM TO SERVE 6 TO 8
SPECIAL EQUIPMENT: CANDY THERMOMETER, FINE-MESH SIEVE, ICE CREAM MAKER

SESAME ICE CREAM

- 8 large egg yolks (5 oz, 149 grams), at room temperature
- ¾ cup sugar (5.25 ounces, 150 grams)
- 3 cups whole milk (25.5 ounces, 726 grams)
- 1 cup heavy cream (8.12 ounces, 232 grams)
- 2 teaspoons toasted (Asian) sesame oil (5 grams)
- 2 teaspoons vanilla extract (8 grams)
- ¼ teaspoon salt (1.25 grams)

CARAMEL SAUCE

- ½ cup sugar (3.5 ounces, 99 grams)

TAHINI SAUCE

- ½ cup heavy cream (4.06 ounces, 116 grams)
- ⅓ cup tahini (see Sources, page 276) (4 ounces, 113 grams)
- 1½ tablespoons medium-flavored honey such as orange blossom or clover (1 ounce, 32 grams)
- ¾ cup crumbled halvah, packed, for serving (see Sources, page 275) (5.25 ounces, 150 grams)
- 8 sesame crunch candies, broken into pieces, for serving (see Sources, page 275) (1.5 ounces, 45 grams)

FOR THE ICE CREAM

1. In a bowl, whisk the egg yolks with 1/4 cup of the sugar. Attach a candy thermometer to the side of a saucepan, and bring the milk, cream, and remaining 1/2 cup sugar to a boil. Whisking constantly, pour a little of the hot milk mixture into the yolks to warm them. Then drizzle the yolk mixture into the saucepan, whisking constantly.

Recipe continues

Halvah Sesame Sundae.

2. Cook over medium-low heat, stirring, until this custard is thick enough to coat the back of a wooden spoon, about 5 minutes. The mixture should reach 170 to 180°F. Strain the custard through a fine-mesh sieve into a bowl and stir in the sesame oil, vanilla, and salt. Let cool, then refrigerate for at least 3 hours or overnight.

3. Freeze in an ice cream maker according to the manufacturer's instructions.

FOR THE CARAMEL SAUCE

Place the sugar in a small, heavy saucepan and heat over medium heat, swirling, until all the sugar is melted. Let the sugar cook until it is a deep amber caramel (356°F), about 2 minutes. Pour in 1/2 cup water (be careful, it will spatter) and whisk until smooth, about 1 minute. Keep warm or reheat before serving.

FOR THE TAHINI SAUCE

Pour the cream into a saucepan and cook until boiling. Add the tahini and honey and cook, whisking constantly, until smooth and frothy, about 1 minute more.

TO SERVE

Serve scoops of sesame ice cream drizzled with caramel and tahini sauce, with crumbled halvah and sesame candy scattered on top.

Asian Trifle with Lime Yogurt Cream.

ASIAN TRIFLE WITH LIME YOGURT CREAM

I decided to come up with a trifle to suit the lighter, sunnier flavors of lychee, orange, passion fruit, and mango, which are available during the winter. Any of these colorful fruits works beautifully in the trifle. (See page 265 for a guide to Asian fruits.) The lime and yogurt, in place of sherry and custard, make this a more refreshing finish after holiday meals.

This dessert travels wonderfully, since it's made all in a bowl, and it gets better as it sits in the fridge. The bowl itself is a design component. Layering the elements in it so they are attractive from the outside is a fun decorating project.

MAKES 1 TRIFLE TO SERVE 12 TO 15

SPECIAL EQUIPMENT: ZESTER, CANDY THERMOMETER, DOUBLE BOILER, ELECTRIC MIXER, LARGE GLASS BOWL FOR ASSEMBLY AND SERVING

FRUIT

1½ cups sugar (10.5 ounces, 300 grams)

Freshly grated zest of 1 lime

½ vanilla bean, split lengthwise, and seeds scraped and reserved, or ¼ teaspoon vanilla extract (1 gram)

1 small pineapple, peeled, cored, and cut into ½-inch dice (about 2 cups, ½ pound, 8 ounces, 225 grams)

Dragon fruit, lychee, passion fruit, mangosteen, mango, rambutan, and oranges, skinned and sliced horizontally

LIME YOGURT CREAM

½ teaspoon powdered gelatin (1.6 grams)

4 large egg yolks (2.4 ounces, 74.4 grams), at room temperature

½ cup sugar (3.5 ounces, 99 grams)

Freshly grated zest and strained juice of 2 limes

1 cup heavy cream (8.12 ounces, 232 grams)

1 cup whole-milk plain yogurt (8 ounces, 227 grams)

1 cup crème fraîche or sour cream (8.5 ounces, 242 grams)

ASSEMBLY

2 (8- or 9-inch) sponge cakes, each layer sliced in half horizontally to make 4 layers total

9 kiwis, peeled and cut into ½-inch dice (22.5 ounces, 638 grams)

1 package Savoiardi biscuits (see Sources, page 275)

FOR THE FRUIT

1. To a medium saucepan over medium heat, add 3/4 cup of the sugar, half of the lime zest, half of the vanilla bean seeds with half of the pod or 1/4 teaspoon of vanilla extract, and 1/2 cup water. Heat, stirring until the sugar dissolves, then simmer for 5 to 7 minutes until very syrupy, about 254°F on a candy thermometer (soft-ball stage).

Recipe continues

2. Add 1 1/2 cups of the pineapple or mango to the syrup, reserving the rest for garnish. Adjust the heat as needed to simmer gently until the fruit is glazed and softened but holds its shape, 2 to 3 minutes. Remove the vanilla bean pod, if using. Transfer the fruit to a bowl and let cool.

3. In a saucepan, combine the remaining 3/4 cup sugar, the remaining lime zest, and the remaining vanilla seeds and the pod or the remaining vanilla extract with 1/2 cup water. Heat, stirring, until the sugar dissolves, then simmer for 5 to 7 minutes until thick and syrupy, like maple syrup. Add 1 1/2 cups of the lychee, mango, or pineapple to the syrup, reserving the rest for garnish. Cook gently until the fruit is glazed and softened, but holds its shape, 2 to 4 minutes. Remove the vanilla bean pod. Transfer the fruit to a bowl and let cool.

FOR THE LIME YOGURT CREAM

1. Attach a candy thermometer to the side of a double boiler and bring an inch of water to a simmer in the bottom of the pan. In a small bowl, combine the gelatin with 2 teaspoons of cold water and set aside. Place the egg yolks, sugar, and lime zest and juice in the top of the double boiler. Whisking constantly, heat the yolk mixture over simmering water until thickened, 5 to 7 minutes. The mixture should reach 170 to 180°F. Take the yolk mixture off the heat and whisk in the gelatin until it dissolves, about 20 seconds.

2. In the bowl of an electric mixer fitted with the whisk attachment, whip the cream at medium-high speed until it is thickened and soft peaks just begin to form. Whisk the yogurt and crème fraîche or sour cream into the yolk mixture, then fold in the whipped cream.

TO ASSEMBLE AND SERVE

With a scissor, trim the 4 sponge cake layers so they will fit into a large glass bowl or footed trifle dish. Place one cake layer in the bottom of the bowl. Starting at the edge of the bowl so that the fruit shows through the glass, arrange the pineapple in one layer on the cake. Spread a quarter of the yogurt cream over the cake, then stand the Savoiardi upright on end against the glass and top with a second cake layer. Using a slotted spoon, spread a layer of mango on the cake, pressing the fruits against the sides of the bowl so they show through the glass. Spread another layer of the yogurt cream on the fruit and place orange slices standing up against the glass, then top with a third layer of cake. Top all with the pineapple or lychee, extending the fruit over the entire cake layer (always making sure the fruit touches the glass). Spread another quarter of the yogurt cream on the fruit and top with the final cake layer. Spread the remaining yogurt cream on top. Cover the trifle with plastic wrap and refrigerate for at least 3 hours and up to 3 days. Before serving, press pieces of the reserved tropical fruit on top. Garnish with matchstick slivers of lime zest.

ASIAN FRUITS

LYCHEES
Sold fresh or canned in syrup, lychees bring a delicate flavor and texture to the combination of tropical fruits in the trifle. If using fresh, simply peel and remove the stone. If using canned, drain the syrup.

DRAGON FRUIT
Crunchy and sweet, dragon fruit tastes like a cross between kiwi and pear. The fruit has black, edible seeds like a kiwi. Cut the dragon fruit in half and remove the flesh from the skin using a spoon.

LONGAN
The flesh of this fruit is juicy and sweet. Longans grow in clusters; their shells change from orange to brown as they ripen. Split the fruit open at the stem, peel the shell, and remove the stone.

PASSION FRUIT AND SINGAPORE ORANGE
Scrape the extremely fragrant passion fruit from its thorny shell. Singapore orange, more like a tangerine in flavor, is a traditional gift to bring when visiting family for Chinese New Year. Called *kam* ("gold") in Cantonese due to their deep color, they symbolize prosperity and luck.

MANGOSTEEN
Cut around the center of the mangosteen peel and then divide into sections like an orange. Select fruit with purple skin.

RAMBUTAN
This fruit—often used like a lychee—can be peeled by slicing open and removing the flesh from the shell. Select rambutans with light reddish skin and green spikes.

EQUIPMENT

With the basic minimum (see the sidebar below), the occasional baker can accomplish a lot. This chapter is for the devoted baker or tool-obsessed individual who cannot sleep for thinking there may be some twisted piece of metal he or she doesn't own. Tool envy aside, the following equipment can make the job easier, more precise, and more fun.

THE BAKER'S MINIMUM

Wooden spoon

Rubber spatula

Metal spatula

Wire whisk

Electric handheld immersion blender, or stand mixer

Food processor

Liquid measuring cups

Dry measuring cups

Measuring spoons

Assorted mixing bowls

Pastry brush

Wire cooling rack

Rolling pin

Handheld or box food grater/zester

Paring knife

Serrated knife

Kitchen timer

Oven thermometer

Heavy-bottomed saucepan (1 or 2 quart)

10- or 12-inch sauté pan

Baking Pans

Springform pan, 9 inches round, 3 inches deep

2 to 3 (9-inch-round, 2-inch-deep) cake pans

9-inch square baking pan

10-inch cake pan with high sides

10-inch Bundt pan

9-by-13-inch rectangular baking pan

9-by-5-inch aluminum or glass loaf pan

12-cup muffin tin

9-inch fluted tart pan

9-inch Pyrex or heavy-duty-metal pie plate

12-by-17-inch jelly roll pan

11-by-17-inch rimmed baking sheets

Great Extras

Tongs

Pie weights

Pastry blender

Marble pastry board

Kitchen scale

Madeleine pans

Cookie cutters

Spice grinder (or coffee grinder)

8- and 10-inch round cake pans

Cake Testers

Long and thin, these are very useful for testing done-ness in a deep cake, when toothpicks just don't have the reach. You could use the straws from a clean, unused broom (and there are even some cute ones made specifically for this task, though any broom will work), or a long, thin wooden skewer. But testers strike me as more convenient.

Cake Turntable

If you're into cake decorating (or you just want to do things right when you do go all out on a cake), get yourself a raised cake stand that spins like a lazy Susan and will enable you to work around a cake smoothly and evenly. There are inexpensive plastic versions of this gizmo that are quite satisfactory.

Cardboard Rounds

Sold in bakeware stores, these come in the same sizes as standard cake pans. Turning a cooled cake onto a stiff round will allow you to move it around and decorate it much more easily. These are also used, in conjunction with dowels, to support a large, multi-tiered cake.

Cookie Cutters

There are an endless variety of cookie cutter shapes. The most basic are the round ones, and it's nice to have a set of these that ranges in size from 1/2 inch to 6 inches in diameter, with either smooth or fluted sides. You can use them for everything, from shaping linzer cookies to cutting out rounds of baked genoise. If you are using fancier shapes, keep in mind that thin appendages (say, an elephant cookie with a trunk) will need to be watched carefully in the oven and handled with extra care once baked to avoid burning or break-ing. Choose cutters that look like they'll actually cut (not dull, thick ones), for crisper shapes, and make sure they're thoroughly dry before you put them away, since some can rust. One solution to this problem is to place the washed cutters on a large cooling rack and

dry them in the oven as it cools. In a pinch, Grandma's trick of using an overturned glass in lieu of a cookie cutter still works.

Dessicant Packs

To keep cookies crisp even in humid weather, Grand-ma's cookie tins leave something to be desired. Little packages of silica gel, a sandlike substance that can absorb a great deal of moisture, keep crispy things crispy longer. These packs, sealed and marked "do not eat," are often found in vitamin bottles. In fact, you can use the ones in your vitamin bottles if they haven't been damaged. Silica gel should not be used if children will be exploring the contents of the con-tainer.

Graters and Zesters

The box grater is a standard workhorse (well, in the grating department), but since we often use citrus zest for dessert recipes, it's good to equip yourself with a rasp-style Microplane zester as well, which allows you to zest right over a bowl and picks up just the right depth of zest, which is to say the minimum to the exclusion of pith. The Microplane is also useful for grating fresh ginger and shaving chocolate and can be used as a nutmeg grater.

Ice Cream Machine

This is one of the most enjoyable toys a pastry chef can have, and it opens up a whole new world of smooth frozen desserts. There are a number of good models for nonprofessionals (without the bulk, and price tag, of a small European car). For sheer charm, the wooden, crank-type machine, made by White Mountain Company, recalls the front-porch halcyon days gone by. Unfortunately, it also recalls the muscle aches of yore. White Mountain Company does make a version with an electric motor, which works well, though it's quite noisy.

The sleeker, modern designs now offered fall into two camps: those that contain a special bowl that needs to be put in the freezer overnight before you can make ice cream (so you'll want to own two bowls if you ever plan on making more than one flavor in twenty-four hours) and the larger, more expensive, self-freezing models that actually freeze the mixture as it churns. In either camps look for good design, such as a bowl that will be easy to remove and clean, and larger churning blades, which make smoother ice cream faster. Salton, Gaggia, Krups, and Cuisinart all make reliable machines.

The finished product that emerges from an ice cream machine has the consistency of soft serve. It is one of the world's great pleasures to spoon this lightly frozen stuff up right then, but if you want to serve nice, round scoops, it's necessary to freeze the ice cream a little more. Use a plastic spatula to transfer it to a sturdy, good-quality plastic container with a lid (such as Rubbermaid or Tupperware) and pack it down tight. If the lid is not touching the ice cream, lay a piece of plastic wrap on the surface. You should have ice cream firm enough to scoop in 4 to 6 hours, depending on your freezer, but of course you can store it for longer. Homemade ice cream is a fresh product and will start to lose its smooth texture and wonderful freshness after a few days.

Kitchen Scale

I cannot recommend measuring by weight strongly enough—it's simply more precise and efficient than bothering with multiple measuring cups and guessing how tightly packed the ingredients should be. Once you start measuring by weight you will have more confidence as a baker. In all my recipes I give weight measurements in grams and ounces. Either one is fine to use, as long as you choose one or the other and stick with it throughout the recipe, as switching your scale back and forth is sure to lead to confusion and possible mistakes.

There are inexpensive digital scales that do not take up much room and lie flat on the counter so you can place a bowl right on them to hold the ingre-dients. Most have a counterweight button or "tare," which sets the scale back to zero so you don't measure the receptacle's weight. You can tare the scale after adding each ingredient, as long as you take care not to go over—it's impossible to scoop that extra ounce of sugar out of the flour, or extra gram of salt out of the sugar once you've sprinkled it in! Avoid nondigital spring scales, which often get out of whack after a few uses. Better to measure by volume rather than trusting one of these. (For the best scales at reasonable prices, see Sources, page 275).

Knives

For making desserts, the essentials are a 4- to 6-inch paring knife for preparing fruits and garnishes, a chef's knife for chopping nuts or chocolate, and a long, serrated slicing knife (at least 12 inches) for slicing cakes into layers. I recommend stainless steel or high-carbon stainless steel knives, since these do not rust.

Mixers

If you are going to do a lot of baking, a good electric mixer is a worthwhile investment. A big, heavy stand mixer will free up your hands, which makes it much more efficient than a handheld. A well-built one, such as a KitchenAid (or any number of other good brands such as Krups and DeLonghi), can also take on stiff batters and bread dough more easily than a handheld. You'll find both the whisk and paddle attachments for stand mixers highly useful, and the dough hook will come in handy if you bake breads.

But if the cost is prohibitive or you don't have the counter space, a strong handheld mixer will certainly do. Handhelds usually offer only a beater attachment.

Nonstick Liners and Pans

In the dessert maker's kitchen, stickiness is a force to be reckoned with. Sticking during baking occurs when the proteins in foods seep into the microscopic crannies of the cooking surface and solidify upon exposure to heat. Or it can happen when a mixture like caramel finds other materials to bond with—that means nearly everything it touches! So when nonstick coatings were invented in the first half of the twentieth century, it was a great boon for cooks. Nonstick surfaces are made of a material that simply will not bond with anything and is resistant to high temperatures.

Nonstick pans are recognizable because they have a dark-colored lining sprayed onto their interiors. On sauté pans and saucepans, these can work well when you are cooking foods that need to be easily removed from the pan, such as omelets. When it comes to standard, basic bakeware (see sidebar), however, I tend to prefer well-greased, traditional surfaces, such as aluminum, since nonstick pans create a very dark crust.

For everything else, silicone is a miracle.

To line baking sheets you can use parchment paper, which is perfectly fine for basic butter-based cookies, but won't repel extremely sticky mixtures like pralines and some meringues. A nonstick silicone liner, like the ones produced by Silpat (see Sources, page 275), works much better. These silicone sheets are very efficient heat conductors and can withstand freezing and baking (though not broiling). Mine last for six months with constant daily use, so in an occasional baker's kitchen, they will serve for years before the ends get ragged and brown and the sheets begin to lose their power to release foods.

Silicone also comes in mold shapes of every design, allowing you to make cakes or candies in shapes like domes, pyramids, scallop shells (for madeleines), hexagons, and more (see Sources, page 275). Turning out a confection from these flexible "pans" is delightfully easy—no knife to release the sides, no inverting and thumping, and no applications of warm compresses in a desperate attempt to unstick whatever is holding to the bottom of the pan.

Pans / Bakeware

Heat is pretty predictable (provided you have an oven thermometer!), but baking pans are not. Good results hinge on the size, shape, and material of the pan you use. Generally, the pan should be equal in height to that of the finished cake, and the batter should fill it to between half and three-quarters full. If the pan is underfilled, the heat will not reach down enough and the top of the cake will be dry and pale. An overfull pan may cause the batter to run over the sides as it begins to rise.

If you want to substitute for the pan indicated in the recipe, make sure its volume is the same and be ready for a different baking time. For example, a cake batter spread out into a sheet pan has a lot of exposed area and will absorb heat and bake faster than it will in a 9-inch round pan. Smaller items, like individual cakes baked in muffin tins, will also take a shorter time to bake, since they absorb heat from all sides and the heat reaches the center of the cake sooner than it would in one large pan. The difference in baking time can be dramatic if you are changing the shape of the pan—it's a good idea to check on the cake frequently after the first 10 minutes of baking. Square pans, or those with unusual shapes (novelty pans shaped like cartoon characters, for example) have thinner edges, corners, and protruding areas, and these will bake first. Be sure to rotate such pans regularly to encourage even browning. (Of course, be gentle and don't keep the oven door open for longer than necessary or slam it shut, as the cake is not fully risen and set until it is done.)

Not all metal cake pans are equal. Dark metal absorbs heat more quickly and efficiently, may speed baking time, and produces a darker crust. An oven-proof glass baking dish takes longer to transfer the heat to the food, so lower the baking temperature by 25°F and expect a browner, thicker crust and a longer baking time. Brushed aluminum is a good heat conductor and is very lightweight; it's the standard in which most recipes are tested. Avoid stainless-steel baking pans, however shiny and attractive they look, as this metal is a poor conductor and will reflect heat away from the pan, slowing things down.

Pastry Bags

When choosing a pastry bag, seek out something flexible yet impermeable. An old-fashioned, stiff canvas bag is not as easy to handle as the newer, more supple, plastic-lined varieties sold in cookware shops, and will also be harder to clean. For fine work I recommend the Matfer nylon bag (see Sources, page 275) if you want to invest in something that will last. Remember, it's important to clean it very well with soapy water and dry it completely after you use it. Few things are as unpleasant as a pastry bag fermenting in the back of a cupboard for weeks on end. Too large a bag is difficult to hold, so stick with the 12- to 14-inch bag, refilling it as needed. And for most jobs, disposable zippered plastic bags—the resealable Ziploc type—certainly make my life easier.

Pastry Brush

Just like painters, bakers prefer the feel and texture of natural bristles, and if cleaned and maintained, these can last as long as the synthetic versions. Wash the brushes in warm soapy water, then shake them out and stand them bristle side up to air dry completely. Use separate brushes for sweets and savories, since garlic oil residue has no place in desserts. Natural brushes from a hardware store are fine to use and are often cheaper than those sold for pastry. If you can, choose a brush with dark-colored bristles so you'll be able to see and remove those stray bristles that inevitably end up falling out and sticking to your dessert. A round brush is useful for buttering small round molds, and a flat brush is best for larger surfaces. Softer bristles are more delicate and won't tear your strudel dough, and they tend to be a bit more absorbent as well.

Pastry Tips

A set of about twelve tips ranging in size, half of them star-shaped, half round, should be sufficient for most bakers. That said, there are some wonderful shapes that make unusual and special effects. These are usually sold one at a time and are not a huge investment. If you are into piping or icing, buy a few of the wacky tips and play around with fancy shapes. The most useful are those numbered 8 to 10, but on tiered cakes some very small (and tedious) decorations will look best. (See Sources, page 275).

Pizza Cutter

This rolling blade is a nice tool for slicing straight through raw dough, marzipan, rolled fondant, cookie dough, and even pizza! You can also get fluted cutters especially for cutting pastry into frilly, decorative shapes. And if you have more than one rolling cutter, everyone will know you're gadget-obsessed.

Reading Lamp

Useful for illuminating the fine details of everything from crimped edges to icing flourishes, a bright spotlight on your workspace is a sine qua non, and is guaranteed to make every job easier, whether it's reading the recipe or post-baking cleanup.

Rolling Pins

Most of us are familiar with the "American" model of rolling pin, which is a cylinder with two handles on ball bearings, and this is fine for most doughs, although you can't use it to soften a cold dough by banging away on it or you will ruin the ball bearings. The "French" version is just an unadorned cylinder—no handles—and is usually smaller in diameter. I prefer the French kind because it allows for a better and closer feel of the dough, but if you are used to the ball-bearing kind, by all means stick with it. I also love the new breed of silicone plastic rolling pins, which are lightweight and less likely to peel away bits from your pastry or tear away chunks of it as you roll. In addition, the plastic ones come in small sizes and are very useful for cookies, or, if you're a pastry chef, rolling out sugar paste for flowers.

Avoid fancy marble rolling pins, which are often heavy, or the ones that you fill with ice water to chill as they roll—this tends to cause condensation and stiffen the dough, which makes them more troublesome than beneficial for tender dough. Working quickly on a floured surface in a cool room is a better option. And if sticking is a problem, roll the dough between pieces of waxed paper or plastic wrap.

Scrapers

To scrape out a bowl with aplomb, invest a few bucks in a bowl scraper, a flexible, thin, yet strong, crescent of plastic that you hold in your hand and swoop through the bowl to get that last gooey drop of batter. A bench scraper, a stainless steel rectangle with a handle, is useful in the kitchen for lifting large, delicate objects, dividing yeasted doughs, and scraping up stuck-on caramel or dough from your work surface.

Sieves

Mesh stainless-steel sieves are useful for sifting dry ingredients. A very fine mesh is good for straining the seeds out of berry purees, jams, and jellies, while a somewhat coarse sieve is more useful for sifting dry ingredients, since sugar and salt crystals can be too big for the tightest mesh. I prefer sifting in a sieve rather than a sifter because it's easier to clean, but either is fine.

Spatulas

There is more than one kind of spatula, and most cooks will want to own several varieties for folding, smoothing, scraping, flipping, and dividing. There are two main categories: flexible rubber spatulas and inflexible spatulas made of metal, plastic, or wood.

In the flexible category, the rectangular type is a great tool for folding batters and scraping down bowls. These can vary from slightly floppy and pliable to quite rigid. The softer spatulas are useful for getting every last drop of batter out of the bowl, and their flexibility helps in folding, but they have the disadvantage that if you leave them in a pot on the heat, you may return to find half the spatula melted

away and your sauce imbued with rubber! Hard rubber spatulas withstand heat up to 800°F but are stiff and less useful for folding, so I recommend buying one of each. The standard size (about 2 by 3 inches) is most practical, though a long, thin one is great for scraping the peanut butter out of a narrow jar, and the enormous, 2-foot-long ones are useful for those of us who make very large recipes (probably not a common occurrence in a home kitchen). The "spoonula" is a hard rubber spatula with an indented spoon side for thick batters that need a strong arm to mix them, and it can be used for scooping up batter.

As far as inflexible spatulas go, the thinner the blade the easier it is to slide under cookies and such, so thin metal is usually the best material for the job. These can either extend straight from the handle or can have an elbow bend in them (this type is called an offset spatula). An offset spatula is useful for spreading batter or dough in a pan with edges that would interfere with your hand movements if you used a straight spatula. These come in a wide variety of lengths and flexibilities. You will reach for your 8-inch sized one when transferring cakes and cookies, icing cakes, or spreading large amounts of butter into a pan. A tiny, 3-inch offset spatula is perfect for finessing those little corners when icing stacked cakes, for spreading brownie and other cake batters evenly into pans, and for transferring delicate cookies like tuiles. A tiny offset with a pointed tip is called a palette knife and is used for fine work and decorations on cakes. The flexibility is important depending on the use. For lifting cakes and icing in wide sweeping strokes a firm spatula is helpful. For finishing touches where even edges are important, a more flexible spatula is best.

Squeeze Bottles

This handy tool, just a plastic bottle with a nozzle (like the red and yellow ones that ketchup and mustard are sometimes served in at diners) is mostly used for plated desserts when you want to make Jackson Pollock–type splatters, or the ubiquitous heart squeezed from two different colored sauces. Go wild and be creative—think Rorschach inkblots. Fruit coulis, chocolate sauce, and herb oils are ripe for this treatment.

Sugar Shaker

Also called a dredger, this is like an oversized salt shaker and is perfect for that pastry chef's failsafe trick, sprinkling confectioners' sugar over a dessert to hide imperfections and make it look delicious and vaguely Austrian. The shaker portions out a fine, even coating, with no lumps, and it can be used one-handed, unlike a sieve, which you need to shake in one hand while banging against the other.

Thermometers

In dessert making, the most pressing need for a thermometer is in situations when you are heating a sugar syrup to a specific temperature (making Italian meringue, for example), and for this you'll need a candy thermometer (also called a confection, sugar, or deep-fry thermometer) with a clip to attach it to the side of the pot and a foot to keep the thermometer from hitting the metal base of the pot (which will be at a much higher temperature than the syrup above it). These thermometers can register temperatures between 80 and 420°F, taking you straight up to the hottest of caramels. Without this tool, cooking sugar syrups requires a fair amount of guesswork.

Instant-read, probe-type thermometers that give a digital reading are useful for measuring syrups and can be used to judge the interior temperature of breads, and roasts, as well.

A good oven thermometer that hangs from an oven rack and can be easily read (so you don't have to stick your head in the oven and squint at the thing for several minutes) is useful, since it's not uncommon for the calibration of an oven to be off by a few or many degrees.

There are now high-tech thermometers that bounce a laser ray off the surface of the object being measured and give an instant reading. This is a quick and sanitary method—but it only gives a surface reading, which can be inaccurate for sugar syrups and most other situations in baking when you'd want a thermometer.

Whipped Cream Maker

Whipping with this is more fun than whipping cream in an electric mixer, and it makes a great splash at parties. It is also handy for creating the trendy flavored foams that keep cropping up on restaurant menus. You do need to stock up on the little gas cartridges, though, and don't use the seltzer cartridge unless you want your dessert to taste like club soda.

SOURCES

ACACIA HONEY: www.localharvest.org / 831-475-8150

ALMOND FLOUR: www.bakerscatalogue.com / 800-827-6836

ALMOND PASTE: www.bakerscatalogue.com / 800-827-6836

ASCORBIC ACID: www.luckyvitamin.com / 888-635-0474

BAKING EQUIPMENT: www.nycake.com / 877-692-2538

BERGAMOT OIL: www.naturesflavors.com / 888-704-4900

BEURRE ÉCHIRÉ: www.gourmetfoodstore.com / 877-591-8008

BLACK SESAME SEEDS: www.penzeys.com / 800-741-7787

BOTTLED SOUR CHERRIES: www.earthy.com / 800 367-4709

CHESTNUT HONEY: www.localharvest.org / 831-475-8150

CHESTNUTS IN SYRUP: www.buonitalia.com 212-633-9090

CHESTNUT PASTE: www.lepicerie.com / 866-350-7575

CHOCOLATE/COCOA: www.bakerscatalogue.com / 800-827-6836

CITRUS OILS: www.boyajianinc.com / 800-965-0665

COFFEE EXTRACT: www.spicebarn.com / 866 670-9040

CREAM OF COCONUT: www.asianfoodgrocer.com / 888-482-2742

DRIED SOUR CHERRIES: www.bobsredmill.com / 800-349-2173

DULCE DE LECHE: www.igourmet.com / 877-446-8763

ESSENTIAL OILS: www.aftelier.com/store.html / 510-841-2111 and www.naturesflavors.com / 888-704-4900

ESPRESSO POWDER: www.kingarthurflour.com / 800-827-6836

FLEUR DE SEL: www.penzeys.com / 800-741-7787

FROMAGE BLANC: www.igourmet.com / 877-446-8763

GRAPEFRUIT OIL: www.naturesflavors.com / 888-704-4900

GREEN TEA POWDER (MATCHA): www.teanobi.com / 415-992-7550

HALVAH: www.russanddaughters.com / 800-787-7229

HAZELNUT PASTE: www.bakerscatalogue.com / 800-827-6836

HIBISCUS FLOWERS: www.serendipitea.com / 888-832-5433

KAFFIR LIME LEAVES: www.importfood.com / 888-618-8424

KUMQUATS: www.kumquatgrowers.com / 352-588-0544

LAVENDER HONEY: www.localharvest.org / 831-475-8150

LEMON GRASS: www.importfood.com / 888-618-8424

MAPLE SYRUP: www.bakerscatalogue.com / 800-827-6836

MARRONS GLACÉS: www.latienda.com / 800-710-4304

MASCARPONE: www.igourmet.com / 877-446-8763

MEDJOOL DATES: www.nutsonline.com / 800-558-6887

MUSCOVADO SUGAR: www.indiatree.com / 800-369-4848

ORANGE FLOWER WATER: www.naturesflavors.com / 888-704-4900

ORGEAT: www.naturesflavors.com / 888-704-4900

PASSION FRUIT PUREE: www.naturesflavors.com / 888-704-4900

PEACHES: www.froghollow.com / 888-779-4511

PEARL SUGAR: www.bakerscatalogue.com / 800-827-6836

PEARL TAPIOCA: www.kalustyans.com / 800-352-3451

PECAN FLOUR: www.bakerscatalogue.com / 800-827-6836

PISTACHIO FLOUR: www.santabarbarapistachios.com / 800-896-1044

PISTACHIO PASTE: www.bakerscatalogue.com / 800-827-6836

POMEGRANATE MOLASSES: www.kalustyans.com / 800-352-3451

QUARK: www.igourmet.com / 877-446-8763

ROCK CANDY: www.thechocolatestore.com / 888-467-4513

ROSE SYRUP: www.kalustyans.com / 800-352-3451

ROSE WATER : www.naturesflavors.com / 888-704-4900

SAVOIARDI: www.citarella.com / 212-874-0383

SESAME CRUNCH CANDIES: www.halvah.biz / 866-442-5824

SCALES: www.myweigh.com

SPICES:

    ALLSPICE BERRIES: www.penzeys.com / 800-741-7787

    ANCHO CHILE POWDER: www.gourmetsleuth.com / 408-354-8281

    CARDAMOM PODS: www.penzeys.com / 800-741-7787

    SAFFRON: www.penzeys.com / 800-741-7787

STAR ANISE: www.penzeys.com / 800-741-7787

SWEET BASIL SEED: www.importfood.com / 888-618-8424

WHOLE NUTMEG: www.penzeys.com / 800-741-7787

TAHINI: www.kalustyans.com / 800-352-3451

TAMARIND CONCENTRATE: www.kalustyans.com / 800-352-3451

UNSWEETENED COCONUT MILK: www.asianfoodgrocer.com / 888-482-2742

WALNUT OIL: www.igourmet.com / 877-446-8763

WILDFLOWER HONEY: www.localharvest.org / 831-475-8150

INDEX

Note: Page numbers in **boldface** type refer to recipes themselves; page numbers in *italics* refer to photographs.

ABOUT THE AUTHORS

Bill Yosses has over thirty years of experience as a pastry chef. A native of Toledo, Ohio, Bill began his career at La Foux, a bistro in Paris, working under chef-owner Alex Guini. Upon returning to New York, Bill completed his culinary studies at New York City Technical College and, at the age of twenty-three, was cooking at The Polo Restaurant alongside esteemed chefs Thomas Keller and Daniel Boulud. As his interest in pastry grew, Bill spent Saturday afternoons in the kitchen of his friend Jean-Pierre LeMasson of Le Perigord Park in New York. Then he returned to France and began working at La Maison du Chocolat and with the renowned pastry chef Pierre Herme at Fauchon.

Bill first held the title of pastry chef in New York's Montrachet restaurant, where he teamed up with David Bouley. Bill moved with David Bouley to his four-star restaurants Bouley and Bouley Bakery, before becoming the pastry chef at Joseph Citarella's in New York City.

Bill has taught courses in baking and pastry-making as a visiting instructor at the Napa Valley branch of the Culinary Institute of America, as well as at the New School for Culinary Arts in Manhattan. One of the foremost pastry chefs in the world, Bill is currently the executive pastry chef at the White House and divides his time between New York City and Washington, D.C.

Melissa Clark, a James Beard Foundation award winner, writes about cuisine, wine, travel, and other products of appetite for numerous publications such as the *New York Times*, *Bon Appetit*, *Food & Wine*, and *Martha Stewart Living*. In addition, Clark has written twenty-six cookbooks, including *Braise*, a collaboration with chef Daniel Boulud, and *The Last Course*, with pastry chef Claudia Fleming. She recently completed a cookbook/memoir based on her popular *New York Times* dining section column, "A Good Appetite." Clark was born and raised in Brooklyn, New York, where she now lives with her husband, Daniel Gercke, and their daughter, Dahlia.